AGING AND DEVELOPMENT

D0468743

The psychology of aging usually focuses upon cognitive changes, with a particular focus on dementia and other forms of cognitive decline. But getting older is about more than simply changes to the brain and related health issues. Changes to our social and emotional lives are also hugely significant as we adapt across our lifespan.

The second edition of *Aging and Development* is the only textbook available that responds to the growing interest in social, personal and emotional development in older age. Ideally suited to complement texts on cognitive change, the book provides a holistic developmental perspective on aging. It highlights a range of issues, including the development of personal meaning and spirituality, improvements in emotional control, uses of reminiscence and life review, the importance of healthy attitudes to aging, as well as the maintenance of close personal relationships. It does not avoid the difficult issues of late life decline, but illustrates how even in circumstances of physical and mental frailty a positive sense of self can be created and enhanced.

Fully updated to provide the most cutting-edge overview on this burgeoning topic of interest, *Aging and Development* includes a glossary and list of useful websites both on the study of gerontology and the psychology of aging. It will be essential reading for all students of developmental psychology, as well as anyone either training to work or already working with older people.

Peter G. Coleman is Emeritus Professor of Psychogerontology at the University of Southampton, UK. He has made major research contributions to the developmental study of aging, particularly in the fields of reminiscence and spirituality, and has been teaching specialist courses on aging to psychologists, social workers, doctors and other health professionals for over forty years. In 2015 he was given the 'Outstanding Achievement Award' of the British Society of Gerontology.

Ann O'Hanlon is a psychologist and CBT therapist, who has directed several European Union projects on aging. She works in the South Eastern HSC Trust in Northern Ireland, and leads a transnational project promoting kindness initiatives at all levels of society. In 2014 she was given an Excellence Award with the British Association of Behavioural and Cognitive Psychotherapy for her work addressing social anxiety with older adults.

International Texts in Developmental Psychology

Series editor: Peter K. Smith, Goldsmiths College,
University of London, UK.

This volume is one of a rapidly developing series in *International Texts in Developmental Psychology*, published by Routledge. The books in this series are selected to be state-of-the-art, high-level introductions to major topic areas in developmental psychology. The series conceives of developmental psychology in broad terms and covers such areas as social development, cognitive development, developmental neuropsychology and neuroscience, language development, learning difficulties, developmental psychopathology and applied issues. Each volume is written by a specialist (or specialists), combining empirical data and a synthesis of recent global research to deliver cutting-edge science in a format accessible to students and researchers alike. The books may be used as textbooks that match on to upper-level developmental psychology modules, but many will also have cross-disciplinary appeal.

Each volume in the series is published in hardback, paperback and eBook formats. More information about the series is available on the official website at: https://www.routledge.com/International-Texts-in-Developmental-Psychology/book-series/DEVP, including details of all the titles published to date.

Published titles

The Child at School: Interactions with Peers and Teachers, 2nd edition
By Peter Blatchford, Anthony D. Pellegrini and Ed Baines

Children's Literacy Development: A Cross-Cultural Perspective on Learning to Read and Write, 2nd edition
By Catherine McBride

Childhood Friendships and Peer Relations: Friends and Enemies, 2nd edition
By Barry Schneider

Aging and Development: Social and Emotional Perspectives, 2nd edition
By Peter G. Coleman and Ann O'Hanlon

I'm feeling angry right now, but don't worry. I'm not going to attack you. But I do need your help.

Is this a good time to talk?

VERSES TO MEMORIZE

"A fool gives full vent to his anger, but a wise man keeps himself under control." (**PROVERBS 29:11**)

"An angry man stirs up dissension, and a hot-tempered one commits many sins." (**PROVERBS 29:22**)

"A quick-tempered man does foolish things." (**PROVERBS 14:17**)

"A patient man has great understanding, but a quick-tempered man displays folly." (**PROVERBS 14:29**)

"'In your anger do not sin': Do not let the sun go down while you are still angry, and do not give the devil a foothold." (**EPHESIANS 4:26–27**)

FIVE STEPS TO HANDLE VALID ANGER

1 *Consciously acknowledge to yourself that you are angry.*

2 *Restrain your immediate response.*

3 *Locate the focus of your anger.*

4 *Analyze your options.*

5 *Take constructive action.*

AGING AND DEVELOPMENT

Social and Emotional Perspectives
Second Edition

Peter G. Coleman and Ann O'Hanlon

LONDON AND NEW YORK

This edition published 2017
by Routledge
2 Park Square, Milton Park, Abingdon, Oxon OX14 4RN

and by Routledge
711 Third Avenue, New York, NY 10017

Routledge is an imprint of the Taylor & Francis Group, an informa business

First edition published in 2004 by Routledge

British Library Cataloguing in Publication Data
A catalogue record for this book is available from the British Library

Library of Congress Cataloging in Publication Data
Names: Coleman, Peter G., author. | O'Hanlon, Ann, PhD, author.
Title: Aging and development : social and emotional perspectives /
    Peter G. Coleman and Ann O'Hanlon.
Other titles: Ageing and development
Description: 2nd edition. | Abingdon, Oxon ; New York, NY : Routledge,
    2017. | Series: International texts in developmental psychology |
    Earlier edition published as: Ageing and development : theories
    and research / [by] Peter G. Coleman, Ann O'Hanlon. | Includes
    bibliographical references and index.
Identifiers: LCCN 2016035115| ISBN 9781848723269 (hardback : alk.
    paper) | ISBN 9781848723276 (pbk. : alk. paper) |
    ISBN 9781315726946 (ebook)
Subjects: LCSH: Aging—Psychological aspects. | Age (Psychology) |
    Adaptability (Psychology) in old age. | Aging—Social aspects.
Classification: LCC BF724.55.A35 C65 2017 | DDC 155.67—dc23
LC record available at https://lccn.loc.gov/2016035115

ISBN: 978-1-84872-326-9 (hbk)
ISBN: 978-1-84872-327-6 (pbk)
ISBN: 978-1-315-72694-6 (ebk)

Typeset in Bembo
by Swales & Willis Ltd, Exeter, Devon, UK
Printed and bound by CPI Group (UK) Ltd, Croydon, CR0 4YY

To the memory of Jim Birren (1918–2016),
mentor extraordinary

CONTENTS

ILLUSTRATIONS

Figures

Tables

Boxes

PREFACE

The psychological study of aging has developed strongly in the twelve years since the first edition of this textbook, including greater attention to the developmental aspects of growing old. The subject also shows signs of moving beyond its North American and European origins. This is greatly needed because Western culture with its deeply rooted negativity to aging provides an inadequate basis on which to generalise about the potentials of later life. Fresh perspectives are required.

A number of changes have been introduced to this edition. Perhaps the most significant is the greater consideration we have given to research findings on the role played by emotions in older people's lives. This reflects the remarkable progress of research programmes examining age changes in emotional processing, led primarily by American and German psychologists. The important theory of socioemotional selectivity underlies much of this research.

Our first edition aimed to draw attention to the need for increasing attention to the later stages of aging, but thirteen years ago we could draw on relatively little developmental theory and research applied to people beyond the age of 80 and 90 years. There is at last much greater interest in involving very old people in all forms of research and we are pleased that we can title the third part of this book 'Development and adaptation in advanced old age' without employing more tentative terms.

I thank Ann O'Hanlon for her willingness to continue as co-author. Her areas of expertise complement my own and together we are able to present a more balanced consideration of the developmental psychology of aging. We have maintained the first edition's focus on the research process and have selected particular topics for more detailed presentation. Thus chapters overviewing a large field of study alternate with chapters providing accounts of recent research projects within that study area. The topics selected are ones in which we have either conducted research ourselves or taken a close personal interest. As we aim to give an impression of current research activities we have selected most of our illustrations from studies conducted in the last decade or so. This means that even where we have chosen the same topic as in the first edition our account of it is largely new.

Naturally we think that all the subjects we have selected for special attention are important ones – others may disagree – but, as the topics we have chosen are inter-related, we hope that we have produced a more coherent and integrated account than would have resulted from a more representative but less connected selection of research areas. The developmental psychology of aging is potentially a very large subject. Ours is only one perspective. We look forward to future advanced texts in this field that will improve on our work.

The years of life referred to variously as 'old age' and 'late' or 'later life' are not only quantitatively an important part of the lifespan. They are and have always been an essential and meaningful part of the lifespan. It is not necessary for every-one to reach this stage of life, but it has probably been important for the stability and vitality of human culture that a significant minority of society did so in every period of history.

Now increasing proportions of the world's population live to experience their own old age, and for them as for previous generations it is important to use the opportunity of these additional years not only to continue previous activities but to reflect on the life they have experienced so far and to give witness to lasting values. Later life can be a time for continued achievement and for fresh understanding, but above all it is a time for appreciating what life means, even as the conditions that sustain life become more precarious.

I remain grateful to Peter Smith for his invitation to contribute to this devel-opmental psychology series and to Routledge for proposing a second edition. Hopefully in the future this series or future like-minded series will contain a variety of developmental books on aging. For the present it is sufficient that a developmental perspective on aging is recognised as important to the study of developmental psychology.

This book is dedicated to Jim Birren, a mentor extraordinary to so many both in and outside the field of the psychology of aging. But I would also like to acknowl-edge the help and support of the many psychologists I have studied and worked with, including Pat Rabbitt, Sheila Chown, Dennis Bromley, Joep Munnichs, Paul Remmerswaal, Jan-Erik Ruth, Tony Gale and Bob Woods. I would also like to thank friends and colleagues in psychology in Southampton during the past few years who have helped provide me with new perspectives on aging and development, especially Rik Cheston and John Spreadbury.

Peter G. Coleman,
Southampton, March 2016

1

INTRODUCTION

Aging and development

This book describes psychological theory and research about aging from a developmental perspective. This may seem an unusual way of approaching a subject more commonly associated with physical and mental decline, but if so this is because we have adopted Western culture's exaggeratedly negative stance towards what it is like to grow old. Especially now that aging has become such a common experience we need to look at it afresh, and with eyes widened by new considerations of the benefits and potentials of the gift of a long life. Even though it can be defined precisely in biological terms, aging is also from another perspective a social construction. How we perceive age varies from culture to culture and from one historical period to another.

A principal value of theory in the social and human sciences is that it provides new ways of considering human life which we may think prematurely that we already understand. Of course we do know a lot about life just by being part of it, but we are always in need of new insights that allow us to imagine new possibilities. Despite the subsequent criticisms of the detailed content of his theory, Sigmund Freud's emphasis on the early origins of human emotional difficulties has made us see childhood in a way that is different to those of previous historical periods. As a result we are more ready than our predecessors to accept the importance of sensitive periods in people's lives. Yet theory can at the same time also be a hindrance to fresh thought. An over-deterministic view of the consequences of childhood trauma and deprivation for the remaining parts of the life course may have made people overly pessimistic about the possibilities for therapy and effecting positive change in adulthood. Even after the substantial research endeavours of Michael Rutter and others outlining the redemptive effects of positive relationships in adolescence and young adulthood on those abused in childhood, the legacy of childhood determinism still looms large in psychology and in society generally.

Theory then is a double-edged sword. It points in new directions while at the same time barring the way along alternative paths. It is for this reason that we are always in need of new theoretical input. Scientific understanding is always provisional, the best approximation until the next more comprehensive system is developed. A little humility is appropriate therefore about any one theory, and safety is better in numbers. Keeping company with a number of theories, appreciating their strengths, recognising their weaknesses, observing how they get on together, taking others on board as one can, is the best recipe for continued growth. Also since we want to understand better the psychology of the individual person, we benefit from a wide range of perspectives. No one theory is likely to satisfy our curiosity about the complexities of human behaviour and experience.

Theory and research share an intimate relationship. Theory is the starting point for research. Research can also produce new theory, but without at least some interpretative framework it is impossible to make coherent observations. We need to take our stand on some basic assumptions. In psychology, for example, careful observation of the individual person can provide ideas that form the assumptions for subsequent larger-scale investigations. It is often assumed that quality of research methodology is the main test of useful research. The choice of theoretical ideas to test, their origin and rationale, are seen as less controversial. But ideas too have their history and require nurturing as well as critical examination. It is important not to be misled by unproven propositions, but equally we should not raise barriers to prevent us from acknowledging additional perspectives that may be helpful.

As part of a developmental series, this book is concerned to introduce readers to ways of thinking about growing old as continued growth, in which persons in later life continue to develop new capacities and adapt successfully to the physical and social problems that arise, such as increasing likelihood of health problems and experience of loss. It is not a book about the psychological decrements of aging. This is not to deny that these issues exist and that they are worthy of study. In fact most of the early work in the psychology of aging was of this character, for example in the performance comparisons between different age groups pioneered in Britain by Francis Galton. Their subsequent dominance of the field has made it almost natural to associate the psychology of aging with the psychology of decline. There are excellent introductory books available on cognitive aging that detail findings on changes in performance with age in various fields such as memory, reaction time and problem solving. This book is about the emotional, relational and internal responses to living a long time that reveal the more positive side of the experience of aging.

'Aging' itself is an ambiguous term. Strictly speaking it refers to the accumulation of time that one lives. But often it is used to imply decline, as when we talk about a machine that ages, or when we refer to biological processes of deterioration in functioning. Psychological aging is a different matter. Processes of loss and gain take place throughout the life cycle. Children's more spontaneous approach to the world around them tends to disappear as intellectual and social developments proceed. This is also a form of aging, but we accept it as part of child development.

If the losses of later life impress us more than the gains, it could be because in the Westernised world we exaggerate the losses and do not sufficiently value the gains. This does not have to be the case. Other cultures have a better appreciation of the spiritual developments that physical decline and changing social roles in fact help make possible.

The study of aging has long suffered from an inadequate cultural and societal basis to the data on which social and psychological theorising is based. Although there have been noticeable advances in recent years, particularly in Asian societies, the vast majority of major studies have been conducted in North America and Western Europe. A good example of the limitations arising from this restricted data base have been shown by recent European Union data that highlight differences in the relationship between age and well-being even within the relatively small part of the world constituted by European countries. Analysis shows that the relatively late peaks of well-being, in the seventh decade and beyond, reported in younger older persons within North American and Western European societies are not paralleled in less wealthy Eastern European societies. In the latter countries declines in levels of expressed happiness already begin in middle age and continue into old age (Morgan et al., 2015; Steptoe et al., 2015). There is also considerable variation even among Western European countries in older people's expressed well-being (Ploubidis and Grundy, 2009). These findings remind us that psychological change with age occurs in a social context.

Nevertheless, it is good to see that the literature on developmental issues related to aging is expanding, but as a result this book has to be more selective than its predecessor. We cannot do justice to all current theoretical ideas, let alone all important research findings. Our text has been constructed in three parts, the first dealing with the study of developmental change with age, the second with processes of adaptation to physical and social aging and the various resources older people employ to do this successfully, while the third concentrates on the later stages of aging considering issues relating to both development and adaptation. Each part contains a chapter on development of thinking and theory construction followed by a chapter on selected research projects conducted over the last twenty years on topics relevant to the theory already described.

In Chapter 2 we consider what have now become classic developmental accounts of aging written by psychodynamic theorists, particularly Erik Erikson's psychosocial model of successive life tasks, as well as currently influential theories based on systematic observation, including Laura Carstensen's socio-emotional selectivity (SES) theory, and more recent developmental hypotheses such as Lars Tornstam's theory of gerotranscendence. It is possible to regard some of these theories, such as SES theory, as normative accounts of average trends with age, but others, such as gerotranscendence theory, as ideal models of adult development and aging that provide descriptions of what is possible and also desirable in advanced age.

Such theorising may seem too prescriptive in contemporary postmodern societies that prefer to leave value choices to the individual. But they contain important notions about aging that continue to have resonance. They can be considered in historical terms as reactions to the denigration of age that had become a habitual thought pattern by the early twentieth century. Psychodynamic thinkers such as Jung and Erikson and succeeding theorists of adult development have sought to provide guidance on the purpose and meaning to living a long life. Many of them have found inspiration in studies of traditional cultures outside of the Western mainstream.

In Chapter 3 we present three distinct areas of current research investigation on normative development in later life. The first is 'emotion regulation', a field of research on age changes that has grown considerably in recent years. In contrast to the study of cognition it presents the experience of aging in a much more favourable light. Much of the work has been inspired by the developmental theory of socio-emotional selectivity, but in turn has also given rise to further more specific theorising about what distinguishes the emotional responses of younger and older people. The second topic we have selected is 'generativity', Erik Erikson's original focus on midlife development, a subject relatively neglected until reawakened at the end of the twentieth century, particularly by the US personality theorist and researcher Dan McAdams. We consider attempts to operationalise and measure this concept, as well as recent research that examines generativity's role in adult development and its implications for well-being in later life.

The final developmental topic we have chosen to highlight is an area of research with many practical implications, influenced by Erikson's concept of 'integrity', but even more so by Robert Butler's theory of the 'life review'. This reflects a powerful traditional myth, the replaying of life's key scenes in the mind's eye preceding death. However, empirical investigation suggests that reminiscence has various other functions too, and that life review itself is not a universal phenomenon. Much of our discussion of reminiscence focuses on the conceptual clarification that often has to take place before research can progress further. But we also give attention to the progress recently made by researchers evaluating reminiscence and life review interventions.

Chapters 4 and 5 constitute the second part of the book and consider approaches to aging and development that have become more popular since the 1970s. These are mainly attributable to the rise of the study of lifespan developmental psychology, associated especially with the pioneering work of researchers in the United States and Germany. This school of researchers has come to eschew what it would regard as over-simplistic normative developmental theory in favour of a more plastic view of adult development. It has followed Erikson though in showing a preference for an interdisciplinary view of human development, in which social, historical and cultural influences play a key influence. However, these external influences act not just to support or inhibit intrinsic psychological strivings and potential, but determine in a more direct way the structure and goals of life by establishing societal life patterns that guide development.

This is not necessarily a more deterministic view of aging. Theorists working in this field stress human plasticity right until advanced age, and the possibilities for adaptation to change that exist both at the individual and the social level.

Generalisation, however, is difficult, except at the more abstract level of defining the limits of human competence and adaptability. Interesting questions arise about the different trajectories people can follow through life. Differentiation, not standardisation, is the norm and becomes greater with age. Thus there is no one path to 'successful aging', but rather different styles of living, managing change, and surviving. The previously popular concept of 'adjustment' has been superseded by less value-laden concepts such as adaptation and coping. However, we have kept a link with developmental theory by including consideration of attachment styles as important influences upon adaptation to aging.

In Chapter 5 we illustrate research in this area with three further distinct topic areas. The first is attitudes to aging. This was a neglected area of research until recently but one that we consider to be of great importance to developments in research on adaptation to aging. Anxiety about aging appears to be on the increase in many Western societies. We pay particular attention to the factors that influence people's prospective views on their own personal futures, as well as the importance of combatting ageist attitudes within society towards older adults. The second topic is the supportive role of relationships, and the challenges faced by older people who experience distressing levels of loneliness in the absence of such relationships. Also reviewed are caregiving challenges within close relationships, and recovery from the loss of close relationships following bereavement.

The final topic in this chapter is meaning, spirituality and religion, a relatively new but rapidly expanding area of research activity. As many novels on the theme of aging illustrate, questions of meaning, both of one's own life and also of life in general, become critical in the later years. This is an area of research where conceptual issues are particularly complex and where generational differences are most marked. We therefore give attention to both these issues before reviewing recent research on associations with well-being and coping in later life.

The third part of the book (Chapters 6 and 7) focuses on advanced old age. This is the period of life that has come to be called the 'fourth age', when the optimal conditions for self-determination that distinguish the 'third age' begin to be seriously diminished by the biological limitations of aging. This is not typically thought of as a time of development, but in fact very late life provides some of the most remarkable illustrations of adaptation, and of successful coping with very taxing life situations. Perhaps because we find it more difficult to identify with those facing massive loss of control and of energy at this stage of life, we do not appreciate as we should the sometimes dramatic behaviour changes that older people display in the face of these challenges.

As Paul Baltes has emphasised, extreme old age, in its present pervasive character and duration, is a relatively new stage of life, and we do not yet have adequate conceptual frameworks with which to understand it. The early developmental theories of the lifespan did not include consideration of the fourth age. Yet by the middle of this century the numbers of the very old will have greatly increased. In the more wealthy parts of the world the numbers over 85 years of age may well exceed those aged under 5 years. This was an issue that both Erik Erikson and his wife Joan wrestled with at the end of their lives. Erik Erikson himself lived to 92 years and spent his last period in a nursing home. An extended life in some form of care or assisted-living setting is to be expected by most of those who live to a great age.

The models of coping that have been found helpful in understanding adaptation at earlier periods of life seem less than adequate when applied to the fourth age. More close observation and reflection are needed. Fortunately for this new edition we have been able to draw on the greatly increased research activity regarding the psychology of late life that has taken place since the beginning of the century. In Chapter 6 we give particular attention to what is known about the psychological characteristics of the very old as well as to theorising about the benefits to them of processes of accommodation and self-transcendence in facing the seemingly inevitable declines of late life. We also give particular attention to the study of well-being both in care settings and living with dementia.

In Chapter 7 we examine examples of research in three areas. The first concerns maintenance of sense of self, one of the longest studied topics in the psychology of aging, but now needing to be extended to the ages of 90, 100 and beyond. We consider recent studies on the benefits of processes of accommodation in late life. We also examine the extension of socio-emotional selectivity theory in studies that reveal the greater emotional complexity in the psychology of very old people. A further research example illustrates the value of individual case analysis in studying adaptation to the later stages of aging. The second topic examines examples of recent research illustrating the importance of meeting need for both autonomy and relatedness of residents in care and assisted-living settings. In the final part we describe two areas of current research activity both of which are helping to promote living well with dementia: first understanding and encouraging processes of adaptation to a diagnosis of dementia, and second adjusting the care provided to the needs of each person. In this last example we illustrate how well-conducted research can lead to improvements in quality of life in its last stages.

In our concluding Chapter 8 we draw some brief lessons from our survey of theories and research on developmental aspects of aging. We indicate some of the special features that we consider necessary to further development of studies in this field. We also give some advice on further reading, as well as a list of useful websites and a glossary explaining important terms in the study of gerontology that may not be immediately understood by all our readers.

PART I

Developmental perspectives on aging

Wisdom is detached concern with life itself, in the face of death itself . . .
(Erikson et al., 1986)

2

THEORIES OF ADULT DEVELOPMENT

Midlife to old age

From relatively small beginnings the study of aging has come a long way in the last fifty years. The importance of the subject has been recognised over a large range of academic disciplines, particularly biology, sociology and psychology, but also demography, geography, anthropology and economics, as well as the humanities and arts. This broadening of interest has led to new questions. We can see better now that the experience of aging is the product not only of inevitable biological and psychological processes, nor even of the individual's particular life history and circumstances, but also of the attitudes, expectations, prejudices and ideals of the societies and cultures in which people develop and grow old. Some present-day investigators have been led to explore how certain images, models and assumptions about the nature of aging lie behind everyday speech, and how the very language we use may encourage or inhibit older people, and even promote their decline (Coupland, 2004).

It is important therefore to begin this account of theories and ideas on development in later life with a reflection on the importance of attitudes towards aging. Not so long ago it would have been thought paradoxical to say the least to include a chapter on 'development' in a book about aging, let alone publish a whole book with that title. A simplistic perspective of the lifespan as 'rise and fall' is deeply embedded within Western culture. It is most graphically depicted in the medieval and later representations of the ages of man, in which the path of later life is one of remorseless decline (Burrow, 1986; Cole, 1992; Thane, 2005). It is important to bear in mind that such taken-for-granted assumptions about the course of life may be very different in other cultures. For example, Hindu culture traditionally speaks of stages of life not in terms of rise and fall but of a forward cyclical movement (Tilak, 1989; Ram-Prasad, 1995).

As a consequence of the social changes brought about in the historical period we call the 'Enlightenment', with its emphasis on reason rather than tradition, and the subsequent industrial and technological revolutions, attitudes to older people seem to have become more disrespectful (Fischer, 1978). Their expertise was seen as based on outmoded ways of behaviour and therefore less relevant to a fast-changing society. This change was also accompanied by a declining concern for the spiritual meaning of aging (Cole and Edwards, 2005). It is not surprising therefore that when the first attempts were made in the nineteenth century to study scientifically the behaviour and performance of people of different ages, it was natural to adopt a pessimistic stance. Even a thinker as imaginative as Freud conformed to the pattern, viewing people above the age of 50 as too inflexible to be able to benefit from the practice of psychoanalysis (Biggs, 2005). Such thinking about age is so ingrained in our culture that we are hardly conscious of what we say. It lies behind many of our casual comments about age, such as 'being over the top' and 'past it' and the unflattering depictions in birthday cards designated for older people.

With the rise in the numbers of older people within the populations particularly of Europe and North America in the latter parts of the twentieth century, a change in attitudes to age was demanded. The term 'ageism' has been coined to refer to the unjustified attribution of characteristics to persons on the basis of their chronological age (Butler, 1987; Bytheway, 1995, 2011), and legislation introduced to prohibit unfair discrimination on the basis of age. As Figure 2.1 illustrates,

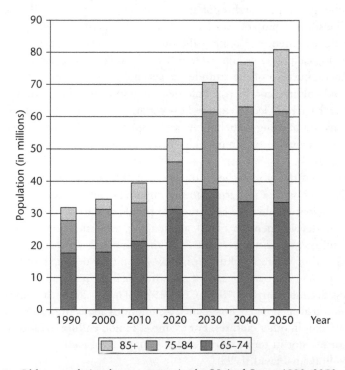

FIGURE 2.1   Older population by age group in the United States 1990–2050.

Source: Poon et al. (2005, p. 347): reprinted with permission, Cambridge University Press.

the number of older people has been rising steadily in Western societies such as the United States, with attention now being focused both on the increase of those over retirement age and those in the oldest age groups more likely to require support. Notable increases are projected for all regions in the world with the highest proportion of over 65s (25.2 per cent) and over 80s (8.8 per cent) expected to arise in Europe in 2050, followed by the Western Pacific region and the Americas (Peace et al., 2007). We will focus on the issue of support services to the very old in Chapter 6.

The encouragement of positive and constructive attitudes to older people is one of the main themes of this book. We now have the evidence that older people are capable of much more than we sometimes imagine, and that they can be flexible and learn new things. What often holds them back are the negative expectations of others and, perhaps even more importantly, of themselves. But we must also avoid going to the opposite extreme, by almost demanding new qualities from individuals regardless of their circumstances and particular experience of life. As the French historian of old age Minois (1989) noted, some of the cruellest societies to the old have been those in which the highest standards of wisdom, serenity and maturity were expected of them. The questions surrounding growth and decline, change and development throughout life are very complex.

In this chapter we will consider some of the theories and models proposed over the last century about ideal patterns of psychological aging. We will first present the developmental concepts of Carl Jung, Alfred Adler and especially Erik Erikson, all practising psychotherapists from a psychoanalytic tradition, who were some of the first psychologists to show interest in exploring personality development in later life even though their primary involvement was in working with younger persons. We will then chart the history of more systematic empirical study of age differences in social and emotional behaviour in the post-Second World War years, beginning with the research work conducted by the University of Chicago Committee for Human Development in the 1950s and 1960s. The subsequent expansion of lifespan developmental studies will be described both in North America and in Europe. This will include some of the newer developmental models and theories of aging, including 'gerotranscendence' and 'socio-emotional selectivity theory'. We conclude with a discussion of attempts to study the intriguing but difficult concept of wisdom in relation to age.

Psychodynamic theories

Modern psychological theorising about human development began in central Europe in the late nineteenth century. Whatever one may think of the detail of his theories, Sigmund Freud (1856–1939) revolutionised thinking about human behaviour by proposing a dynamic model for human motivation and opened up interest in much broader fields of psychology than cognitive performance alone. He stressed that people did not always act in rational ways nor were they necessarily aware of the bases of their action. Freud and his immediate followers were not strictly speaking psychologists but clinicians involved in the treatment of mentally disturbed people, but in a short period of time at the turn of the century they produced a wealth of ideas about human motivation, often conflicting and so broad ranging that they have not yet been properly examined.

Freud himself did not consider the processes of human aging in any detail, and his description of developmental stages is limited to the very early periods of life. But his one-time colleague Carl Jung (1875–1961), who broke away from Freud to establish a rival school of psychoanalysis, did give much greater importance to what he called the second half of life. For him midlife was a crucial turning point when the individual was provided with opportunities for new developments. These were less to do with involvement in the outside world than with more interior processes that he referred to with the term 'individuation'. A person could achieve a new balance in personality, a man accepting his 'feminine' as well as 'masculine' aspects for example. Jung laid great stress on the value of symbolic and religious experience in creating a state of harmony between the individual and the world around, and derived evidence for his theories from his wide-ranging knowledge of other cultures and societies (Jung, 1972). Jung's ideas on development in midlife have been very influential and have been reflected in the work of later psychologists of adult development such as Daniel Levinson (Levinson et al., 1978; Levinson, 1996).

Another of Freud's associates, Alfred Adler (1870–1937) also came to stress different aspects of human motivation (Adler, 1927). Disagreeing with Freud's stress on the overriding importance of sexuality he proposed instead that the prime motivating force in all people's lives is a feeling of inferiority. All individuals have this feeling to some extent because of the weak position they once occupied as children, when power and privilege were exerted by adults. Some feel this more strongly than others, for example as a result of physical defects or heavy-handed parenting. Adler saw subsequent developments of an individual's lifestyle as a means of compensating for feelings of inferiority. In extreme examples this could take the positive form of remarkable achievements by people with handicaps, but could also be expressed negatively in excessively self-assertive behaviour. Adler himself saw the most successful resolution of problems of inferiority to be in involvement with others, in the development of 'social interest'.

The particular relevance to psychogerontology of Adler's theory is that he realised feelings of inferiority and loss of self-esteem could become major issues again in later life, as a result of changing status with retirement from work, bereavement, bodily decline and loss of capacities. At the same time possibilities for developing new close friendships to sustain identity and self-esteem tend to diminish. In Adlerian terms rigid, prejudiced and rejecting attitudes on the part of older people could be seen as resulting from a fear of comparison with younger people. The perspective of an Adlerian approach to therapy was essentially constructive. Inferiority feelings and neurotic lifestyles could be overcome by helping the individual to develop a wider interest in others, including the younger generation, and to cultivate a sense of belonging again.

Erikson's model of developmental tasks

Like Jung and Adler, Erik Erikson's primary focus was not on old age per se, but he argued that all stages of development, including early life, could not be studied without reference to the whole lifespan. One of his main contributions to developmental psychology was his recognition that child development had to be understood within the context of the child's particular social environment, and that this was peopled by adults who were confronted by their own developmental tasks. In his book *Childhood and Society* (Erikson, 1950/1963) he provided a highly influential framework for the study of the lifespan, which he described in terms of a series of psychosocial tasks to be fulfilled. Thus the child's, or rather baby's, first psychological task in life Jung describes as developing a sense of trust rather than a sense of mistrust. The ensuing childhood stages are characterised in terms of 'autonomy', 'initiative' and 'industry'. In adolescence the issue is the development of 'ego identity' versus 'identity diffusion' – Erikson is probably best known for his formulation of the concept of 'identity crisis' as something particularly characteristic of modern man – and in early adulthood the development of 'intimacy' versus a sense of 'isolation'.

In middle age the issue becomes one of 'generativity', a term coined by Erikson himself but which has now become widely accepted. He describes it as 'primarily the interest in establishing and guiding the next generation'. This can mean a focus on one's own family but it can also include broader interests and concerns in the society in which one lives. The opposite state Erikson calls 'stagnation' for which he offers a succinct illustration: 'individuals, then, often begin to indulge themselves as if they were their own – or one another's – one and only child' (Erikson, 1963, p. 259). The task of the last stage of life is to attain 'ego integrity', an assured sense of meaning and order in one's life and in the universe, as against despair and disgust. This involves 'acceptance of one's one and only life cycle as something that had to be and that, by necessity, permitted of no substitutions' (Erikson, 1963, p. 260). Despair may be expressed in a feeling that one has failed and does not have the time to attempt another life or an alternative road to integrity, and also in disgust with other people, especially the young.

In Erikson's theory the developmental stages are conceived as hierarchically arranged, the next stages presupposing the development of the previous stage. But even if the next stage is built upon the previous stage it does not replace that earlier stage. So when a person's development through the life cycle is coming to a completion in old age, that stage represents the summation of all earlier stages, including the psychological strengths (or weaknesses) that the person has acquired. Throughout life the developmental phases come together creating a whole. They arise in turn, each part having its time of special ascendancy, until all parts have risen to form a functional whole. In the end, a person may reach the highest stage of ego-integrity, gaining wisdom through pondering upon the life that has been lived and pulling the various parts of life's puzzle together, or, at the opposite pole, experiencing despair at what life did not bring. Although he argues for a universal genetic blueprint, Erikson acknowledges that individuals can proceed through the stages in varying tempo and intensity.

Achieving ego integrity does not only involve reflecting on one's own life. It also involves an acceptance of the society that will continue after one's own death. Ill health and the other stresses of later life may lead to self-absorption with one's own problems unless interest in the world outside can be maintained. Yet if society is to be so different from the one known, if it appears likely to overthrow or indeed had already overthrown the values that were so important in guiding one's own life, it can be harder to die. It needs courage and imagination to see through the different manifestations of human interests and activities and to perceive an underlying constancy. Erikson refers to 'the comradeship with the ordering ways of distant times and different pursuits' and the 'relativity of all the various lifestyles which have given meaning to human striving' (Erikson, 1963, p. 260). These developments bring about in his view a new way of being, which he characterises as 'truly involved dis-involvement' whose product is wisdom. Acceptance of death is also central to this stage of life. In fact Erikson brings his account of the life cycle full circle with the closing statement 'it seems possible to further paraphrase the relation of adult integrity and infantile trust by saying that healthy children will not fear life if their elders have integrity enough not to fear death' (Erikson, 1963, p. 261).

Erikson's interest in the whole of the human lifespan was also reflected in his contributions to psychobiography. His earlier theories were based in large part on the narrative case studies he had written on his clients. But he later came to write two major books analysing important historical persons, Martin Luther and Mahatma Gandhi. His analysis of the latter, which won the Pulitzer Prize throws particular light on the passage from identity to generativity concerns, and how in Gandhi this generativity became gradually broader in its scope (Erikson, 1970). Later in his career Erikson returned to the subject of aging. Together with his wife, Joan, and psychologist Helen Kivnick he elaborated on the personal qualities people brought to their old age as a result of successful completion of each developmental stage: 'hope', 'will', 'purpose', 'competence', 'fidelity', 'love', 'care' and 'wisdom' (Erikson et al., 1986). Helen Kivnick and others have introduced these concepts into care settings with the aim of getting staff to look beyond older persons' problems, to include the 'life strengths' they had developed in their assessments, and to consolidate and build on them (Kivnick, 1991; Pomeroy et al., 1997) (see Table 2.1).

Erikson's theory of adult development has been and remains highly influential (Hoare, 2002). Its central concepts of identity, intimacy and generativity continue to form the theoretical background of research into influences on positive development (McAdams, 2006; Sneed et al., 2012; Jones and McAdams, 2013). His final stage of integrity has also been more investigated in recent years, with particular attention to its key characteristics and associations with other features of well-being in later life (Sneed et al., 2006; Hearn et al., 2012; Westerhof et al., 2016), but its aspect of death acceptance remains neglected. Death in general has been given insufficient importance within gerontology (Neijmeyer and Werth, 2005;

TABLE 2.1 Erikson's model of developmental tasks and resulting life strengths

Stage of emergence	Developmental tasks	Consequent life strengths
Infancy	Trust vs mistrust	Hope & faith
Early childhood	Autonomy vs shame, doubt	Wilfulness, independence & control
Play age	Initiative vs guilt	Purposefulness, pleasure & imagination
School age	Industry vs inferiority	Competence & hard work
Adolescence	Identity vs indentity confusion	Values & sense of self
Young adulthood	Intimacy vs isolation	Love & friendship
Middle adulthood	Generativity vs stagnation	Care & productivity
Old age	Integrity vs despair	Wisdom & perspective

Johnson, 2009).The theories of aging that do consider the significance of death appear exceptional, such as disengagement theory (which we will consider in the next part) and Butler's (1963) concept of the life review, triggered by awareness of death's approach. Joep Munnichs, perhaps more than any other psychogerontologist, has emphasised how the growing awareness and acceptance of finitude is a major developmental task of later life (Munnichs, 1966, 1992).

There have been various criticisms of Erikson's theory, including that he underestimates the significance of biological change and over-stresses psychological development of the individual as part of the social system. Moreover his view of harmony between inner development and external environment, that 'society, in principle, tends to be so constituted as to meet and invite this succession of potentialities for interaction' (Erikson, 1963, p. 270) has been thought too optimistic. In fact it is rather paradoxical that in spite of Erikson's readiness to accept the impact of culture and historical period on development, the theory clearly reflects norms and values from the 1950s. The timing of life events, rights, obligations and roles tied to different ages – the social construction of the lifespan – has changed since then. Erikson has also been seen as paying insufficient attention to negative developments, for example the 'bad products' of human life, how a person can become a mentor of evil, ensuring that the next generation carries on with destruction as the previous one (Kotre, 1996).

As he grew older, Erikson seems to have become more aware of the shortcomings in his earlier descriptions of late life. In his last book (Erikson et al., 1986, p. 336) he raised the question of the need to add further stages to his scheme, but refrained from doing so in the end. After her husband's death Joan Erikson continued to ponder on the need for changing the theory. In a letter to social gerontologist Lars Tornstam, to whose gerotranscendence theory we will refer later, she wrote after becoming acquainted with his work:

> When I got 91 myself, I became aware of the inadequacy of the words 'wisdom' and 'integrity', feeling that they in no way represent what I was

experiencing as an elder . . . So boldly I revised the eight stage . . . including
a ninth and tenth stage, which even attempt to deal with 'gerotranscendence'.

(Cited in Tornstam, 1996b, p. 48)

On the basis of Joan Erikson's and Tornstam's statements some psychologists have
attempted to assess a possible further stage beyond integrity in persons aged in their
eighties and nineties (Brown and Lewis, 2003).

However, there seems to have been no real interest in radically modifying
Erikson's model of the life course to fit better with a changed sociocultural system.
As a result his system remains as it appeared when it was first created in 1950. It
has no real imitators. In regard to the study of aging, its main and lasting contribution seems to have brought to the forefront of gerontological concern questions to
do with the psychological and social conditions necessary for later life to flourish.
Erikson's descriptions of 'generativity' and 'integrity' as the tasks of the latter part of
life have continued to resonate in research on aging, and in the following chapter we
will give detailed attention to recent research on the concept of generativity and its
significance for the mental health and well-being of older people.

Theories based on empirical investigation

The theories of Jung, Adler and Erikson on adult development were based on
a wide range of clinical and other observations, as well as considerable personal
reflection, but were not developed in the context of empirical scientific enquiry.
Of course the long time spans involved make investigating adult development
inherently very demanding. The opportunity for the large-scale research required
to validate theoretical ideas, including the necessary academic infrastructure of
institutional support for such investigation, did not begin to be put in place until
the 1950s. One of the first centres to emerge in the field of aging studies was
established at the University of Chicago, the self-named Committee for Human
Development, a collaborating group of scholars that included both sociologists
and psychologists. The theories that developed from their pioneering work came
to provide more precise ideas on developmental patterns of aging during the
1950s and 1960s (Havighurst and Albrecht, 1953; Cumming and Henry, 1961;
Neugarten and Associates, 1964).

Robert Havighurst (1948/1972) elaborated on Erikson's notion of developmental task, attempting to delineate in more detail the major social-psychological
accomplishments expected of a person in early, middle and late adulthood. For
example, he described the developmental tasks of middle age (35–60 years) as
achieving adult responsibilities within the personal and social sector; maintaining
economic standards of living; relating to one's spouse as an individual; guiding
one's teenage children to become independent and responsible persons; establishing adult leisure time activities; accepting the changes of one's middle-aged body;
and adjusting to one's aging parents. By contrast the developmental tasks of later life
(beyond 60 years) were listed as meeting civic and social obligations and preparing

for retirement; adjusting to reduced income in retirement; arranging for satisfactory living arrangements; making an explicit affiliation with one's age group; adjusting to one's declining physical strength; and adjusting to the death of one's spouse. This statement of 'tasks' has an admirable clarity to it but the limitations of the era in which it was written are evident now, more than fifty years later.

Other Chicago theorists paid particular attention to the impermanence of social structures. For example, Bernice Neugarten pointed out that time had a profound impact on how the life cycle was organised and experienced. In her earlier writings she concentrated on the impact of 'the social clock'; that is, those underlying norms and behaviour expectations telling us when 'the best time' is for different things in life, such as getting a job, bearing a child, or taking retirement (Neugarten, 1968). In her later writings she recognised how the time borders between developmental periods in life were changing. Puberty, for instance, was coming two years earlier (at 12 to 14 years) than in earlier generations. Retirement as well was coming earlier, especially in many Western countries (although this situation has now reversed itself as a result of the difficulties of continuing to provide generous pensions to an increasing aging population). Neugarten was also one of the first to make a distinction between the 'young-old' and the 'old-old' (see Chapter 6).

Moreover, Neugarten also recognised how time limits were not being experienced as so pressing as in earlier generations. The life cycle had become more fluid and various parts of the life cycle were being reorganised (Neugarten and Neugarten, 1987). Whereas childhood and the teenage years formerly meant education, early adulthood and middle-age work and old age leisure, this no longer held true. Many teenagers were taking a year of 'sabbatical' for travelling and gaining experience before they either continued with their studies or made a commitment to a job. Many middle-aged persons were also doing the same, either voluntarily in order to rest, to re-educate themselves or because they had become unemployed for a period of time. Older people in turn might take up adult educational classes or work part time or as a volunteer for some periods of their retirement. Neugarten referred to this phenomenon as the coming of an 'age irrelevant society' where other factors such as education or ability had more impact on opportunities than the person's age.

Other social gerontologists to write about the impact of social change on aging included Matilda White Riley (Riley, 1973; Riley et al., 1999). She was one of the first to use the concept of 'cohort' in addition to 'generation' to draw attention to the fact that even a few years' age difference can affect the experience of development and aging within fast-changing modern societies. Every aging cohort reflects in its attitudes the different conditions within the society, culture and era in which they grew to maturity and aged. What people often mistakenly took for factors reflecting development and aging might to a great extent be reflections of cohort/generational differences produced by socio-historical change. These reflections were clearly contrary to any time-linked, fixed developmental scheme such as those produced by authors like Levinson (Levinson et al., 1978). Awareness of the significance of cohort or generation differences for development over adult life have become even more critical as we have moved into the twenty-first century. Nor are these necessarily equivalent across cultures. As many as six still living 'generations', with distinct attitudes and preferences, have been identified in US society, but of these only the now aging 'baby boomers', born in the post-Second World War years, and perhaps also the 'millennials', who came of age in the new century, are similarly identifiable in Britain (Howe and Strauss, 2000).

The growing awareness of the importance of historical shifts to research on developmental psychology, particularly across adulthood and aging, have necessarily required changes to research methodology. Not only are lengthy longitudinal studies required, rather than cross-sectional comparisons between age groups, but also 'cross-sequential' studies that follow in parallel different cohorts or generations across historical time (see Table 2.2). At the end of such a study it is possible to make comparisons between the experience of persons of the same age in different historical periods, and to come closer to distinguishing universal developmental changes from differences due to generational change. Warner Schaie has succeeded in conducting such a study on change in cognitive performance in persons growing older in the United States (Schaie, 1996), but only a few other examples of comparable research on social and emotional change with age have been undertaken so far (e.g. Gatz and Karel, 1993; Bengtson et al., 2009), and none of equivalent length and sophistication. Such research of course requires sufficient longitudinal funding and commitment from research institutes across generations.

Disengagement theory and its rivals

Besides extending interest in the psychology of aging to include the study of personality change (Neugarten and Associates, 1964), the Chicago group formulated the first major psychosocial theory of aging, the so-called 'disengagement theory'. This was a product of a large-scale cross-sectional study of different age groups carried out in Kansas City in the late 1950s (Cumming and Henry, 1961). It was both a psychological theory of the individual's decreasing involvement with the world around and a sociological theory in that it explained these changes as functional to

TABLE 2.2 Cross-sequential model for research on adult development

	Time of measurement				
Time of birth (Cohort)	2010	2020	2030	2040	2050
	Age in years				
1950	60	70	80	90	100
1960	50	60	70	80	90
1970	40	50	60	70	80
1980	30	40	50	60	70
1990	20	30	40	50	60

the society within which they occurred. The individual withdrew from the major roles of life while society concomitantly ceased to depend on the individual for the performance of those roles.

Disengagement theory aroused immediate controversy. An opposing 'activity theory' was formulated, which argued for the benefits to the older person of continuing to fulfil social roles and activities as opposed to withdrawing from them, and much subsequent research effort was focused on the question of which of the two 'theories' was the more valid perspective. Studies showed that disengagement was not always as voluntary as Cumming and Henry have suggested, but often forced on people by events, and those who remained engaged were often the happiest. Even more damning were claims of the theory's insidious effects on social policy, buttressing custodial forms of treatment in institutions for example. The reaction against the idea of disengagement was so great that it came to be cited as an example of the type of general theorising that gerontology should not indulge in (Achenbaum and Bengtson, 1994).

However, the original theory of disengagement needs to be seen in the context that Cumming and Henry themselves described. It was set up consciously as a reaction to the implicit 'theory' of aging current in American society of the time, that becoming old was intrinsically deteriorative and that successful aging consisted in being as much like a middle-aged person as possible. A healthy old age was seen as a contradiction in terms: anyone who was old was by definition unhealthy. Cumming and Henry challenged this view. The behaviour of an average 5-year-old is different from that of a 10-year-old, and so is that of a 20- and 40-year-old. Yet they are all regarded as normal for that age group. Why do we not treat the average behaviour of a 70- and 80-year-old in the same way? Cumming and Henry argued for a re-evaluation of the changes in behaviour that characterise old people, that they should not be casually labelled 'pathological', but be regarded as normal and healthy.

Typical of these changes, they claimed, was the process of social disengagement. This was so important for them that they gave its name to the whole theory. But they also attempted to characterise other features of normal aging. For example, one neglected part of the original conception is that society at the same time as releasing older people from social obligations allowed them a new kind of licence. Therefore aging could also bring liberation. Perhaps for the first time in their lives, people became free to say what they think about anything and everything. The picture of the old person as a 'free spirit' is clearly a positive element in the original theory that has been neglected by subsequent research. Cumming and Henry failed in their attempt to gain acceptance for the disengagement view of aging. Growing old has continued to be seen as intrinsically negative. A UK survey showed that people resist for as long as possible using the term 'old' to apply to themselves (Thompson et al., 1990). This may be a healthy reaction on older people's part, but it also shows that our concepts for late life need reconsideration (Gilleard and Higgs, 2011).

The need for a re-evaluation of the meaning of old age was first strongly expressed by David Gutmann, who eventually set out an ambitious developmental theory of aging, the culmination of many years' work in diverse societies around the world (Gutmann, 1987, 1997). It is significant that, besides being influenced by Erik Erikson, he was one of the researchers on the original Kansas City study in the team of psychologists directed by Bernice Neugarten, whose own edited collection of the work done, published after Cumming and Henry's book, was relatively neglected in comparison with theirs (Neugarten and Associates, 1964). Her concept of increasing 'interiority' with age has remained a more attractive concept than 'disengagement'. During his work in Kansas City Gutmann developed the use of the personality theorist Henry Murray's 'Thematic Apperception Test' (Murray, 1938, 1943) to investigate personality change. He demonstrated striking age and gender differences. Older men in particular reacted as if they were less oriented towards coping with stress by producing changes in their situation, and more oriented towards accommodating themselves to the environment. As a result adjustment appeared to be increasingly achieved through changes in perceptions of the self in relationship to the environment.

In his subsequent work Gutmann used similar techniques to study older people in a variety of traditional societies around the world. He also succeeded in carrying out longitudinal studies by tracing the same individuals he had interviewed in earlier years. He claimed that the psychological potentials that developed in later life enabled older people to play important roles in traditional societies. The term he adopted was that of 'emeritus parents'. While women became more assertive and powerful within the realm of the extended family, older men appeared to 'disengage' from the world of pragmatic action, but in order to become the tenders of the values of their culture. Their detachment from ordinary affairs freed them to make this advance so that they came to represent the abstract but vital elements underlying their culture. They did this by engaging closely with the moral values and religious practices that underlay their culture. In so doing they gained new meaning in their own eyes and in the eyes of others. In the last two hundred years or more, Gutmann suggests, Western societies have increasingly failed to provide the circumstances for most older people to develop their potentials, and it is vital for the health of the whole of society that we find ways of recovering these potentials.

The link with the previous disengagement theory view of development in late life is intriguing. Gutmann argued that Cumming and Henry too readily associated functional withdrawal from society with the emergence of more accommodative states, and presented examples to show the two can be quite dissociated. In the case of the Druze of Syria, Lebanon and Israel, the greater passivity of the older man was a central component of his greater association with social norms, religious traditions and moral values. 'Instead of being the center of enterprise, he became the bridge between the community and the productive, life-sustaining potencies of Allah' (Gutmann, 1987, p. 225). As previous anthropologists have noted, elders in various societies often become the interpreters and administrators of the moral sector of society. Disengagement from social action is not the end state. Rather it is only the first step in a total process of transition and re-engagement, a process that is interrupted or aborted in a secular society. Gutmann provides a clear answer to

Erikson's question as to the conditions necessary for old age to flourish, namely a stable society where values are transmitted from generation to generation.

The reaction to Gutmann's ideas has been largely muted. Some have acknowledged their imaginative scope; others have queried his methods (particularly the use of projective tests). But there has been little attempt either to integrate his ideas into current gerontological thinking or to be openly critical of them. Although invited to express his views at leading conferences, such as those of the Gerontological Society of America, he has attracted few followers interested in applying lessons from traditional societies to modern American society. Perhaps his uncompromising message that Western society has taken a wrong direction in lessening the power of tradition in intergenerational relationships is just too radical to accept. There is also the fact that Gutmann delineates clearly demarcated roles both to younger and older men and women in modern as well as traditional societies, which fits uncomfortably with contemporary notions of gender equality.

Other writers, both in the United States and elsewhere, have also stressed the need for revaluing older people's role within society. For example, the British social historian Peter Laslett, who recommended adoption of the concept of the 'third age' for flagging the opportunities contemporary society offered older people, urged them to re-engage vigorously within the cultural and educational sphere, seeing them as standard bearers for societal values that are often neglected in the work-dominated 'second' age of life (Laslett, 1989). These views have been much more easily accepted. The idea of disengagement from previous activities in order to pursue higher-order concerns is a long-established model of aging well. It is clearly expressed for instance in early Hindu writings (Tilak, 1989). It continues to be promoted by those who encourage 'contemplative aging' as a way of a being in later life (Tornstam, 2005; Sherman, 2010).

Newer developmental models of aging

Erikson's influence continues to be felt strongly in new developmental models of aging. Perhaps the most elaborated sequential theory of aging has been provided by the psychiatrist Gene Cohen (Cohen, 2005). A student of Erikson's at Harvard University, he became the first head of the Center on Aging at the US National Institute of Mental Health. Through his involvement and knowledge of neuro-scientific research he was able to counteract some of the false assumptions about the aging brain, making use of fresh discoveries showing that the brain was able to grow new neurons throughout life. To have focused on the fact that neurons do not regenerate was to miss the important point that fresh neurons are created out of stem cells. As a result as people aged it was perfectly possible for them to become more creative. The scientific evidence also indicated that they became able to use both hemispheres of the brain more efficiently. This he argued made possible the greater constructive use of personal memories and enhanced reflection observed in the later years. One consequence was the greater sense of self, which was less focused on the self in isolation and more in relationship to the world.

As a result of his investigations Cohen came eventually to expand Erikson's last two stages of life into four 'phases', a term he preferred to 'stages' because it was more flexible and less demarcated. Like Jung he argued for the importance of 'midlife evaluation' in which persons took stock of their lives and set new goals for the remaining years. He regarded it less a time of crisis and more a quest for authenticity. It was in this period, usually occurring in a person's forties or fifties, that they acquired the type of intelligence that formed the basis of a more balanced and wiser view on life. He suggested that these changes were associated with the greater bilateral brain involvement he observed in persons as people entered midlife.

This time of re-evaluation was followed by a period of further experimentation and innovation, for which he employed the term 'liberation' because individuals came to display an even greater personal freedom and a willingness to experiment with new experiences. For most people this phase took place in their sixties, often around the time of retirement from previous work responsibilities. Although showing some similarities to the adolescent's striving for independence, this change appeared to be more driven from the inside and to be less influenced by contact with the peer group. Cohen associated this desire for novelty with new neuron formation that was identifiable in the information processing part of the brain.

The third phase, which Cohen named 'summing up', was characterised by motivations to find meanings in looking back on life as well as sharing this 'wisdom' with others. This could also involve attending more to previously unresolved matters both in personal life and in the wider society. As in Charles Dickens's depiction of the miser Ebenezer Scrooge in his *Christmas Carol* it was never too late to change one's life. He saw the neurological underpinning of this heightened use of memory in changes within the hippocampal regions of the brain. He noted in his studies of 70-year-olds how when telling their life stories both sides of the hippocampus lit up (i.e. the right side of the brain as well), describing autobiography as 'like chocolate to the brain', an optimal experience of 'savouring', which combined curiosity, intuition and passion.

The fourth and last phase he described as 'encore' because of the way in which very old persons often retained the desire to restate and reaffirm their major commitments, as well as to continue reflecting on them, but especially also to celebrate the meaning of life and fellowship. Expressions of such late-life energy, as in the desire to participate in reunions, occurred also in the face of adversity or loss. Cohen even saw brain parallels for these final developments in further changes occurring in the amygdalae, the brain's emotional processing centres, which allowed imagination to flourish despite physical decline.

Also strongly related to Cohen's idea of moving beyond the self in later life is Lars Tornstam's theory of gerotranscendence (Tornstam, 1996b, 2005). Like many of the other previous developmental theories, it presupposes a qualitative shift with age in a person's orientation to the world. According to Tornstam, 'gerotranscendence' involves experiencing a redefinition of the self in relation to time, space, life and death. 'simply put, gerotranscendence is a shift in meta-perspective, from a materialistic and pragmatic view of the world to a more cosmic and transcendent one' (Tornstam, 1997, p. 17). Despite a relative lack of empirical investigation, the concept of gerotranscendence has continued to attract much interest in Western societies over the last twenty years. In part this is because it successfully incorporates elements from earlier theorising while adding other features to produce an integrated picture of an 'ideal old age' (see Table 2.3).

Tornstam refers to Jung's concept of the collective unconscious in describing how the gerotranscendent individual experiences increasing closeness with universal psychological structures that have characterised man in different cultures. His stress on a new feeling of affinity with past and coming generations also corresponds to Erikson's idea that the integrated older person has a feeling of companionship with the past and coming generations. There is a corresponding decreased fear of death. It is not the individual life, but the general flow of human life that becomes important. There is a decrease in self-centredness, again consistent with Erikson's theory, that leads to generativity towards younger individuals and a greater insight into the selfish and unselfish aspects of the self. There is a loss of concern with the aging body, along with a general shift from egoism to altruism. The individual experiences a return to and transfiguration of childhood, and accepts himself or herself as he/she is and the life lived as it has been unfolding. The difference between self and role is acknowledged, with a tendency to abandon roles. Roles are viewed from a comforting distance. A transfiguration of experience towards experiencing a new innocence enhances maturity.

At the same time there is an increase of time spent in meditation, pondering on life and on the past self. This accords with Butler's (1963) conception of life review as a healing process in later life, with Neugarten's emphasis on increased 'interiority' in old age (Neugarten and Associates, 1964) and also with Gutmann's findings that passive mastery of life is typical of old age in traditional societies (Gutmann, 1987). Tornstam draws upon Zen Buddhism in describing how withdrawal into meditation allows the older individual to reach a stage of cosmic transcendence over time where past, present and future become one. A further sign of gerotranscendence, according to Tornstam, is a decreased interest in superfluous social interaction: the individual loses his or her interest in establishing new acquaintances and relies on those already well established. This accords with the theory of

TABLE 2.3 Characteristics of gerotranscendence

An increased feeling of communion with the 'spirit of the universe'
A redefinition of the perception of time, space and objects
A redefinition of life and death, and a decreased fear of death
An increased feeling of affinity with past and coming generations
A decrease in interest in superfluous social interaction
A decrease in interest in material things
A decrease in self-centredness
An increase in the time spent in meditation

Source: Tornstam (1996a, 2005).

age related socio-emotional selectivity, which we describe later in this chapter, for which there is considerable empirical support. Consistent also with recent research interest in studying the development of wisdom in relation to age, which we discuss in the next part, Tornstam refers to the transcendence of the right–wrong duality leading to a more broad-minded understanding of others. As a result older people withhold more from judging and from giving advice. Such changes have been described before in the psychological literature as signs of the maturation of moral thinking (Kohlberg et al., 1983).

Overall Tornstam's depiction of the aging person is an attractive although highly idealised one. He describes an increased 'communion with the spirit of the universe', referring to a feeling of flow of energy coursing through the universe and making the person feel in communion with nature, expressed, for example, in the oceans and the starry night. There is a redefinition of the perception of time, space and objects. The borders of past, present and future are blurred and an affinity with earlier times and other cultures develop in the aging person. The borders between the self and others also become diffuse and lead to a decreased self-centredness and the development of a more cosmic self. There is a decrease in interest in material things: an understanding of the deadening weight of wealth and the freedom of 'asceticism' develops. As a result older people give away personal goods such as sets of silverware, books or larger heirlooms, and money and assets to their younger relatives or for some charitable purpose.

In the theory of gerotranscendence aging has again come to be seen as a normative process of disengagement. Similarly to previous theories of development with age, Tornstam suggests that there is an intrinsic and culture-free transcendence process in old age that is the product of normal living. He explicitly rejects psychoanalytic explanations in terms of a defence mechanism for the aging ego; and to the criticism that few older people seem to display all the characteristics he describes he argues, as Gutmann does, that they are obstructed by the changes inherent in the development of modern Western civilisation, particularly its secular and individualistic features. The process of gerotranscendence may also be inhibited by caregivers (and gerontologists!) who are constantly striving to keep an old person active. This may obstruct the integration of personality necessary at the end of life. Having the time, and energy, available to meditate may be a prerequisite for growth in very late life.

As in both Erikson's and Gutmann's theories, cultural factors appear crucial to development in later life. However, Tornstam also proposes that the inner dispositions in combination with the process of living one's life come eventually to elicit gerotranscendence, even if it is not until very late in life. Similarly to Butler in his theory of life review, Tornstam gives a key role to perceptions of death and finitude. Even a younger individual will develop gerotranscendence if he or she encounters a major life-crisis such as a serious illness that confronts the individual with death. Tornstam (1996b) has given some examples, based on the work of Chinen (1989), of the development of wisdom in old age by referring to biographical analysis of some outstanding philosophers and scientists such as Ludwig

Wittgenstein and Albert Einstein. He has also produced some support for this theory from large-scale surveys in his native Sweden (Tornstam, 1997). He has shown a clear differentiation between his conception of gerotranscendence and depression; that is, gerotranscendence is not withdrawal in a pathological sense. Perhaps, most importantly, Tornstam has also been interested in the possibilities of applying the theory in practice among professional caregivers such as nurses (Wadensten, 2005) (see further Chapter 6). The results showed that a significant minority of them reported that the theory had positively affected their outlook on old age and on their own aging and that the effect was stronger among the better educated professional caregivers (e.g. the registered nurses). Almost every second interviewee reported that the theory gave them new understanding of the care receivers. The care receivers' need for solitude was recognised, as well as a clearer view of the difference between the value-systems of the caregivers and the caretakers; that is, concerning the 'need' for activation. These insights helped in giving higher priority to the desires of the care recipients. The theory also functioned as a stress-releaser for guilt feelings among the staff for not being engaged enough in activating their clients (Tornstam, 1996a).

The theory of gerotranscendence remains influential, reflecting the need for the more positive vision of aging it presents (Sherman, 2010; McCarthy et al., 2015), but there has also been criticism (Jönson and Magnusson, 2001; Dalby, 2006). A major empirical study in the Netherlands (Braam et al., 2006) showed stronger relationships between gerotranscendent attitudes and perceived meaning in life among women, the older-old members of the sample, those who were widowed and those who were not attached to a particular religion, suggesting the importance of context and social factors. Self-reported shifts towards less materialistic concerns among older Americans have also been noted by US researchers (Eisenhandler, 2003; Ingersoll-Dayton et al., 2002). However, the most important evidence for development of gerotranscendence with age should come from longitudinal studies and the limited US evidence here is mixed. For example, findings from the Ohio Longitudinal Study of Aging (Atchley, 1999) suggested that the majority of the sample reported increasing attachment to material things as well as less connection between themselves and past and future generations as they grew older. By contrast the Berkeley California longitudinal study findings do suggest an increasing expression with age of universal moral attitudes and declining reference to group distinctions (Dillon and Wink, 2007).

One has to conclude that the empirical evidence for the main theoretical propositions for gerotranscendence remains weak and the hypothesised obstructive influence of society is perhaps used to explain overmuch. It is also possible to question Tornstam's sharp distinction between gerotranscendence as a developmental rather than a coping process. In coping with serious life distress, a reorganisation of values and behaviour can often be seen after the stress period is over (Ruth and Coleman, 1996). There is the danger moreover of using the theory to create another type of 'elite' aging and demeaning those older people who do not have either the cognitive capacity or sufficient energy to ponder issues of life and death or meditate in isolation. As we pointed out at the beginning of this chapter, we have to beware of the tendency of developmental theory on aging to be over-idealistic and, as a consequence, to neglect those older people in greatest need of support. We will return again to the concept of gerotranscendence when discussing the recent growth of research on aging, meaning and spirituality in Chapter 5.

Socio-emotional selectivity theory

Probably the most influential developmental theory of aging to arise in academic psychology during the last thirty years has been Laura Carstensen's 'socio-emotional selectivity (SES) theory' (Carstensen, 1991; Carstensen et al., 1999; Mather and Carstensen, 2005; Carstensen, 2006). Again there are associations to be made with disengagement theory. SES theory also claims that reductions in social contact across adulthood are volitional, but explains them more specifically in terms of changes in the salience of specific social goals. As persons age, they come to prefer social relationships that promote present well-being and contentment in the present over relationships that may prove to more useful in the longer term. They also prioritise emotional over cognitive goals, feelings of well-being over knowledge acquisition.

The essential premise of this theory is that the relative importance of goals changes as a function of perceived time, in particular a growing awareness that life will come to an end. In this respect too it links with disengagement theory and with Erikson's theory of life stages. When time is perceived as largely open-ended, future-oriented goals such as information acquisition are of paramount importance. When time is perceived as limited, adults adapt by prioritising present-oriented emotion-based relationships. Age is associated with preferences for emotionally satisfying contact over others such as information-rich contact.

To illustrate their theory, Carstensen et al. (1999) compared relationships across the lifespan. The first-year student invests much time and energy in establishing new friendships. Maximising experience allows more satisfying choices to be made. A newly-wed couple, if they are sensible, will devote a lot of time to their relationship and to solving problems as they arise within it. Although this may take considerable effort, this is balanced in the longer term by the lessening of future conflicts. An elderly couple by contrast 'often decides to accept their relationship as it is, to appreciate what is good, and ignore what is troubling, rather than seek new solutions to problems' (Carstensen et al., 1999, p. 167). The difference can be understood in terms of a greater present rather than future orientation, and maximising emotional satisfaction.

The theory also suggests that age-related differences in anticipated future time influences developmental trends in knowledge-related social goals. In childhood and youth, much new information is gained through contact with more experienced and knowledgeable individuals. A teenager is especially dependent on the views and ideas of his or her peer group. As the years go by, social interaction will be needed less and will also be less effective in obtaining information. The individual is better educated in many ways and access to new information shifts to more spe-cialised sources such as books, journals and databanks. Thus the function of social contacts as gateways to information is reduced, and relied on only in some special situations, such as asking a physician friend for advice on some medical symptoms or a lawyer friend for advice on some tax matters. Some information gained from friends thus may be potentially useful, but on the whole Carstensen argues that this kind of 'banking information for the future' is of less use in old age. Lang and Carstensen (1994) have produced evidence to support their view that older people proactively manage the decline in the size of their social network as they age. When time is limited, familiar social partners are preferred because they are best able to influence emotional states in the short term.

We partly disagree with Carstensen concerning this information acquisition aspect of her theory. Some evidence has emerged that confirms the continuous need for information acquisition in decision-making in old age. Older adults, par-ticularly those who are well educated, can be very skilful decision-makers; this skill can be developed through reliance on a large social network of well-educated friends, who can give expert advice in difficult situations. Birren, for example, has shown that age per se does not have the impact on decision-making in consumer affairs that education has. The autobiography groups that he has also pioneered demonstrate the value of forming new reciprocal relationships for self-development in later life (Birren and Deutchman, 1991; Randall and Kenyon, 2001; Birren and Svensson, 2013).

Our identities and self-images are also constructed according to how we per-ceive the way other persons perceive us. Throughout life we get the building blocks for our self-images in the mirrors that significant others provide for us. Expressed in another way, our identities are negotiated with important others in our immediate life-space. As we get older, however, there are fewer and fewer persons who can confirm our long-held views of ourselves. Many social partners cannot provide us with confirmatory feedback, because of differences in experi-ences, values or preferences, or because they hold stereotypic views of how older persons are. Carstensen gives the example of an older woman who has always been interested in the latest fashions and who likes to wear heavy make-up, but who might be viewed as holding up a mask against aging if we did not know her personal history.

Studies have shown that the social networks of the elderly are similar in structure to those of younger age groups, but that contacts within them occur less frequently for older people. They tend to prefer contact with their own children or friends or other familiar persons, whom they contact often. In these relationships there are quite intense emotions invested, and there are few data to support the idea of 'emotional flattening' in old age. However, there does appear to be a reduced interest in interacting with acquaintances or a new partner. The pattern of avoiding initiating new contacts with non-familial persons is clearly visible in nursing homes and other institutions. There might be quite a risk involved in contact-seeking in old age; conversations become more difficult for instance if the other person has difficulty hearing as a consequence of sensory loss. According to Carstensen, withdrawal represents an adaptive response in an overcrowded or unpredictable social environment, and explains why interventions to activate contact-seeking in residential care settings have often had only a temporary effect (but see Chapter 7 on more recent studies in this field). The older person does not perceive the need for increased activities: this need is felt only by relatives and care staff.

A central principle of Carstensen's selectivity theory is the increasing reliance on previous social contacts to maximise the possibilities of positive emotion in encounters with significant people in their lives. Far from being emotionally flattened, older persons appear to be emotionally conscious, making judicious decisions about activities and giving thoughtful consideration to their functions as affect regulators. Aversive social feedback has an even greater impact on their well-being than a passive response. Choosing social partners reflects older people's adaptive efforts to optimise the positive outcome of most if not all social interactions they engage in.

Socio-emotional selectivity theory has if anything become even more influential in recent years, frequently cited by studies of age differences in a wide range of areas such as reactivity to stress, coping with interpersonal problems, evaluation of remembered events, perception of facial expression, empathy and prosocial behaviour, as well as trusting attitudes to others (Stawski et al., 2008; Coats and Blanchard-Fields, 2008; Schryer and Ross, 2012; Johnson and Whiting, 2013; Beadle et al., 2015; Li and Fung, 2013). This is in addition to Carstensen and colleagues' continuing work at Stanford University in California on changing emotional experience with age, for which they have also produced general reviews (Scheibe and Carstensen, 2010; Carstensen et al., 2011). In the following chapter we will come back to SES theory as well as examine related theoretical developments as we review some of the latest research on age differences in emotion regulation.

The study of wisdom

Despite academic psychology's continuing focus on the study of cognitive changes with age, it did, as we have seen, during the last decades of the twentieth century begin to apply scientific research methods to social and emotional aspects of aging. These were areas where developmental theories had suggested more positive changes were to be found with age. One topic that demanded consideration and was also associated with the study of cognition, was the subject of wisdom, which Erikson had described as a product of the last stage of adult development, and was frequently cited by other developmental theorists. Wisdom had long been a focus of interest for philosophers and theologians, but for psychologists and social scientists, it was a new subject, described as one of the most neglected and least studied by some of its first researchers (Sternberg, 1990; Sternberg and Grigorenko, 2005). It seemed a promising antidote to negative stereotypes about later life.

Wisdom traditionally has been thought to be the result of long experience. For example, Erikson placed wisdom at the end of the life course because he believed it to be an attribute that would arise only when other psychosocial issues had been addressed. Associated attributes for wisdom included openness to experience, self-reflection and self-awareness, and recognition and acceptance of the limits of feasible knowledge (Sternberg, 1990). These characteristics were not directly related to biological aging and so did not necessarily decline in later life. The experience and knowledge that adults continued to develop into the latter part of the life course could be a good source of advice for younger adults, particularly in the area of human relationships. Some of the first empirical studies conducted examined the characteristics people associated with wisdom or with people typically viewed as being wise. In one such study, Holliday and Chandler (1986) asked 150 participants (age range 22–86 years) to generate descriptors of wise people (as well as shrewd, perceptive, intelligent, spiritual and foolish people). They found that wisdom was defined in terms of learning from experience, being open-minded, and knowledgeable, being of an older age, and having the ability to consider different perspectives.

The largest research programme to date devoted to wisdom has been undertaken by Baltes and colleagues at the Max Planck Institute of Human Development in Berlin (Baltes and Staudinger, 1993, 2000; Scheibe et al., 2007). Their starting point was the distinction Baltes drew between what he described as the 'mechanics' and the 'pragmatics' of the mind. The mechanics of cognition, which are dependent on the hardwiring (neurophysiology) of the mind, can decline or slow in later life. In contrast, pragmatic features, including culturally acquired information and knowledge, were more likely to increase with age and experience at least into the seventh or eighth decade of life. They argued that wisdom should be defined in terms of a rich factual and procedural knowledge about the 'fundamental pragmatics of life' (Baltes and Staudinger, 2000, p. 122). The fundamental pragmatics of life essentially refers to important aspects of the human condition such as life planning and management, and the reality of death. Wise people are seen as those who have both exceptional insights into human development and good judgement and advice about difficult life problems. Their work on wisdom provides an interesting example of researchers integrating multiple lines of enquiry into a single framework of theory-driven research.

In their empirical work, Baltes and colleagues hypothesised five criteria necessary for this pragmatic acquisition of a knowledge-based state of wisdom, reflecting both content and process aspects of wisdom. Content criteria include factual and procedural knowledge, and are hypothesised to be fundamental to wisdom. Process criteria include lifespan contextualism, value relativism and the recognition and management of uncertainty. They hypothesised a developmental shift in the onset and development of these five criteria, with the acquisition of (factual and procedural) knowledge occurring first, while the three-process criteria develop later alongside greater experience of life and of others.

The strategy used by Baltes and colleagues involved a focused interview in which participants were given vignettes of hypothetical dilemmas which then formed a focus for discussion. These vignettes typically centred on different types of experiential and relational challenges, including career and parental challenges, life crises and gender-role conflicts. One vignette involved a 14-year-old girl who wishes to move out of the family home immediately; participants were asked about what they/she should do and consider. Another vignette involved the receipt of a phone call from a good friend who indicated he/she had decided to commit suicide. After some practice and warm-up exercises in thinking aloud, participants were asked what one should do and consider for each of the vignettes (Staudinger and Baltes, 1996). The method thus allowed the participants freedom in expressing themselves, while the raters scoring responses had criteria they were searching for. This is however very labour intensive compared, for example, to the questionnaire measures other researchers have developed.

Knowledge would seem to be an important criterion for wisdom. It seems unlikely people can make wise choices without some basic level of knowledge about a given issue or experience. Nevertheless, Chandler and Holliday (1990), as well as others who have entered this field of research, have criticised the Berlin school's definition, claiming that it relied too much on expertise, and narrowed rather than broadened people's ideas about the nature of wisdom. Certainly relatively few people display high levels of wisdom-related knowledge on the Berlin wisdom tasks (Kunzmann, 2007). Alternative definitions of wisdom have been proposed which stress that wisdom is not solely the product of knowledge but of its integration with emotional processes (Ardelt, 1997; Kramer, 2000). These definitions also point to the importance of reflexivity. It is only by engaging in reflective thinking and by looking at experiences and phenomena from different perspectives that persons are likely to see reality without the occurrence of distortions, and increase the probability of gaining true insight.

Although there is still no consensus on a universal definition of wisdom, progress has been made. There seems to be agreement that wisdom is a complex construct, involving competence (knowledge, ability to solve problems), reflection (self and other evaluation) and appropriate use of affect (emotion regulation, compassion) (Jeste et al., 2010; Staudinger and Glück, 2011). Some researchers have differentiated between different types of wisdom, between practical knowledge for example and a knowledge that is more spiritual or metaphysical (Wink and Helson, 1997). Others such as Edmondson (2009) have emphasised the social context of wisdom, the cultural settings in which wise people express themselves. Certainly it seems essential to wisdom that the lessons learned not only benefit the individual concerned but also contribute to the common good. This means that, in assessing wisdom, judgements made by others need to complement self-report scales and performance assessments. The characteristic 'wise' is appropriately attributed to others but not to oneself (Redzanowski and Glück, 2013).

What have research findings indicated about the relationship between wisdom and age? Some have supported an association between the two. For instance, Wink and Helson (1997) found that practical wisdom was higher for adults in their early fifties than adults in their late twenties. The early work of Baltes and colleagues also suggested that older people are well represented among those few scoring highest on the wisdom tests they developed (Baltes et al., 1995), although declines occurred in the oldest age groups (Baltes and Staudinger, 2000). However, Webster (2003), in examining age differences in wisdom as measured by his Self-Assessment Wisdom Scale (SAWS) (a forty-item questionnaire with five components: presence of critical life experiences; reminiscence/reflectiveness; openness to experience; emotional regulation; and humour), found no significant effect for age. The consensus of subsequent studies is that wisdom tends to increase from childhood through adolescence to adulthood, but that further development into later life is not normal (Richardson and Pasupathi, 2005; Jordan, 2005). But greater sensitivity to the possibility of curvilinear relationships to age have allowed one of the most recent research studies in this field (Webster et al., 2014) to demonstrate in a Dutch sample that middle-aged adults (30–59 years) scored higher on the SAWS than younger or older adults. Empathy, an important component of wisdom, has also been shown to have a similar curvilinear relationship with age (O'Brien et al., 2013).

It seems then that wisdom does increase with lived experience in the same way that knowledge-based intelligence does, but the physical, psychological and social losses of late life lead to a decline in both. Openness to experience, one of the factors in the SAWS measure, has also been shown to decrease in later life (Donnellan and Lucas, 2008; Stephan, 2009). The concept of wisdom therefore, at least on most current definitions used in psychological research, does not appear to be the antidote to negative depictions of aging that it was once hoped to be. Subsequent research by the Berlin group has considered other more specific features of human development that may show stronger associations with aging. Integration of goals – related both to wisdom and to Erikson's concept of integrity – is one on which they have shown positive age trends (Riediger et al., 2005; Riediger, 2007) (see Box 2.1).

BOX 2.1 AGE DIFFERENCES IN INTEGRATION OF LIFE GOALS

Riediger, Freund and Baltes at the Max Planck Institute for Human Development in Berlin carried out two investigations on the subject of development of personal goals through adulthood. In the first – a cross-sectional study – younger adults between 20 and 30 years and older adults 59 to 77 years were asked to describe four goals they had for the near future, their degree of involvement in pursuing them, as well as the amount of mutual interference or incompatibility they experienced between the separate goals. The older participants reported more intergoal facilitation between their separate goals, and also, partly as a result of this, a higher level of goal-pursuit intensity.

In the second study, which was longitudinal, the researchers investigated age differences in the pursuit of one particular goal, namely maintaining an

(continued)

(continued)

exercise routine. Older participants again reported more facilitation between achieving this goal and the other goals they were seeking in their lives at the same time. Objective attendance performance showed that older participants maintained their exercise adherence longer, and diary information also indicated that they were more engaged in pursuing this goal than were younger participants. These differences could not be explained by other differences in educational level, reasons given to exercise or greater time availability.

The authors conclude that older adults are more likely than younger adults to have goals that are consistent with one another. Why should this be so? Is it because older people are more experienced in choosing goals that interrelate? Could it also reflect the fact that they have more freedom than younger people in deciding the goals they want to pursue?

(Riediger et al., 2005)

However, there are also other approaches to the study of wisdom which allow old age to have wisdom of its own. For example, Randall and Kenyon (2001) have disputed the 'elite' perspective on wisdom current in so many psychological studies on the subject. They used biographical interviews to explore wisdom as being more broadly and regularly manifested in the lives of 'ordinary' people. They also distinguished various dimensions of wisdom in daily life, including practical, interpersonal, ethical and spiritual wisdom. In documenting 'narrative wisdom', they have argued that wisdom can be discovered in all our lives and at every stage, by exploring the lives we have lived so far, the challenges that have been addressed and the choices that have been made. Also Edmondson (2009, 2015), on the basis of her close observations of expressions of wisdom in daily life, has encouraged a more sympathetic view of the different types of wisdom older people can and do offer from their experience of a long life. Even Thomas and Kunzmann (2014), writing from within the context of the Berlin wisdom model, have noted that the oldest age groups may acquire particular wisdom-related knowledge around the theme of loss and retention of meaning in life. This is very important knowledge to impart to others.

In a recently published study Ardelt and Edwards have produced evidence to suggest a relationship between wisdom, broadly conceived, and subjective well-being in later life (Ardelt and Edwards, 2016). Ardelt has been one of the first to criticise over-restricted conceptions of wisdom and has devised a measure that comprises assessment of its affective and compassionate as well as cognitive and reflective dimensions (Ardelt, 1997, 2003). Most importantly, in this latest study she demonstrates a significantly stronger relationship between this broader concept of wisdom and well-being in older people living in nursing homes and hospices. This appears to be mediated by the greater sense of purpose in life her wiser old people possessed. We will return to this subject as we consider processes of adaptation to the experience of aging in later chapters.

3

CURRENT RESEARCH ON DEVELOPMENTAL ASPECTS OF AGING

In this chapter we consider in more detail research on three subjects in the developmental psychology of aging: first, age changes in regulation of emotion; second, the meaning and impact of generativity in older people's relationships with others; and third, the functions of reminiscence and life review in later life. All three illustrate how psychological development in later life benefits not only older people themselves but also the families and communities to which they belong.

For each topic we provide a brief background to research on the topic and then describe examples of studies published in the last ten to twenty years. Every well-constructed research study involves a number of elements: the setting of objectives including the possible formulation of hypotheses around the research question; the choice methods of enquiry appropriate to the research question; the analysis of results whether using statistical methods in quantitative studies or detailed consideration of the content of interviews in qualitative studies; the summarising of findings, and extracting of conclusions as well as implications for further investigation. It is not possible of course for us to provide such a detailed account of every study we discuss but we intend our accounts here (as well as in Chapters 5 and 7) to give at least an impression of the important features of the research we describe.

We begin with the subject of emotion regulation because this has become in recent years the most researched topic in the psychology of aging after the study of cognitive change. Moreover, unlike the study of mental performance, it also shows results which are generally favourable to age. Older people are often distinguished by their improved ability to control their emotions. It is this development in later life which may provide the basis for other positive age-related changes observed in older people's lives.

We then turn to Erikson's conception of 'generativity' and his proposal that as adults mature they must move from a preoccupation with establishing their own identity to a concern with guiding the next generation. This was a relatively neglected part of Erikson's total theory of lifespan development until the close attention given to it in the 1980s by the personality theorist Dan McAdams. His studies demonstrated the importance of rigorous definition and operationalisation if theories are to be adequately tested and an empirical knowledge base constructed.

The final topic we have selected for this chapter is reminiscence and life review, an area of developmental theory that came into prominence in the 1970s and 1980s. The study of reminiscence suggested possibilities for intervening positively in older people's lives by drawing on their capacity to remember or at least to recognise important features of their past lives when reminded of them. Life review by contrast is a concept related more closely to Erikson's last stage of achieving integrity, but also relevant to developmental theories which emphasise the importance of reconciliation with past experience. Studies on life review have recently produced results with important therapeutic implications.

A major limitation of research on psychological change with age is the lack of longitudinal study. Most of the studies conducted in this field have been cross-sectional comparisons of groups of persons of differing ages. As we stressed in the previous chapter, by their very nature the age differences reported in these studies are open to explanation in terms of generational changes in attitudes as well as possibly reflecting genuine developmental changes with age. This limitation needs to be born in mind when considering the research findings reported in this chapter. However, more longitudinal studies are presently being conducted despite the extra demands they put on researchers and grant funding bodies. There is greater appreciation of the necessity for such long-term research commitment as only studies that follow the same people through their lives can provide the necessary depth of understanding into the processes of adult development.

Regulation of emotion

Emotion was a neglected aspect of research on aging. The vast majority of empirical studies comparing younger and older people from the later nineteenth century onwards chose to concentrate on cognitive performance, and especially memory, problem solving and general intelligence. As noted in Chapter 1, these still remain the major topics in psychological research on aging (Stuart-Hamilton, 2012). Although understandable in terms of concern about the increasing prevalence of forms of dementia as the world's population ages and the need to distinguish normal from abnormal cognitive decline with age, a focus solely on cognition tends to foster an overly negative and fearful image of aging. By contrast, the study of emotional change presents an altogether more encouraging perspective on the compensating strengths that people develop as they grow older.

The study of emotion has also been neglected in general psychology. There is a vast imbalance of literature in favour of the study of cognitive processes. Yet emotions are perhaps an even more important and essential part of what makes us human. Western culture, from Aristotle through to Aquinas and the philosophers of the seventeenth and eighteenth century Enlightenment, has been inclined to define humans in terms of their rational component. Emotion driven responses tended to be regarded as part of the lower 'animal' order. Even Darwin, whose observations provided a fresh impetus to the study of the functions of the emotions, regarded emotional expression as vestiges of patterns of action that once were useful but were perhaps no longer so. He gave support to an attitude already strong within society that emotions were suspect, subvertors of reason, and scarcely to be approved of. The result can be seen in twentieth-century science fiction's vision of future super reasoning but emotionless beings.

It has taken a different more respectful attitude to human and animal emotions, stimulated especially by the work of ethologists, to realise how emotions are our way of responding to important life situations. According to this view (Oatley and Jenkins, 1996), emotions happen when certain events affect our striving after goals. Our various emotions can be understood as based on distinctive mental states that go with readiness for action, and arise when we evaluate an event in relation to our goals. Thus the primary emotions (and their corresponding moods in brackets) appear to be: happiness (contentment) at the achievement of goals including solving problems; sadness (depression) at the loss of a goal or a particular avenue leading towards it; anger (aggression) at the frustration of a plan to reach a goal; fear (anxiety) because of a conflict between goals, including the important goal of self-preservation; disgust (aversion) at perceiving something (or someone) to be harmful.

Whereas emotions arise suddenly, and last for seconds or minutes, moods are emotional states that may be vaguer, and they can last for hours or days. The distinction between emotions and moods is like that between two types of muscular activity: contractions, which change the pattern of a limb, and muscle tone, which maintains a posture. Discrete emotions are concerned with changing a situation, and moods with maintaining it. Negative emotions in particular have the function of interrupting ongoing behaviour, but in turn through the production of mood states create new patterns of behaviour or thought, concentrating the attention, ensuring that we think about making sense of what has happened, constructing new plans about what to do about it, and perhaps modifying our goals in relation to the new events.

Over the last ten to twenty years there has been a major development of research interest in age differences in emotion (Mather, 2012). A review of research on emotional aging by Scheibe and Carstensen (2010) has highlighted three common findings: older people's high levels of affective well-being, their increased sensitivity and attention to positive information (and decreased sensitivity to and avoidance of negative information), and their greater confidence in their ability to control their own emotions. Studies in this area continue to expand. In the five years since Scheibe and Carstensen's review article was published further empirical studies on age differences in emotion have appeared in the two premier journals covering the psychology of aging, the American Psychological Association's *Psychology and Aging* and the Gerontological Society of America's *Journal of Gerontology: Psychological Sciences*.

In their ability to regulate emotions older people often appear superior to younger people. In practice this means that they are better able to generate positive affect in the face of difficulties, and to reduce negative affect after failures or negative events (Kessler and Staudinger, 2009). In general as people age they impress by their ability to master negative emotions and not to over-react to changing circumstances. Altogether the evidence suggests that the occurrence of negative emotions decreases with age while the experience of positive emotions remains at least constant (Charles and Carstensen, 2010). Although not as large as the decrements found in research on age differences in cognition, the findings on improvements in emotion regulation with age are generally significant and noteworthy. For example, a US Gallup survey of 340,000 adults found increases from midlife (forties and fifties) to the earlier stages of aging (sixties and seventies) in enjoyment and happiness and decreases in worry and expressions of both anger and sadness (Stone et al., 2010). Other studies have shown that older adults described less anger and more detachment in response to spoken criticism (Charles and Carstensen, 2008) and could predict their own emotional response to situations better than younger adults, as a result being in a better position to consider whether to enter them (Nielsen et al., 2008).

At least some of these findings can be explained in terms of socio-emotional selectivity theory. As discussed in the previous chapter this proposes that older individuals put greater emphasis on maintaining the positives in their lives, and become less concerned about promoting more distant possibilities or identifying and removing threats which may never materialise. Younger adults by contrast become more willing to accept short-term drops in well-being because they serve long-term goals such as gaining knowledge or independence. But there are clearly other factors at work such as enhanced experience at controlling or inhibiting negative emotions. The age positivity effect has also been linked to neurological changes, especially in the amygdala and frontal cortex (St Jacques et al., 2009), which, as we noted in Chapter 2, Gene Cohen (2005) referred to in the developmental theory of aging which he proposed.

However, there are at least five reservations to be made in regard to generalising, on current evidence, about improvements with age in regulating emotion. First, there are some circumstances where older people in fact struggle more than younger people to retain their calm. Novel and demanding situations for example may disturb them more. Therefore it may be more important for an older than a younger person to be able to predict their environment beforehand. In other words, older people may be better at dealing with usual and expected problems but not with the unexpected. A theory which has recently been put forward to explain this difference is Susan Charles's 'strength and vulnerability integration model' (SAVI) (Charles, 2010). This posits that aging is characterised both by improvements in the use of strategies that serve to avoid or limit exposure to negative stimuli, but also by greater vulnerability in situations that elicit high levels of sustained emotional arousal. This is due to reduced physiological flexibility. As a result high-arousal situations can become particularly aversive to people as they grow older, and any advantage older adults might show in regulating their emotions would likely disappear in situations of intense sustained emotional arousal.

Second, in conducting studies in this area, it is important to consider each emotion separately. For example, Kunzmann and Thomas (2014) have found that older adults report anger much less frequently, but sadness at an equivalent level to younger people. (Later on we will consider contrasting findings from experimental studies on this topic.)

Third, data for those in the oldest age groups (over 85 years) is often missing from such studies and where present suggest a marked decline in ability to control emotions in the later stages of aging (Gerstorf et al., 2010). This is a further argument for giving separate attention to the increasing numbers of those living to advanced age (as we do in the final part of this book). Charles's SAVI model, mentioned above under the first reservation, may help to explain changes in emotional control which occur in late life.

Fourth, most of the research that has been conducted so far has only taken place in a limited range of societies, in the case of emotion regulation mainly in the United States and Germany. This is an insufficient basis for generalisation as we stressed in Chapter 1, where we cited as an example recent studies showing large variation in relationships between aging and well-being across different European countries (Morgan et al., 2015).

Fifth, as already emphasised at the beginning of this chapter, there are still few longitudinal studies in this area. These are needed to overcome the limitations of cross-sectional designs and rule alternative explanations such as generational differences in attitude and behaviour as well as differential survival rates. For example, those better able to regulate their emotions may live longer as a result of better cardio-vascular health. There appear to have been only two studies of changes in positive affect over a long period of time, a US study over twenty years (Charles et al., 2001) and a recently reported French study by Gana et al. (2015) (see Box 3.1).

BOX 3.1 CHANGES IN POSITIVE AFFECT WITH AGE

Although many studies have produced evidence for changes in emotional experience with age, there have been few substantial longitudinal studies published. A recent journal article by Gana, Saada and Amieva reports the findings of a twenty-two-year longitudinal study on expressions of positive affect with a sample of initially 3,777 older people (aged 62 to 101 years) living at home in the Gironde and Dordogne in the southwest of France. The average age of the sample at outset was 75 years. The study had ten assessment points over the 22 years.

(continued)

(continued)

Expressions of positive emotion increased with age, reaching a peak as the sample's average age reached 81 years (n = 1,566). The proportion of those with a maximum 'happy' score on the scale (35 per cent) also peaked at 81 years. Subsequent decline was slight and even at the average age of 90 years (n = 68) the remaining sample still scored more positively than at the original baseline average age of 75 years. Good self-perceived health was a significant predictor of expressed happiness at each assessment point.

The findings suggest a high quality of life of those growing old in this area of France.

(Gana et al., 2015)

In the rest of this part we will describe some detailed examples of recent research on age differences in emotion regulation. We consider three areas of study each characterised by its own distinct research methods: interviews on coping with stress in daily life; laboratory-based experiments on reactivity to stress; and experience sampling of emotional preferences recorded over time.

Coping with stress in daily life

Differences in emotional functioning between older and younger people were first systematically studied in the 1980s by the prominent US stress researchers Richard Lazarus and Susan Folkman. Their pioneering work had already high-lighted how styles of coping vary, from seeking to remove or solve problems by direct action to controlling emotional reactions to the stress caused by problems (Lazarus and Folkman, 1984; Lazarus, 1999). Their investigations of age differences showed that older adults compared with younger adults tended to deal with stressful situations more by controlling their own internal reactions. At the same time Folkman and Lazarus and colleagues were aware that people of different ages tended to face different stresses which might account for these different responses. Younger people experienced significantly more hassles in the domains of finances, work, personal life, and family and friends. Older men and women reported pro-portionately more stressful situations related to environmental and social issues, home maintenance and health. The researchers therefore analysed these categories of stress separately, but still found consistent age differences. Older people tended to use more emotional control and less problem solving within each problem area (Folkman et al., 1987).

Subsequent studies have continued to find less emotional stress reported in the daily life of older people than in younger and middle-aged people (Zautra et al., 1991; Almeida and Horn, 2004; Stawski et al., 2008). These findings can now be explained in terms of socio-emotional selectivity (SES) theory as reflecting a shift in motivation with age towards greater acceptance of the present situation as well as greater avoidance of negative emotions (Carstensen et al., 2003). But it is also possible that older people avoid emotional stress because of its consequences for them. Greater familiarity and experience with stress may have taught older people that it was more sensible to use emotional control in situations where problems were difficult to resolve. At the same time declining resources in their own physical health and ability to call on social support may have weakened their ability to solve problems by confrontation.

New methods have now been applied to this area of research, including closer examination of actual responses to stressful situations in daily life. For example, Schilling and Diehl (2014) studied reaction to stressor pile-up over a week among people of varying ages, in the course of which they completed thirty assessments. Every evening the participant was required to complete a diary about the day's events. They also received telephone interviews asking about any stressful events they had encountered. The numbers of stressful events were summed and their severity rated on both positive affect and negative affect scales. They found that there was an additive effect of stressor accumulation on negative affect, but that this effect was less in the group of people aged 60 years and over, which suggests that older adults had developed effective emotion regulation skills for handling stressor pile-up, even though there was no difference in their response to acute stress on individual days.

Birditt (2014) focused her comparative study on negative social interactions, which are some of the most frequently mentioned and distressing of daily stressors mentioned by every age group. She conducted daily interviews for fourteen consecutive days. She found no differences in the way that older people reacted emotionally to unpleasant social encounters; they did not use more avoidant and minimising coping strategies. This might seem surprising in the light of previous studies. However, as Lazarus (1999) himself had emphasised it is important to distinguish between emotional and behavioural responses to stress. Older people may experience just as much negative emotional reaction as younger people to stressful social encounters but respond differently in their actual behaviour. It may be that older people in the previous studies under-reported their emotional reactions precisely because they were not followed by negative behavioural responses such as shouting and persistent arguing.

In the same study Birditt also distinguished between the responses of the young old (70–79) and the older old (80 and above) in her sample. The latter appeared to be more negatively affected by their emotional reactions, such as hurt, irritation and annoyance, and found it less easy to use avoidant strategies. Their inability to do so may have intensified the reactions they felt. Their greater reactivity is in line with Susan Charles's 'strength and vulnerability integration model' (SAVI) (Charles, 2010) referred to earlier. At one and the same time very old people may show both superior regulation of emotions and increased physiological vulnerability to stress. We will return to this subject in Chapter 7.

Experimental studies on emotional reactivity

Emotional regulation is one area within the developmental psychology of aging where experimental research methods can usefully be employed. The laboratory situation allows for measurement of behavioural and physiological reactions as well as self-report. One of the first of such studies compared younger and older adults' emotional arousal in watching sad and amusing films, and found less emotional reactivity in the older adults to both kinds of films (Tsai et al., 2000).

Subsequent studies have become more sophisticated both in the kinds of stimuli presented and the hypotheses investigated. Shiota and Levenson (2009) showed that older adults were more successful in following instructions to reappraise situations positively after watching negative emotion-eliciting films and pictures. Johnson and Whiting (2013) studied reaction to briefly presented facial expressions, demonstrating again a positivity age effect, with older participants tending to see 'happy' rather than 'neutral' expressions, and 'neutral' expressions rather than 'fearful' ones. In both cases younger people showed a bias for seeing 'neutral' expressions. The experimenters compared results under two conditions of short (60 ms) and long (2,000 ms) duration of presentation. The fact that the response biases were more pronounced at the shorter presentation suggests that some degree of automatic processing is responsible for the age positivity effect in emotional perception.

Contrasting results were found as predicted in relation to perception of information related to death by De Raedt et al. (2013). As in Johnson and Whiting's study this material was presented briefly as words on a screen. Older people showed less attentional avoidance than middle-aged participants, suggesting that they were more prepared to receive such information. The lessening of death-associated threat with age could also be considered a positivity effect according to socio-emotional selectivity theory. In this study the investigators attempted to control a little for generational effects by taking into account differences between the two groups in religiosity and belief in an afterlife, and still found the same age effects on attentional avoidance of death-related material.

The importance of including physiological measurement in research in this area is illustrated in another study by Wrzus et al. (2014). They proposed distinguishing a person's emotional reactivity during stress situations from subsequent recovery time. They devised an unpleasant experimental situation for their participants comprising not only difficult mental arithmetic tasks but also an unsympathetic experimenter who interacted with them 'demandingly, briefly and sternly' and 'avoided comforting' them. At the same time their heart rate was monitored, in beats per minute, via electrocardiogram (ECG) electrodes. They found that though heart-rate reactivity was less in the older participants, their recovery time was greater. The researchers offer an explanation of age differences found both in this and previous studies by proposing the following argument. The flexibility of the physiological system diminishes with age. This explains why older people try to avoid unpleasant situations. It also suggests that when confronted with stress they respond with less intense and slower heart-rate activity if they are able to. As a result the lower heart-rate reactivity shown by older people is related to a longer recovery time. As the authors conclude, 'older people may indeed be less easily annoyed, but take a longer time to cool down' (p. 574).

In the same paper Wrzus and colleagues make a further distinction between the differential impact of varied emotions. They note that experiencing sad emotions may lead to relatively stronger reactions in older people, because of the associations aging has with loss (Smith and Lazarus, 1993; Streubel and Kunzmann, 2011). By comparison anger-inducing situations may produce less of a response. The comparison between anger and sadness emotions across age has been the subject of another intriguing US study, in which the authors Haase et al. (2012) investigate the interesting hypothesis that responding with sadness may in fact become more adaptive in later life.

In their study Haase and colleagues showed their participants a series of film clips, all of which were clearly aimed at eliciting definite emotions apart from one film, the stimulus of interest, which was both emotionally neutral and thematically ambiguous. It showed two men conversing in a way that had no evident purpose, and was not obviously aimed at eliciting any particular emotion. Their results were striking. Older adults (aged 60–69 years) showed stronger sadness reactions to all films than younger (20–29 years) and middle-aged (40–49 years) adults. More importantly, responding to the emotionally neutral film with sadness was positively associated with subjective well-being in those in the older group but not in other groups, whereas responding with anger was associated with higher well-being in the middle-aged groups but not in the younger and older groups.

Why should this be so? The authors employ lifespan developmental theory to argue that a tendency to anger, because it fosters higher control beliefs and goal seeking, is likely to peak in midlife (Lachman, 2004). Sadness on the other hand, because it promotes lower control beliefs and encourages goal disengagement, is more adaptive after loss and also elicits support from others (Andrews and Thomson, 2009; Wrosch and Miller, 2009). In the young group on the other hand – where no reactivity bias was found – neither anger nor sadness may be adaptive because they do not yet usually have access to the social status and financial resources to make anger effective, and there is no need for goal disengagement. Of course as the authors acknowledge, because the data are cross-sectional, the results may at least in part reflect generational differences in upbringing or other factors.

Although only an initial study in a complex area of research, this study makes the valuable point that individuals do not always seek to minimise negative emotions. It also does well to engage with lifespan developmental theory. It raises interesting questions about the usefulness of the different emotions, and their possible variation across the lifespan.

Affect preferences in later life

It is well established that individuals – and perhaps also cultures – differ in the types of positive affect states that they ideally prefer (Tsai et al., 2006). However, recent research evidence also indicates that aging brings a shift in preference away from high-arousal to low-arousal emotions. Kessler and Staudinger's (2009) self-report study in Germany was one of the first to show that compared with younger and middle-aged participants older participants seemed to have a stronger preference for low-arousal positive emotions, scoring higher on items such as 'serene', 'relaxed', 'resting' and 'at ease'. They did not differ on high-arousal positive affect items such as 'elated', 'delighted', 'excited' and 'euphoric', and as previous studies had shown reported less negative emotions both of high and low arousal. These effects could not be explained by the other factors the investigators examined such as education, health or personality traits, although of course they could be explained by generational differences.

Other studies have obtained comparable findings. In a large Australian study participants were asked to indicate the frequency of experiencing different emotions over the preceding four weeks: whether they felt calm and peaceful, were full of life, feeling down, or nervous. Older people reported higher levels of low-arousal positive affect (Windsor et al., 2013). However, the more recent US self-report on regulation of positive emotions conducted by Scheibe et al. (2013) had the added advantage of being explicitly designed to test Charles's (2010) recently formulated strength and vulnerability integration (SAVI) model.

In this study adults aged 18–93 years were asked to describe their ideal positive-affect states as part of an extensive experience sampling procedure. They were provided with an electronic pager and instructed to complete an emotion response sheet each time they were paged. Over a period of a week they were paged five times each day during the daytime. They were required to indicate not only how they felt at the time but also how they would ideally like to feel on a range of twenty-eight emotions. Two facets of positive affect were distinguished: feeling calm, peaceful and relaxed versus feeling excited and proud. Among their four age groups (under 40; 40–59; 60–79; 80 and over) it was older participants, and especially those over 80, who showed the greater preference for low affect emotions. Their daily experiences were also more consistent with this pattern. A further interesting finding was that meeting individual goals for lower-arousal positive affect was associated with better health.

What is the significance of this increasing preference for feeling calm and peaceful as people grow older? Charles's SAVI theory suggests that with age high physiological arousal becomes increasingly uncomfortable. But again we have to bear in the mind the possibility of an explanation in terms of generational differences. For example, there has clearly been a change in child-rearing values over the course of the twentieth century from emphasising restraint to encouraging emotional expression (Consedine et al., 2002). However, it seems more likely that these changes reflect the different situation people face as they age, with increased vulnerability leading to greater cautiousness and avoidance of demanding situations, but also to the more peaceful adaptation to life suggested by earlier developmental theorists as Jung, Erikson and Neugarten (Labouvie-Vief, 2009).

Scheibe and colleagues' finding of an association between achieving ideal levels of arousal and individual health is of particular significance. It is consistent with evidence for the effect of calm, relaxed and peaceful emotions on immune and neu-roendocrine processes which promote resistance to illness (Cohen and Pressman, 2006). But more important is this recent study's emphasis on the benefit of achiev-ing the individual's desired affect. People differ in their need to rest physically and mentally in order to be able to deal with the stresses of their lives. With age the need for quiet periods in life appears in general to increase.

Generativity

Generativity is the seventh of eight successive stages in Erikson's (1950, 1963) life course theory of human development and refers to the vital role adults play in establishing and guiding the next generation (Erikson, 1950). According to Erikson, the human life cycle incorporates eight successive challenges, each involving a conflict between two opposing factors. The successful resolution of each psychosocial challenge then offers an integrated set of skills and virtues that enable ongoing development and well-being at later ages and stages including advanced old age. For Erikson, these eight challenges are psychosocial in nature, because the needs of both the individual and society are dynamically interwoven and interrelated in a continual exchange. The seventh challenge and the focus of this part, is the challenge of *generativity versus stagnation*, with the associated virtue of care.

Generativity can manifest itself through any of a wide range of activities aimed at securing the survival and well-being of future generations, while leaving a positive legacy of the self (Kotre, 1984). The most obvious ways many adults actualise their generative potential is by bearing and/or raising children. However, generativity can also manifest itself through a variety of family, friend, teaching, community and political roles. For instance, generative adults may engage in practical activities such as building or creating things to benefit others such as new schools or parks for children. Generativity can also manifest itself culturally or politically, in activities aimed at maintaining and improving experiences for larger groups of people. Such activities can include passing on social values and ideals to upcoming generations (Hunter and Rowles, 2005). For most researchers, generativity is distinct from altruism; although young adults can make important contributions to society and to future generations the latter may not necessarily be directed towards supporting or helping the next generation.

Research on generativity is important for a wide range of reasons. Generativity challenges negative images and stereotypes of aging, because it highlights the vital role that adults in mid- and later life have in supporting and caring for others. Generative activities are also crucial for the well-being of individuals and whole communities, as younger generations need the insights and skills that older peo-ple have accumulated with time and experience. This is especially the case given that other sources of information often available to younger generations, such as books or the Internet, cannot offer individualised advice or support tailored to their particular circumstances and needs.

Recently, researchers have examined the onset and occurrence of generativity, and whether it is an issue most salient for adults in midlife. Also queried is the nature of the relationship between health and generativity. Before discussing this research, we will examine the ways researchers in this field have sought to measure generativity. Measurement is a central issue for quantitative researchers and the measures we use can profoundly shape the ways a given experience or entity is viewed.

Measuring generativity

Erikson first developed his lifespan theory of development in the 1950s, but he did not offer any systematic way to measure or examine his theory empirically. As such, there were very few empirical studies in this field (for exceptions see Ryff and Heinke, 1983; Vaillant and Milofsky, 1980) and few measures that enabled research into the nature, origins or consequences of this construct.

McAdams and colleagues developed a detailed conceptual and measurement framework for the scientific study of Eriksonian generativity. Although other researchers have worked on aspects of Erikson's theory (Kotre, 1984; Ochse and Plug, 1986; Vaillant and Milofsky, 1980), McAdams and colleagues were the first to put forward a model of generativity as a configuration of seven different but interrelated psychosocial features (McAdams and de St. Aubin, 1992; McAdams, de St. Aubin and Logan, 1993).

Within their model, see Figure 3.1, they suggest that inner desires for symbolic immortality and the need to be needed, alongside cultural expectations or demands, lead adults towards a concern for the next generation. These generative concerns will ideally be underpinned by a belief in the goodness or value of human beings. Generative concerns are hypothesised to then lead to generative commitments and generative actions.

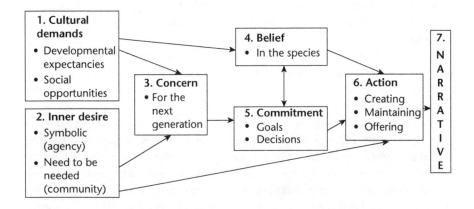

FIGURE 3.1 McAdams' model of generativity.

Source: McAdams and de St Aubin (1992); McAdams et al. (1993).

Generative commitments are recognised through the formulation of plans and goals aimed at assisting the next generation. In contrast, generative actions are defined as any action that the individual is typically or characteristically trying to do or accomplish, which are directed towards helping, guiding or teaching the next generation. Examples of generative actions include bearing/raising children (e.g. biological or parental generativity), teaching someone a skill (e.g. technical generativity), or behaving in a particular way for the benefit of the community (e.g. cultural generative acts) (Kotre, 1984). These aspects of generativity are all believed to be underpinned by generative narration which refers to the larger life story or narrative that contributes to the individual's identity.

McAdams and de St. Aubin (1992) have developed scales to measure generative concerns, generative commitments and generative actions. To measure generative concerns they developed a twenty-item self-report scale, the Loyola Generativity Scale (LGS). Participants rate each item on a four-point scale from 0 (the statement item never applies) to 3 (the statement applies very often). Items for the generative concern scale were based on earlier empirical literature; possible items were discussed and amended via many different researchers and as a consequence of data from their first study (McAdams and de St. Aubin, 1992). Internal reliability scores for this scale were acceptable (alpha = .70).

To measure generative commitments, they use a sentence-completion test; participants describe each of ten personal strivings, defined as things the individual 'typically or characteristically is trying to do each day'. For each striving, participants compete the sentence 'I typically try to . . . '. Responses are coded and scored with reference to involvement with the next generation, providing care, help or guidance to others, and creative contribution (McAdams et al., 1993). Scores are then summed across the three coding criteria and across the ten personal strivings. The generative commitments measure is thus more open-ended; rather than focusing on any specific pre-conceived ideas of the researcher, participants are free to report their own plan and commitments; this may give this scale greater validity.

Finally, generative actions can be measured by a behavioural checklist of fifty items, including ten distracter items which are not related to generativity. Examples of generative behaviours within this measure include 'invented something', 'donated blood' and 'did volunteer work for a charity'. Participants are asked to rate how often they carried out each behaviour within the previous two months. Scores range from 0 (not carried out) to 2 (carried out two or more times). Although not as sophisticated as the earlier two measures, this generative actions checklist was found to be correlated with the other two measures.

A strength of the work by McAdams and colleagues is the way they have grounded their model in the work of earlier researchers; these include Erikson (1950), Browning (1975) and Kotre (1984). In the model of McAdams and colleagues, cultural demands and inner desires are seen as being motivational sources for generative concerns, commitments and actions. In the context of culture, society places certain expectations on individuals to support, help and guide younger generations through young adulthood and into midlife. These motivational concepts draw on Erikson's views about 'the need to be needed' and Kotre's (1984) thinking about the quest for symbolic immortality; that is, acts and experiences that live on in others.

Erikson also believed that generativity was grounded in adults' beliefs about the goodness and worthwhileness of human beings. He strongly believed in human growth and potential into advanced old age. He took a life-history perspective to focus on the more hopeful and active aspects of human lives and choices, and the ways these interconnected through the life course and within an ever-widening radius of family, organisational and community relationships. Belief in the worth-whileness of human beings, and the self, also underpins the model of McAdams and colleagues. They hypothesise a belief as an internal representation that then influences concerns, commitments and actions towards generativity (McAdams et al., 1993).

By basing their model on earlier work, McAdams and colleagues have high-lighted a wide range of factors encompassed by generativity; that is, researchers need to distinguish and define the component of generativity of interns to them. These components could include generativity as a developmental need, an internal motive, a cultural expectation, concerns or thoughts about others, commitments or plans for others, and particular behaviours. Additionally, their measures are easy to use, grounded in theory and have good psychometric properties. They also allow refined insights of the different dimensions of generativity. By comparison, an early scale by Ochse and Plug (1986) has good internal reliability, but this one measure focuses on a general notion of generativity, rather than focusing on distinct dimensions of Erikson's theory.

Although the framework and measures developed by McAdams et al. remain in wide use (see Einolf, 2014; Hofer et al., 2014; Penezić et al., 2008; Schmitt et al., 2015), recent researchers have also contributed survey measures. For instance, Schoklitsch and Baumann (2011) built on Kotre's four types of genera-tivity to develop three specific types of generative concern measures: generative concerns over the whole adult life, generative concerns in the present, and genera-tive concerns as parents. Similarly, Cheng (2009) describes the development of a twenty-item scale measuring generative acts or actions; these items do not include actions towards idea or product creation, but instead focus on attempts to pass on moral and behavioural codes. In contrast, generative goals or strivings can be assessed by the GOALS questionnaire, where participants rated goals from differ-ent life domains on a five-point Likert-type scale (Hofer et al., 2014). All of these newer scales have evidence to support reliability and validity, but all of them need further testing, including as wide a range of samples as possible in order to test these psychometric properties under different conditions and contexts.

The type of research question being addressed however, may lead some researchers to adapt a more qualitative or biographical approach to explore genera-tivity, which includes the use of case studies (e.g. McAdams and Guo, 2015). In an interesting study, researchers developed legacy mapping, a one–page map articulat-ing what professional nurses intend to be better in healthcare due to their efforts;

this tool was found to help participants achieve their goals and in a very meaningful way (Hinds et al., 2015). Other researchers have also sought to analyse open-text responses or comments for generativity-related themes (e.g. Liddle et al., 2013).

Nevertheless, one of the limitations of the work of McAdams and others is that of defining and measuring generativity from a largely individualistic and Western perspective. Although most of the research on generativity to date has been carried out in the United States, the way in which generativity is being conceptualised can vary by culture (Cheng, 2009; Hofer et al., 2014; Penezić et al., 2007). Specifically, although Erikson took a predominantly psychological and developmental perspective to generativity (1963), others have examined this construct as a societal and cultural phenomenon (Alexander et al., 1991; Black and Rubinstein, 2009; Hofer et al., 2014).

Additionally, other researchers have sought to contribute additional psychosocial conflicts that could add breadth and detail to Erikson's central crisis of generativity versus stagnation (see Slater, 2003). The more detailed conflicts include inclusivity versus exclusivity, pride versus embarrassment, responsibility versus ambivalence, career productivity versus inadequacy, parenthood versus self-absorption, being needed versus alienation, and honesty versus denial. Each conflict will necessitate development and testing of measures, and further research will be needed to examine the relationships between these and both their predictors and consequences on health, well-being and development.

Many other questions remain for future studies. It is not clear for instance what level of generative action is needed before an individual can be said to be behaving generatively. This is especially puzzling as people can be generative in some roles (e.g. as parents), but not in other roles or settings (e.g. in taking care of the wider social community). It is also important to develop measures for other components of generativity, for example a measure of faith in the species, or faith in the fundamental goodness or value of human beings. Some exciting future studies may also combine methodologies, for example use of interviews alongside survey measures to get detailed qualitative insights, alongside information on relationships and generalisability available with a quantitative or survey approach.

Predictors of generativity

Erikson places generativity most firmly in the middle adulthood years, assumed to be around age 35 to 65 years. He believed that it was only when adults had made progress with earlier life challenges including establishing identity (the fifth stage) and long-term bonds of intimacy (the sixth stage) that they are ready to focus their energies towards the betterment of the next generation and leaving a positive legacy. Placing generativity in the middle adulthood years, however, does not mean that generativity is restricted solely to this life stage. For instance, Kotre (1996) argues that different behavioural expressions of generativity can peak at different points of the life cycle, with biological generativity being most salient for younger adults, and cultural generativity, defined as passing on of culturally relevant ideas and values, being most likely to peak later in life. Additionally, in later theorising, Erikson (1997) acknowledges that generativity may change into advanced old age but should not disappear, as he strongly cautions against stagnation and withdrawing fully from creativity, involvement and caring or guiding others. Understanding whether generativity is age related rather than being culturally or personality dependent is important if we are to understand better the occurrence of generativity, and its potential for understanding and promoting the well-being of individuals and communities.

There is disagreement in the literature about the onset and course of generativity, and whether indeed it is something most salient for adults at midlife. On the one hand, some researchers have found high levels of generative concerns among midlife adults (McAdams et al., 1998; Ochse and Plug, 1986; Peterson and Stewart, 1990; Valliant, 1993). For example, Keyes and Ryff (1998) found statistically significant age differences in generativity with those aged 40–59 years scoring higher than those aged 24–39, or those aged 60-plus years. More recently, Freund and Blanchard-Fields (2014) examined generativity as a facet of altruism, and found that older people were more likely than their younger counterparts to behave altruistically. However, although the above results suggest that generativity increases with age, other researchers have found either no relationship between generativity and chronological age (e.g. Van de Water and McAdams, 1989) or mixed evidence (e.g. McAdams et al., 1993).

Discrepant findings can be explained by a range of factors including differences in recruitment and sampling, differences in measurement, and limited attempts to replicate studies. Differences between cross-sectional and longitudinal research may also provide important insights. In an early classic study, Stewart et al. (2001) examined the potential confounds of decade and historical time. This confound can be problematic because adults in particular age groups can have certain experiences (e.g. the Second World War for current generations of older people) which impact on their lives, irrespective of their current age. This would mean that what is true for one generation is not necessarily true for another generation. In the Stewart et al. study, there was a ten-year age difference between participants recruited in the Michigan and Mills samples, yet both were assessed when they were in their forties, which was in the 1990s for the Michigan sample and the 1980s for the Mills sample. No significant effect was found; that is, both samples reported the same feelings at the same ages although they were rating their experiences at different time points in different decades. These results provide evidence that findings were a consequence of development rather than cohort or particular generational social experiences.

One of the strengths of the Stewart et al. (2001) research is their attempt to analyse the onset of generativity over time and across different sample groups. Longitudinal designs also enable researchers to distinguish between factors which are best considered in terms of individual difference variables rather than a variable best associated with a particular time or stage in life. However, this study is also biased towards women and towards adults with more educational and material resources. More research is therefore needed examining the onset and occurrence of generativity, with other sample groups including adults with particular responsibilities (such as caregiving to frail parents) which may impact significantly on the occurrence and course of generativity.

However, McAdams et al. (1998) and Stewart and Vandewater (1998) have argued that generativity is too complex and multifaceted to be a discrete developmental task in the adult lifespan, and that instead, aspects of generativity may occur at different time points through the life course. Additionally, although generative concerns can remain stable into late life, generative actions or behaviours may decrease. Freund and Blanchard-Fields (2014) attribute the latter to there being fewer opportunities, and fewer resources in later life to be generative given ill health, retirement and also children leaving home. Consequently, across four studies, they report making sure that all adults of all ages had the same opportunities to be altruistic.

However, far from being a time of fewer opportunities for generativity, Cheng (2009) believes that continuing advancements in longevity and healthcare, along with a desire to provide childcare to working adult children, can mean that many more older adults are in fact spending increasing amounts of time with grandchildren and great grandchildren. Therefore, while midlife generativity may be dominated by themes of parenting, generativity for many older adults may extend far beyond the family to include unrelated or distant groups and themes, including civic engagement. These views offer a challenge to researchers to develop sophistication in their designs that ideally enables multiple variables to be examined at one time. For instance, to examine not just age by generativity effects, but also the context or environment which may influence results. Building on awareness of this complexity of environment, plus the different facets of generativity, findings by Freund and Blanchard-Fields (2014) across different studies and methodologies, indicated that older people were more generative than their younger counterparts.

Nevertheless, further research is needed, given the plethora of potential predictors or antecedents of generativity that can influence generativity at any age or stage. These include family and community relationships (Peterson and Stewart, 1996; Hart and McAdams, 2001), personality-type characteristics such as agreeableness or conscientiousness known to influence prosocial behaviours (see Courbalay et al., 2015), compassion and empathy (Moore et al., 2014), setting (Kessler and Staudinger, 2007) or simply the availability or resources which can differ between age groups and generations. If/where the latter reduces from midlife into later life, this would mean that both capacity and opportunities for generativity into later years may become more constrained by comparison with younger age groups. Biography and narrative identity (Adler et al., 2015; Jones and McAdams, 2013; McAdams and Guo, 2015) can also shed light on events, relationships and ways of thinking that may shape development towards generative capacity.

At any age, gender and ethnicity can also influence the occurrence and course of generativity through inequality, and reduced social and health opportunities (e.g. Black and Rubinstein, 2009). For instance, many studies have reported higher levels of disability among older women by comparison with men and greater financial dependence among women who typically were forced to give up working and financial independence when they married. Statistically, women are also more likely than men to have experienced violence, to have lower levels of education, to live alone, and to be without a carer often after spending many years providing unpaid care to family or friends (European Union, 2012). Older women are also much more likely than men to be disadvantaged in terms of health status and mobility, and to live in residential settings (European Union, 2012; Hyde and Jones, 2007). However, the UN flagship report (2015) focuses on economic and social dimensions of gender inequality to change lives for the better (see United Nations, 2015); this includes putting in place policies and pensions to ensure that gender inequality does not continue, and does not perpetuate heath, education, economic and political unfairness.

Generativity and well-being

Just as younger generations need older adults, Erikson hypothesised that older adults need to be generative for their health and well-being, and for continuing development towards integrity and wisdom. Indeed, Erikson recognised that the conflict and tension inherent in each of the eight life challenges can be sources of substantial growth, strength, self-respect and commitment (Erikson and Erikson, 1998). A substantial body of literature in personality and developmental psychology has built on Erikson's ideas to suggest that generativity represents a hallmark of successful aging (Hofer et al., 2014; Versey et al., 2013; Reichstadt et al., 2010), resilience (Landes et al., 2014), and psychosocial maturity (see Ryff and Migdal, 1984). For some people, however, the resolution of earlier conflicts may not be towards generativity, but towards a persistent sense of stagnation and personal impoverishment, evident in lower levels of self-esteem, confidence, and physical health (Erikson, 1950). To shed light on Erikson's model, we now examine the relationship between generativity and health in more detail, and offer some suggestions for further research.

Several studies have examined the link between generativity and psychosocial well-being, often getting mixed results with some aspects of generativity, namely generative concerns being the most strongly associated with health and well-being (see McAdams et al., 1993; Grossbaum and Bates, 2002). It is possible that generative concerns and thoughts can leave a person feeling good, but actually getting involved can be more demanding, particularly where individuals do not feel sufficiently skilled or supported. Nevertheless, helping and supporting others is associated with improved health, including better coping (DeGrezia and Scrandis, 2015), and a substantially reduced risk of mortality (Okun et al., 2013). Declaring a professional legacy (or what they intend to be better in health due to their efforts) resulted in nurses being more likely to achieve meaning and this legacy (Hinds et al., 2015).

Using sophisticated statistical analyses, and a longitudinal design of one year, Cheng (2009) hypothesised that generative actions would not be related to well-being, unless those generative actions were valued and respected by others. They also sought to examine whether a lack of respect would lead to demotivation and disengagement from generative goals. At baseline a convenience sample of 190 adults aged 60-plus years were recruited from social centres for older adults. Participants ranging in age from 60–89 years (n = 190, mean age 73, sd = 5.93, 68 per cent female, 34 per cent living alone, 47 per cent married, 38 per cent with no formal education). They were surveyed at two time points, twelve months apart. Surveys used included an adapted and back-translated measure of generative concerns and actions (McAdams and de St. Aubin, 1992), four subscales from the Ryff Psychological Well-being Scales (Ryff, 1989; positive relations, purpose in life, personal growth and self-acceptance), and a specifically developed measure of perceived respect. Consistent with other studies, generative concerns were most predictive of well-being. Generative behaviours were also moderately to strongly associated with well-being at a bivariate level. Additionally, perceived respect was found to predict generative concern over time, and to mediate the relationship between generative behaviour and well-being; that is, unlike midlife generativity, where strong cultural expectations towards generativity may override the reactions from younger generations, later life generativity attempts were found to be statistically influenced by participants' perceptions of others' willingness to listen.

This study raises some interesting issues about the social context in which generativity can occur (see also Pilkington et al., 2012). However, the generalisability of the findings needs further investigation, particularly in relation to adults in midlife rather than later life, and to other non-Chinese/Western populations. Additionally, and as noted by the researchers, it is possible that respect from a range of sources (e.g. children, professionals, community others) might carry different effects, and each should be studied further separately and together. The study also used one measure only of respect, and that was from the perspective of older people; while this may be the most relevant in terms of later well-being, an interesting line of research could examine the relationship between felt respect, and self-respect. Or between respect, and other factors known to impact on quality of life or well-being, including attitudes to aging, physical health status or the availability of practical or economic resources.

In another complex but unique longitudinal study, researchers sought to examine the relationship between early adversity, midlife generativity, and later life health and adjustment to aging (Landes et al., 2014). Data were analysed from 635 white men from both the Harvard Sample and Inner City Cohort in a seventy-three-year longitudinal Study of Adult Development. They hypothesised that childhood adversity would have an enduring inverse effect on positive aging among those who were not generative in midlife, whereas those who did become generative would be unaffected by childhood adversity. The Harvard sample were first interviewed in their late teens, and then when they were on average around 25, 30, 50 and 65 years of age; they also had follow-up questionnaires every two years, and physical health exams every five years from age 45 years. The Inner City sample were interviewed at ages 14, 17, 25, 32 and 47, with follow-up questionnaires also every two years, and physical health exams every five years from age 47 years. Childhood adversity was defined in terms of harsh parenting and social economic status. Generativity was assessed via two-hour interviews by researchers blind to other data; participants had to demonstrate 'a definite capacity for establishing and guiding the next generation beyond raising their own children, through their actual sustained responsibility for the growth, well-being and leadership of other adults' (p. 945). Thirty-eight per cent met this criterion, with all interrater disagreements resolved through discussion and consensus. Physical health at different time points was assessed blind to other data, and coded from 1 (deceased) to 7 (excellent health). Adjustment to aging was assessed via participants' sense of meaning, and their subjective well-being. For generativity to mediate the relationship between childhood adversity and later life outcomes, generativity had to be associated with both childhood adversity and adjustment to aging and health status at age 60–75.

Findings demonstrated the enduring and protective function of generativity in helping to counter early adversity, and in promoting positive adjustment and well-being in later adulthood. Specifically, results showed that childhood adversity was negatively and proportionally associated with the achievement of generativity at midlife (age 50–65 years); that is, the more childhood adversity, the less likelihood there was of achieving generativity. The authors suggest these findings may be explained by the role of inequalities of early socio-economic disadvantage that can accumulate through the life course (see also Brandt et al., 2012). However, findings also showed that midlife generativity reduced the negative effects of childhood adversity, and that this was associated with health in later life. Additionally, there was a trend for generativity at midlife to mediate the relationships between lower social childhood class and later-life health outcomes. Generativity also moderated (neutralised) the association between lower social childhood class and later adjustment to aging; that is, despite early adversity, those engaging in positive growth through the life course experienced more favourable health and adjustment outcomes in later life.

A significant strength of this study was the use of a longitudinal data set spanning more than fifty years. This contrasts greatly with other studies using less detailed and less reliable cross-sectional designs, or retrospective assessments of earlier ages and stages (e.g. Black and Rubinstein, 2009). This research also provides a unique opportunity to study whether generativity mediates and/or moderates the relationship between childhood adversity and later life outcomes. However, this study is based on data collected a long time ago beginning in the 1930s, and it is not clear how replicable the findings would be to more recent cohorts. Additionally, the study is limited to Caucasian men in the United States, and its generalisability to the lives of women or other cultural groups remains unclear.

The role of women featured strongly in a recent study on generativity and compassion; the latter is potentially an important but under-researched feature of generativity and the maintenance of relationships (Moore et al., 2015). While empathy involves the capacity to understand and share the feelings of another, compassion includes a desire to help others, lessen their suffering and change this suffering towards a more hopeful legacy for the future. Moore et al. (2015) examined the relationship between compassion and well-being, in a large community survey with those aged 50-plus years (n = 903, mean age = 77). Even when statistically controlling for other explanations, the biggest predictors of compassion were resilience, being female and having a higher number of significant life events. However, further research is needed in this area using a range of generativity-specific measures, and more comprehensive health measures compared to the one-item health measures used in this study.

Much more research is needed on generativity given the huge potential benefits of this positive and proactive contributor to our understanding of adult development, and also well-being, relationships and even mortality (Okun et al., 2013). Future research could examine the relationships between generativity and a range of lifestyle and situational characteristics (e.g. caregiving), and psychological factors (including compassion, or a 'belief in the species'). Indeed, research to facilitate generativity may also be very urgent given that the desire to leave a legacy or mark can become increasingly important as the finitude of life becomes more salient. For example, enhancing identity by identifying more with the contribution which one's own generation has made to the world may be one important way of promoting a sense of generativity (Weiss, 2014). However, regardless of research question or methodology, participants to future studies may need to be given incentives for participation to manage possible selection biases towards those already generatively oriented.

Reminiscence and life review

The last field of research activity we examine in this chapter is investigation into the functions and benefits of reminiscence, the process of recalling past events and experiences, and in particular life review, a focused consideration of one's past life as a whole. Research on reminiscence not only has a long history within the developmental psychology of aging but has also contributed a great deal to improving attitudes to and care for older people. Encouraging older people to reminisce is seen as a natural activity nowadays, and very much part of life within assisted-living settings. Fifty years ago attitudes to reminiscence tended to be dismissive. Although there has also been a general cultural shift in favour of remembering the past, much of the impetus has come from gerontological theory, research and practice (Webster and Haight, 2002; Kenyon et al., 2011).

Reminiscence work owes a particular debt to Erikson's definition of integrity as 'the acceptance of one's one and only life cycle as something that had to be and that, by necessity, permitted of no substitutions' (Erikson, 1963, p. 260), but even more to Robert Butler's concept of 'life review' (Butler 1963). Writing from his experience as a practising therapist in a psychiatric journal, Butler put forward the view that life review is a normative process which all people undergo as they realise that their life is coming to an end. This article had a considerable impact, containing many literary references to illustrate its points, while being rooted in the author's own clinical observations. It led directly to the development of research on the value and functions of reminiscence and life review and to the more purposeful use of reminiscence in working practice with older people (Bornat, 1994; Birren et al., 1996).

However, as reminiscence came to be promoted in practice with older people in the 1970s and 1980s, a major credibility gap emerged in that, despite plenty of anecdotal accounts of the benefits of reminiscence, controlled studies of its efficacy did not produce significant results (Thornton and Brotchie, 1987). This issue could not begin to be resolved until researchers started making distinctions between different functions of reminiscence. Because of the continuing importance of this issue we will first review research on the differential functions and effects of reminiscence. We will then focus on the concept of life review, and consider a longitudinal study examining its antecedents and consequences. Finally, we will examine recent research on the evaluation of reminiscence and life review interventions with older people.

Types and functions of reminiscence

Constructing a fruitful typology of uses of reminiscence became vital to defining the subject area. By the late 1960s there were at least three quite distinct sets of theoretical frameworks proposed for understanding the benefits that reminiscence brought to older people. The first was identity maintenance. This was mainly based on observation of older people's behaviour in threatening situations, particularly in the demeaning circumstances of American nursing homes of the 1960s and 1970s (Lieberman and Tobin, 1983). It was this conception of reminiscence that was seized on by those wanting to enliven elderly care settings. By promoting the natural defence of reminiscence they hoped to combat apathy and depression in institutionalised and otherwise neglected older people.

A quite different notion was that of life review. The idea of reintegration of the self following the midlife crisis was strongly present in Jung's writings, as also in Erikson's, but it was Butler's discussion of the topic that was seized upon as a means of justifying and giving dignity to older people's reminiscences. However, whereas the identity maintenance function of reminiscence concerned the role of the past in promoting stability of the self, the life-review function pointed to possibilities for change and development. These differences in function were minimised in subsequent studies of the frequency and benefits of reminiscence, and it is likely that the full implications of the concept of life review were not properly considered by most of those who promoted reminiscence practice in care settings.

A third more social aspect of reminiscence was also present in the early literature. It existed within both the disengagement theory of aging and the contrasting theory of social and cultural re-engagement, described in the previous chapter. In disengagement theory terms, reminiscence was seen as part of natural withdrawal from social responsibilities with age. It was a way of obtaining solace for the self while impacting less on the world around. But at the same time anthropologists were noting the ways in which elders in traditional societies actually invested themselves with authority by drawing out teaching from their life's experience. A study of veterans of the late nineteenth-century Spanish-American war illustrated this point well in describing the strengths and vitality of this particular group of older people (McMahon and Rhudick, 1967).

One of the first comparative studies of reminiscence functions was conducted in London (Coleman, 1974). This study developed criteria to assess different categories of reminiscence and quantify their presence in transcripts of conversation. Reminiscence with an analytical and questioning character was shown to have positive associations with morale in those who declared themselves dissatisfied with their past lives, thus supporting Butler's notion of the benefits of life reviewing. Culturally informative or transmissive reminiscence was significantly associated with well-being, at least among the men in the sample. Longitudinal study of the sample illustrated how, by contrast, other types of reminiscence might be maladaptive, especially repetitive rumination and painfully nostalgic memories (Coleman, 1986).

In a subsequent Canadian study, also based on systematic observation of older people's reminiscence, Wong and Watt (1991) showed that 'integrative' reminiscence – corresponding to Butler's life review – was related to independently assessed markers of aging well. Their observations on the negative associations of obsessive or compulsive reminiscence proved particularly influential. They recognised the links with symptoms of post-traumatic stress disorder (PTSD) where memories linked to experience of overwhelming fear can become intrusive presences with lifelong consequences. The study of the continuing role of traumatic memories in later life, the factors that influence them and the optimum methods of diminishing their harmful influence has become an important field of research in its own regard (Hunt et al., 1997; Hunt, 2010; Burnell et al., 2011).

Necessary to progress in research on reminiscence was the development of psychometrically sound self-report instruments. Whereas the previous method of rating conversation transcripts had led to many fresh insights, it was costly in interview time. The development of valid questionnaires allowed for large-scale studies which could test more sophisticated hypotheses. Webster's 'Reminiscence Functions Scale' (RFS) (Webster, 1993) has proved particularly successful. This is a forty-three-item questionnaire in which subjects indicate on a six-point scale how often they reminisce for different purposes. The items are presented as completions to the stem 'when I reminisce it is to . . . '. As well as functions of 'identity building', 'teaching/informing', 'problem-solving', 'intimacy maintenance' and 'conversation', the measure assesses some previously little studied functions of reminiscence: 'boredom reduction', 'bitterness revival' and 'death preparation'.

The eight dimensions identified by Webster have stood the test of time and his scale is now in widespread use in North America, Western Europe and Australia, with a recent comparative study extending its use to Israel (O'Rourke et al., 2013). Analysis of the latter data set has confirmed a model of relationships between the various forms of reminiscence and well-being developed in previous studies by the same team of researchers (Cappeliez and O'Rourke, 2006; O'Rourke et al., 2011). The model proposes three latent constructs underlying the eight functions of reminiscence: 'self-positive' functions (comprising identity building, problem-solving and death preparation); 'self-negative' functions (comprising bitterness revival, boredom reduction and intimacy maintenance); and pro-social functions (comprising conversation and teaching/informing). In samples of older people, the self-dimensions have the predicted positive and negative relationships with indicators of well-being such as life satisfaction, absence of psychological distress and positive attitude to own health over a time period of more than a year. The pro-social functions effects have more indirect effects on well-being conditional on the nature of the social interactions involved. As Wong and Watt's (1991) study had suggested, the benefits of 'transmissive' reminiscence are largely dependent on the presence of a properly appreciative audience for the older persons' conversations and teaching.

The inclusion of reminiscence for intimacy maintenance among the maladaptive functions may appear at first sight surprising but it is characteristic of prolonged grief reactions and has been linked previously to lowered morale (Coleman, 1986). More recent studies of the course of older people's adjustment to bereavement have shown how persistent feelings of regret in particular are predictive of maladaptive grief responses (Torges et al., 2008). They impede integration of past and present and prevent the construction of a meaningful future. Along with bitterness revival and boredom reduction, reminiscence for intimacy maintenance often fails to produce genuinely constructive results. An interesting finding from a comparative study of Canadians and Israelis (O'Rourke et al., 2013) was that bitterness revival appeared a more significant component of self-negative reminiscence for the latter, whereas boredom reduction was more evident in the former group. The authors suggest that these differences reflect the greater threats to security of existence that older Israelis have experienced during their lives, and the relative uneventfulness of life by comparison for older people in Canada.

Webster (2002) has also considered the issue of racial differences in reminiscence function. He confirmed earlier work by Merriam (1993) that certain ethnic groups – African Americans, Chinese Canadians and Native Indian Americans – used reminiscence more. Further research needs to examine to what extent this finding reflects a stronger oral tradition among these groups and/or a greater need to use reminiscence to promote self-understanding, preserve identity and teach younger generations. Reminiscence now has a protean presence in studies of aging, showing links with some of the key concepts we will consider in later chapters, such as attachment and personal meaning. Negative correlations with variables such as purpose in life, life control and will to meaning suggest that a struggle to find meaning may underlie much reminiscence in later life (Cappeliez, 2002; Korte et al., 2012). A high level of reminiscence activity may not necessarily be a positive sign. It could indicate a person caught in negative ruminations and needing therapeutic assistance.

Life review, its antecedents and associations

Despite the proliferation of different reminiscence functions, 'life review' – or 'integrative' reminiscence – remains the foremost developmental concept in the reminiscence literature. It suggests a distinct task for later life in achieving a rounded evaluation of the life that has been lived. However, life review's universal character as originally proposed by Butler has been questioned by interview studies which suggest that well-being in later life is not dependent on reminiscence (Coleman, 1986; Sherman, 1991), also by evidence that life review demands an inner propensity that is not characteristic of all or even most older people (Wink and Schiff, 2002), and even by theoretical considerations of the self's bias towards continuity (Parker, 1995). Reminiscence, in adulthood, appears to be more often used to reassert previous patterns of self-understanding, for example in response to threat or challenge, than to create the new understanding arising from life review.

Nevertheless, life review in the radical sense enunciated by Butler remains a fascinating concept, perhaps even more so because of its special developmental character. It implies a search for meaning through reflection on one's life's experience (Randall and Kenyon, 2001), and may lead to transformation of goals and changed values (Freeman, 1997, 2010). Other recent studies have reaffirmed the developmental aspect of life review, specifically linking it to later life, in reconstruction of the self. Tornstam (1999) has associated it with his concept of gerotranscendence (see Chapter 2) in arguing for an increased use of reminiscence in later life to unify across time, linking the living with the dead, the past and the future.

Susan Bluck, in arguing for greater interaction between the study of reminiscence and of autobiographical memory (Bluck and Levine, 1998; Bluck and Habermas, 2000), has pointed to the reconstructive role of memory throughout life in addition to its stabilising role. The self is largely constant over time, and reminiscence certainly often serves the function of maintaining stability, but it is also being constantly revised through the selective accession and modification of memories. It is important to recognise and respect both functions, especially in intervening in people's lives. There are times for reassuring those we seek to help but times also for helping them to move on in their level of self-understanding.

The study of life review like other emergent features of aging should be placed in a lifespan perspective. We need to identify the developmental precursors and antecedent conditions which foster its expression. Placing it in this context also encourages attention to the different facets of reminiscence. An example of such a study of the life review has been published by Wink and Schiff (2002). It is based on the Berkeley (California) longitudinal study whose original sample of newborn babies and pre-adolescents was collected in 1928–9 and 1931 respectively. Having been investigated intensively in childhood and adolescence, they have been interviewed in depth on four occasions in adulthood. Wink and Schiff were able to base their analysis on 172 participants while they were in their late sixties and mid-seventies. These constituted 90 per cent of the cohort still available (neither dead nor lost). They derived an assessment of life-review activity from the interviews conducted at that time and related it to ratings of personality collected earlier in life. In-depth interviews on psychological and social functioning, lasting on average three-and-a-half hours, were conducted with the participants. Two independent judges rated the material for signs of life review using a five-point scale adapted from the work of Sherman (1991). Only 22 per cent of the sample showed clear evidence of striving for a new level of self-understanding, 20 per cent were unclear and the remaining 58 per cent showed no signs at all of striving for new understanding or integration.

Although life review was not associated with self-ratings of life satisfaction, it was positively rated to ratings of other characteristics, notably creativity, spirituality and generativity. It is to the great credit of this study that it included such characteristics. Considered in terms of its social relevance, creativity, spirituality and generativity are much more significant outcomes than well-being. Gerontological research has perhaps been impoverished by an over focus on individual subjective well-being as the primary outcome variable. The contribution older people make and the example they set to the rest of society from the witness of their lives are certainly as important.

As one might expect, life review was also related to ratings of 'openness to experience', one of the 'big five' personality traits (Block, 2010), personal growth and to using reminiscence (on Webster's reminiscence functions scale) for identity exploration and problem solving. Most interesting are the links found with psychological characteristics assessed earlier in life, such as observer-based indices of introspection and insight. Life review was also related to a global measure of past negative life events, such as a major off-time bereavement, other personal crisis or illness. Wink and Schiff's thesis, consistent with that of previous commentators (Coleman, 1986; Parker, 1995), is that life review is an adaptive response to aging in those who have encountered marked difficulties in life, but that for the majority of older persons it is not a necessary adaptation. They take their analysis further by describing in detail and contrasting two individuals from their sample, both with high acceptance of their lives, but the one high and the other low in life-review involvement.

Case-study analysis is a neglected method of research in psychology but one that can be used not only to illustrate but also to validate theory. Ultimately psychological propositions have to make sense at the level of the individual person, and need to be employed in understanding individual behaviour (Bromley, 1986; Coleman, 2002). Such analyses are also likely to raise questions about existing theory and provide suggestions for further hypothesis testing. Particularly valuable are longitudinal case studies that base their conclusions on data collected over a substantial period of the person's life (see Chapter 7 for further examples). The nature of Wink and Schiff's study means they can draw on data on self-reflection collected throughout the persons' lives.

'Melissa' and 'Frank' are two such cases, with contrasting features, drawn from their study (see Box 3.2). Interviewed for the last time at 69 years Melissa had been through many difficulties in her life, including with her parents when she was young and subsequently with her husband whom she had divorced in midlife. However, she had succeeded in working through the various problems she had encountered and created from it a cohesive story. She had, in Erikson's terms, accepted the 'inevitability' of her life. Moreover, she had been able to apply the lessons she had learned in her current work as an artist and counsellor, and rated her current life satisfaction very highly. Frank was also very satisfied with his life but, despite his rather introverted personality and in strong contrast to Melissa, had never felt the need to analyse his life. It had been relatively straightforward. When young he had followed his parents' advice to go into a safe and remunerative occupation rather than pursue his literary interests and had been successful in work and family life. He had been able to retire early, and subsequently taken up his original interests. He seemed never to have felt the need to fuse his interests into a cohesive whole.

BOX 3.2 CONTRASTING CASES: LIFE REVIEW AND ITS ANTECEDENTS

'Melissa'

Interviewed at 29 years, Melissa was estranged from her parents and her marriage was disintegrating. A year earlier she had begun psychotherapy in response to her distress. She described in detail the difficulties she had growing up with a controlling mother and hostile father, and an abiding sense of betrayal and feeling barely alive. Despite her insecurities about sexuality and about men, she had left home, got pregnant by and married the man who had come close to her in her difficulties. But he turned out also to be as emotionally needy as she was, and became more and more controlling and abusive of her.

Only after many years trying to improve the situation and finally realising that he would not change did Melissa separate from him. Her subsequent development as an adult involved a lot of hard work and painful adjustments in order to become financially and emotionally independent.

Interviewed at 69 years, Melissa was continuing to work on herself. For the first time she had been able to pinpoint her basic sense of betrayal at being sexually abused by her father at the age of 3 or 4, a fact that she believed was subsequently covered up by her mother. She never confronted her father with this accusation, but described a cathartic scene shortly before he died when she had shaken him with rage and yelled at him to behave. Back in her car afterwards she had suffered a panic attack. But as a consequence of her

(continued)

(continued)

understanding of both her father's and mother's behaviour she had begun to understand her own problems in relationships with men. She was now a productive artist with many other interests, including counselling, for which she had recently undergone training, and was open to finding another partner.

'Frank'

Interviewed at 36 years, Frank indicated how he had wanted to pursue his early interests in literature and writing, but his parents counselled him to find a stable occupation. He had accepted their advice and did not regret it.

His career in banking was hugely successful, thanks to a combination of making right decisions, and having good colleagues and clients. He astonished his friends and colleagues by his decision to retire early in his mid-fifties. But there was no financial or other need for him to work further and he and his wife had other outdoor as well as indoor interests, including literature, which they wanted to develop.

Interviewed at 76 years, Frank explained how he had retired early to concentrate on his passion for writing literary criticism that he had left behind at college. He had only been moderately successful at this task but he still enjoyed it immensely. He did reminisce at times, for example, to relive experiences with his wife or tell stories to the grandchildren. However he accepted his life story without feeling the need for any further analysis.

(Wink and Schiff, 2002)

As Wink and Schiff analyse the two cases they show that the focus of Frank's reflections during his interviews had remained firmly on things outside of himself, whereas Melissa's focus had been on her own personal life experiences. Frank's successful life had been virtually conflict free. Melissa had experienced abuse, betrayal and rejection in great measure and had needed to learn to cope with a range of conflicting feelings as a consequence. In conclusion they suggest that Frank's case is a counter-example to the adage that an unexamined life is not worth living, while Melissa had experienced pain to the degree that it is perhaps necessary for life review to occur in later life. The two cases help not only to illustrate but also to help explain the general finding from their research on the Berkeley sample that life review is not inevitable and is a product of life's difficulties rather than its successes.

Evaluative studies of reminiscence and life review

From its beginning the study of reminiscence has been closely tied to therapeutic practice with older people. This makes all the more important the task of identifying which types of reminiscence should be encouraged and which avoided.

Barbara Haight has been a pioneer researcher-practitioner in this field in the United States. She was the first to develop rigorous evaluations of the time-limited life-review interventions which she developed for use by nurses working in the community and in nursing homes (Haight, 1988, 1992). She also provided regular updated reviews of the reminiscence literature (e.g. Hendrix and Haight, 2002) and helped launch the International Institute for Reminiscence and Life Review as a centre for communicating ideas, practice and research findings (reminiscence andlifereview.org). Interest in the beneficial practice of reminiscence has become worldwide and is well exemplified in the considerable work undertaken in Japan, including Nomura's recent study on the value of reminiscence groups in promoting psychological recovery following the Great East Japan earthquake and tsunami in 2011 (Nomura, 2013).

The field of reminiscence interventions is now so large that it has become necessary to examine more critically the nature of the various interventions employed, and to assess their benefits for different client groups. There are already a number of different procedures in use. The method of life review advocated by Haight for example is a one-to-one approach, but also a time-limited series of six sessions covering the whole life course, including a final integrative session. Both positive and negative themes are addressed. The design of this programme explicitly takes into account the time constraints operating on health and social welfare workers as well as the needs of their clients. By contrast the 'guided autobiography' groups, pioneered by Birren and colleagues (Birren and Deutchman, 1991; Randall and Kenyon, 2001), are much more extensive in the time and social skills (such as written composition and creative listening) required. Participants are typically made up of people who are from the outset well motivated to explore the major themes of their lives in company with others (Ruth et al., 1996). The therapeutic benefit of writing is now a well-established theme in health and clinical psychology (Niederhoffer and Pennebaker, 2002).

Thanks to recent advances in research we can now see more clearly how the specific outcomes of reminiscence will depend on the types of memories recalled (Bluck and Levine, 1998). Accessing some memories will encourage self-acceptance, while accessing others will actually stimulate self-change. Much then depends on the aims of the intervention and the techniques used. Life review in the sense in which Butler originally described it is more concerned with the possibility of self-change than with maintaining present self-conceptions. It would be possible to change one's sense of self by drawing on a different, often neglected and seemingly forgotten, set of memories to the ones on which the present self is based. But this is a difficult and anxiety-raising task, as Butler realised. It is more possible when someone is already dissatisfied with life or is seeking self-growth, but for most people it is hard to give up a theory of the self in which they have long invested.

The major advance in reminiscence work with older people in recent years has been the clearer understanding achieved of the mental-health implications of different types of reminiscence (Westerhof et al., 2010b). Whereas constructively organised reminiscence in group settings can be used to foster group solidarity, personal life review uses the various positive self-functions of reminiscence to enhance self-acceptance and sense of meaning. Westerhof and colleagues' (2010b) further distinction between life review and life-review therapy is of particular interest. The latter relates more to the negative uses of reminiscence such as promoting resentment, sense of loss and dissatisfaction with life with those encountering psychiatric problems as chronic depression. It uses varies therapeutic approaches (cognitive behavioural, psychoanalytic, narrative) to counter these tendencies of the self and to promote more positive attitudes.

Controlled studies on life-review therapies are now well established using samples with clinically significant symptoms. A notable early example was Serrano et al.'s (2004) examination of the efficacy of promoting the recall of positive personal memories which depressed people often find difficult to bring back to the surface. In recent years Dutch psychologists based at the University of Twente have made significant progress in identifying the factors involved in a successful life-review-therapy intervention (Westerhof et al., 2010a; Korte et al., 2012). Like Birren and Deutchman's 'guided autobiography' groups they have tended to run a relatively large number – twelve – of group sessions based on a variety of themes. The content of the sessions was also intentionally developed from more limited themes, such as the houses participants had lived in, through to more challenging themes, such as friendship and turning points in their lives, and finally to more evaluative themes, such as personal wishes, the future and their sense of identity. Participants in such a group were shown to improve more in sense of personal meaning than a control group who simply watched a video about the art of growing older. Moreover, this improvement in meaning predicted a decrease in their depressive symptoms at six months follow-up, and mediated this improvement according to the statistical analysis conducted (Westerhof et al., 2010a). In some of their most recent published research, the Twente group have gone on to investigate the efficacy of 'on-line' life review accompanied by e-mail counselling (Lamers et al., 2015).

The same set of investigators has also considered ways of using reminiscence to tackle the presence of excessive anxiety as well as depression in older people's lives. In an initial study, the reminiscence function of bitterness revival was again demonstrated to be particularly associated with depressive symptoms, whereas problem-solving reminiscence mediated the relation of critical life events with anxiety. This suggested clear lines of approach for a differential life-review therapy approach to the two psychiatric disorders (Korte et al., 2011). However, a subsequent controlled study of life review with a large sample of older people with varying levels of symptoms of depression and anxiety, although showing benefits for both indicators of depression and anxiety, did not clearly differentiate the relative mediating processes (Korte et al., 2012). For both those with depression and those with anxiety the main reminiscence functions to be reduced were bitterness revival and boredom reduction. There was also a significant improvement in sense of mastery and positive thinking. Clearly, further work is needed to understand more precisely the processes of change involved in life-review therapy.

In this as well as the previous chapter we have considered developments with aging which are beneficial not only to the individual but also to the society around and to future generations. It is appropriate to close with a focus on the witness to past truths and future values that older people provide in their reminiscing. What for example makes a good life story? It is important to devise criteria for judging the quality of reminiscence in its own terms, and not only through the consequences for the individual's subjective sense of well-being. Coleman (1999) as well as Habermas and Bluck (2000) have emphasised the importance of coherence as an essential characteristic of an integrated and satisfying life story. Habermas and Bluck proposed four types of global coherence: temporal, cultural, causal and thematic.

Temporal coherence describes the manner in which remembered experiences are temporally related to one another and to external historical events. Cultural coherence refers to the normative cultural facts and events that define conventional life phases (e.g. births, marriages and deaths). Causal and thematic coherence on the other hand refer to the evaluative and meaning-making components of the life story. For example, when causal links are not established, life appears to have been determined by chance and will be experienced as meaningless. However, it is possible to work with people on 'restorying' their lives (Kenyon and Randall, 1997) so that negative experiences become opportunities for development and acquisition of wisdom (Randall and Kenyon, 2001; Kenyon et al., 2011). Even emotionally disturbing events can become an occasion for transformation. The term 'post-traumatic growth', first coined by Tedeschi and Calhoun (1995), has come to be accepted over the last twenty years as an integral part of the science of 'positive psychology' (Snyder and Lopez, 2002).

Studies on lives disrupted by the historical events in Europe in the twentieth century have provided important material for appreciating the developmental possibilities of aging (Andrews, 1997; Kruse and Schmitt, 2000; Hautamäki and Coleman, 2001; Keller, 2002; Coleman and Podolskij, 2007; de Medeiros et al., 2015). They illustrate both how such historical events interfere with normal identity processes, but also their potential for leading to the acquisition of new insights and values later in life, which can then be communicated to others. Emotion regulation, generativity and reminiscence − the three topics we have discussed in this chapter − connect closely with one another. The best uses of reminiscence, such as a life review, can be generative for others, but to be truly creative often depend on the person's ability to grapple with difficult and powerful emotional memories.

PART II

Aging and adaptation

Forming a coalition between the human mind and society to outwit the limits of biological constraints in old age seems an obtainable and challenging goal for cultural evolution . . .
(Baltes and Baltes, 1990)

4

THEORIES OF AGING AND ADAPTATION

Problems, deficits, losses and declines in later life have been well documented in the gerontological literature. Biologically, aging is defined as a deteriorative process. Socially, relationships disappear as older adults lose parents, spouses and other close friends. Previous work and family roles that the individual enjoyed may no longer be salient after retirement and when children leave home. Multiple losses, challenges and problems can pose a significant strain on the individual, particularly if these occur in quick succession (see also Cesari, 2013). It is not surprising that adjustment, adaptation and various expressions used to refer to the individual's experience of well-being are some of the most commonly used terms in social and psychological studies of aging.

However, data from several decades of research shows that adults in later life are not as anxious, depressed or fearful as might have been expected (Kunzman et al., 2000). For example, an early longitudinal study of older people over 10 and 13 years in Southampton, England, showed remarkable stability in self-esteem and well-being. Specifically, rather than becoming more anxious or depressed, these older people generally retained high levels of self-esteem and autonomy (Coleman, 1993). More recent data from a representative longitudinal multi-cohort study in Australia used multiple screening instruments to assess common psychiatric disorders, but found comparatively low rates of depression or anxiety (Kiely and Butterworth, 2015). Specifically, around one quarter of midlife adults had a lifetime prevalence of depression or anxiety, and 8 per cent had a twelve-month prevalence.

Similarly, Raposo et al. (2014) examined anxiety disorders, suicidal ideation and age in nationally representative samples of Canadian and American adults. They found suicidal ideation was less prevalent among older compared to younger adults. Additionally, in a large representative sample of adults aged 50-plus years in Ireland (n = 8,175) 9 per cent had symptoms indicative of depression, while 24 per cent had symptoms of anxiety (Freeman et al., 2016). Therefore, while significant numbers are vulnerable to anxiety or depression, the majority are not as anxious or depressed as might be expected. Understanding the 'resilience' which most older people demonstrate has become a key question in gerontology (Windle, 2011).

The discrepancy between expectation and reality is also known as the aging–well-being paradox. As they age most persons maintain well-being despite the increased constraints and losses associated with growing older, although as we will discuss in Chapter 6 it appears more difficult to maintain well-being with the physical decline often associated with impending death (Gerstorf et al., 2010; Vogel et al., 2013). An interesting methodological point is that participants experiencing a greater level of contact with researchers (e.g. in-person/telephone interviews versus mailed surveys) tend to report less negative and more positive psychosocial functioning (see Luong et al., 2015). However, although this observation sheds light on discrepant results, it does not detract from the overall finding that most people into later life age well and without the distress that might be expected. Additionally, older people in fact can show better emotional functioning by comparison with their younger counterparts; that is, they can score higher on measures of life satisfaction, joy, empathy, positive emotions, and lower levels of anger and depression (Grühn et al., 2015).

Ongoing research is contributing to explanations for the aging–health paradox and ways to add quality of life and health for more people. Certainly if people think predominantly about losses and challenges associated with growing older, they are going to feel anxious and distressed. In contrast, focusing on the parts of life that are more meaningful, or more positive and hopeful, can leave people less anxious and more content. More positive thinking can include downward social comparisons ('others are much worse off than I'), goal disengagement ('this was not the right thing for me'), and gratitude ('I am glad that I have/am able to do X').

Having the correct information about later life can also move people away from pessimistic thinking. For instance, the average total number of years that a person might expect to live, life expectancy, has increased significantly and by around 27 years just in the last century (Hayflick, 2000). In most areas of the world people are also living longer in good physical health than ever before. They benefit from earlier diagnosis of health problems, better treatments and improved quality of care, with expanding use of telehealth and telecare. Of course the greater numbers reaching advanced old age brings its own challenges (see Chapter 6), but a longer expected lifespan brings more opportunities than problems. Additionally, there are many theories outlining the proactive steps people can and do take to manage the difficulties, constraints and losses of later life. These include strategies of selective optimisation with compensation (Baltes et al., 2003), socioemotional selectivity theory (Carstensen et al., 2003), and control strategies (Gerstorf et al., 2014). Where people are distressed, interventions are very useful including cognitive behaviour therapy (see Hughes et al., 2014; Laidlow and Kishita, 2015) and self-compassion (Brown et al., 2015; Allen and Leary, 2013).

The experience of aging involves diverse biological and social influences. The latter can include what European sociologists have traditionally referred to as the structured dependency of older adults (Townsend, 1981; Phillipson and Walker,

1986). For instance, retirement from paid work is very often forced upon older adults in such a way that it weakens both their financial and social status. Older women especially were sometimes pushed into financial dependence on their spouses when they were required to give up paid work when they married. The current policy emphasis however within the European Union remains focused on 'productive aging' by which is meant keeping people longer in the labour market. Whether this is intended primarily to benefit older people rather than to combat ever-increasing pension costs is not clear, but, particularly for older women, taking on paid and unpaid care-giving roles can have adverse consequences in terms of health and well-being (DePasquale et al., 2016). Therefore an aging population offers challenges for societal interventions and policies towards health promotion and improved self-care, improved coordination of care, and new work and pension arrangements to help people to stay healthy and active into their later years (Rechel et al., 2013).

In terms of understanding the aging–health paradox, early researchers in the study of stress assumed that negative effects would be related to the amount of stressful experience. However, as the result of the work of Richard Lazarus and colleagues, a more sophisticated understanding of stress and coping has developed (Lazarus, 1966; Lazarus and DeLongis, 1983; Lazarus and Folkman, 1984). Lazarus argued that the experience of stress could be represented by three processes:

- primary appraisals of the potential threat to the self;
- secondary appraisal of possible responses to the perceived threat;
- coping as the process of responding to the perceived threat.

Consistent with the theories and studies reported in Chapters 2 and 3, the limited comparative research carried out on stress and coping in different age groups suggests that the use of intrapsychic methods, involving the control of emotions, becomes more common with age, and problem-focused approaches decline. However, it has to be borne in mind that sources of stress change with age. Folkman et al. (1987) reported that younger adults experienced significantly more hassles in the domains of finances, work, home maintenance, personal life, and family and friends than older adults. Older men and women reported proportionately more stress related to environmental and social issues, home maintenance and health. Nevertheless, this study did show that age differences in styles of coping remained even within individual areas, which tends to support a developmental interpretation of changes in coping methods with age.

However, age differences in psychological functioning tend not to be large. Even in the limited field of cognitive functioning there is a considerable amount of variation among individuals, and much more so in the field of personality studies. Most striking is the consistency over time within individuals. As a result recent investigators have become less interested in looking for normative age differences than in accounting for the processes of self-regulation which underlie continued stability as well as the determinants of eventual change.

Differential aging

The perspectives on aging of Jung, Erikson and those who followed them in elaborating normative stage theories of adult development were in part a reaction against the negative stereotypes of aging predominant in the late nineteenth and early twentieth century. Their response was to propose positive models of aging. Both views assumed a large degree of generalised age changes. The dominant school of lifespan developmental psychology that has developed over the last thirty years in North America and Europe has come instead to emphasise differential aging as well as the influences of societal and historical factors on age-related expectations (Baltes et al., 1980; Baltes, 1987; Maddox, 1987). Thus it has become possible to better understand why it is that some older adults do show characteristics similar to the negative stereotypes of age, whereas others age much more positively. This has led to the coining of terms such as 'normal', 'pathological' and 'optimal', or 'successful', aging.

The last term – 'successful aging' – has no consensus definition, but broadly refers to optimal physical, psychological and social possibilities for living, or to an experience of aging where health, activity and role fulfilment are better than those found within the population generally (Cosco et al., 2014; Foster and Walker, 2015; Rowe and Kahn, 1998, 2015). Within this framework, researchers are interested in finding ways in which adults can not only offset problems or challenges, but also function to maximum potential in their later years (Baltes, 1987; Baltes and Baltes, 1990). Death is seen to occur at the end of a full and active life, in ways comparable to a clock which simply stops ticking (Baltes, 1991). The opposite model of pathological old age assumes a much more pessimistic outlook for the self in which increasingly poor health and lower levels of psychological and social functioning can be expected. This would include aging with dementia.

The 1990 article by Paul and Margret Baltes from the Max Planck Institute of Human Development in Berlin sets out clearly both their theoretical and research agenda. They stress two concepts as having influenced their thinking about successful aging: interindividual variability and intraindividual plasticity – 'systematic age-related shifts in the extent of variability and plasticity are cornerstones for a developmental theory of human adaptation' (Baltes and Baltes, 1990, p. 1). Significant too is the emphasis they give to beliefs and attitudes about aging: 'Optimism about old age influences research and personal action by directing it toward the search for positive aspects of aging' (Baltes and Baltes, 1990, p. 2). As we will argue in the following chapter this is a key topic for future research. Figure 4.1 shows the shifting balance in gains and losses which adults attribute to the later periods of the lifespan, with an increasingly larger number of losses. But even in very old age, some positive changes are expected, for example in wisdom and in dignity (Heckhausen et al., 1989). Such attitudes are influential on actual outcomes, but also themselves malleable.

Baltes and Baltes cite the essay *De Senectute* (On Old Age) of the Roman philosopher and statesman Cicero as a prototype of productive thinking about aging.

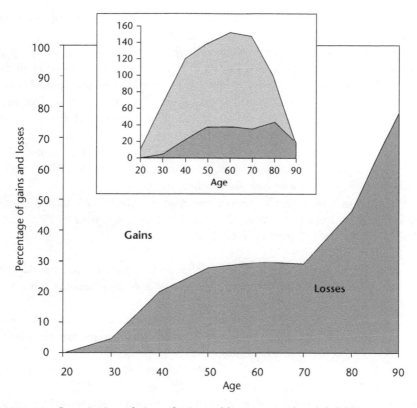

FIGURE 4.1   Quantitative relation of gains and losses across the adult lifespan: percentages and absolute numbers.

Source: Heckhausen (2005, p. 182): reprinted with permission, Cambridge University Press.

In this, Cicero challenges the negative stereotypes of aging in his own time relating for example to illness and forgetfulness as over-generalisations, and points to the importance of motivation, values, good habits and social encouragement for optimising human potentialities in the later years. Baltes and Baltes conclude:

> although his [Cicero's] stoicist optimism about the power of the human mind is certainly an oversimplification of the mind–body interface, forming a coalition between the human mind and society to outwit the limits of biological constraints in old age seems an obtainable and challenging goal for cultural evolution.
>
> *(Baltes and Baltes, 1990, p. 27)*

However, gains and losses accompany each other throughout the lifespan (Baltes, 1987; Dannefer and Perlmutter, 1990), and it is in studying the interaction between them that most insight can be gained into the nature of development. As far as later life is concerned, this means understanding better strategies of adaptation and coping. Successful adaptation and coping with the stresses and changes of life are principal markers of mental and emotional health in people of all ages. The psychology of aging has been defined by Birren and Schroots (1996) in terms of the ability of the individual to adapt to changing circumstances during adulthood. Many adults have concerns about their own future old age and death. That such potential worries are managed is important if individuals are to maintain a sense of well-being. Health professionals also, if they are to help their clients, need to be aware of the strategies that can be used to create a sense of control, predictability and safety. Learning about the different possibilities for adaptation is likely to be useful in helping older adults who are adapting less well.

The ways in which people regulate and manage threats with their own old age are likely to develop over many decades. The following quote by Pearlin and McKean Skaff (1996) illustrates this view:

> Because stress processes and the changes they encompass may unfold over considerable spans of time along the life course, they become inherently intertwined with and indistinguishable from what we ordinarily think of as development and aging. Therefore, when we examine changes prompted by stress, we may at the same time be observing changes that can also be described as life-course developments.
>
> (Pearlin and McKean Skaff, 1996, p. 239)

By understanding better the ways in which adults respond to age-related threats we may also gain more insights into the mechanisms leading to many of the positive attributes that can occur into the latter part of the life cycle, such as wisdom and mature forms of integrity. This is because some of these positive attributes may arise only when potential threats with own old age are successfully regulated. For instance, the attribute of wisdom may arise only when the individual has overcome fears around the finite nature of death and successfully integrated such fears with an appreciation and urgent awareness of the positive things that life has to offer. By understanding better the positive attributes and experiences that can come with age we may be in a better position to encourage the development of these experiences in more people.

The most substantial early study into older people's styles of coping was the Bonn longitudinal study of aging (Thomae, 1976, 1987; Rott and Thomae, 1991). This investigated stresses in the areas of health, family, housing and income, among a sample of 222 people of 55 years and followed up over periods of 20 years and employing in-depth interviews. The investigators developed the concept of 'hierarchies of coping responses' with which to describe their observations over time. Considerable consistencies were demonstrated, but also changes. 'Hope for change' and 'active resistance' diminished, whereas 'revision of expectancies' and 'asking for help' increased. However, differences between areas of stress in the coping methods employed remained significant. For example, 'asking for help' did not increase in regard to problems of income, perhaps because older people, of this generation at least, found it too demeaning a solution to their problems. The investigators also found a significant decline both in 'depressive reactions' and in the number of 'resistance' responses to health stresses in their female group (who had initially scored higher than the male group on both indices) in the course of aging. They postulated a process of learning on the part of these women to cope more effectively with health problems (Rott and Thomae, 1991).

Subsequent studies in Germany have developed further this approach to the study of coping, for example Kruse's studies of persons coping with chronic disease, caregiving, and war trauma (Kruse, 1989; Kruse and Schmitt, 2000; Kruse et al., 2003). These studies, like the earlier Bonn studies, are characterised by careful delineation of typologies of coping. People respond in diverse ways to what appear objectively similar situations. Their coping styles also become increasingly specialised and different from others over time.

In developing theory about aging and adaptation such researchers seek to understand the basis of these differences. The sections to follow examine some of the major theories devised for explaining the way people manage the latter part of the life course. These include selective optimisation with compensation, the shifting balance between accommodation and assimilation, and changing attitudes to relationships and future-time perspective (the developmental theory of socio-emotional selectivity theory already discussed in Chapter 2). Patricia Crittenden's dynamic maturational model of attachment is also outlined as an example of a theory from child developmental psychology, which we believe could be applied with profit to issues surrounding aging. As we emphasised earlier, there is always need for fresh theoretical insights in psychology, and these can often be provided by other, especially adjacent, areas of psychology.

Selective optimisation with compensation

The most prominent and well-articulated theory of adaption is the model of selective optimisation with compensation (SOC) developed by Paul and Margret Baltes (Baltes and Baltes, 1990; Marsiske et al., 1995; Freund and Baltes, 1998). This theory provides a prototype strategy of successful aging, of adapting to the constraints and losses of later life by optimising favourable outcomes for the self. This model remains in wide use, contributing to a range of interventions and insights, including adaption and successful aging (Baethge et al., 2016; Shang et al., 2015; Müller et al., 2013).

The SOC strategy, as its name suggests, proposes that people can manage their lives and limitations in resources more successfully if they apply three strategies. 'Selection' necessitates concentrating on or selecting goals and areas that are of high priority to the individual, and which suit their skills and situation. To focus on specific goals, rather than dividing energy among many goals, focuses behaviour and can help create a feeling of purpose and meaning in life. With growing restrictions on their powers, individuals should select only the most rewarding interests and commitments, ones that can be performed without great effort. However, the choices made should not be determined only by subjective preference but also as a result of objective judgement. Individuals can make the wrong choice, and focus on activities which do not optimise their sense of identity, meaning or even pleasure.

Within the theory, selection is further defined in terms of elective and loss-based selection. Elective selection is defined in terms of 'regulative processes that are involved in selection from a pool of alternative developmental pathways' (Freund and Baltes, 1998, p. 531). Loss-based selection occurs in response to a decline of resources and is defined in terms of a downward shift to less important goals.

The process of selection implies a continual narrowing in the range of alternative options open to the individual. Although this narrowing of options may occur throughout the life course, including childhood, it is likely to be more salient into old age given the pressure of increasing constraints on the self as a consequence of decreases in ability and energy, and the declining effectiveness of the culture in supporting older adults (Baltes, 1997). By reducing activities to high-efficacy domains, the activities can be as enjoyable as before they were reduced in number (Baltes and Carstensen, 1996). The process of selection is initiated by the anticipation of change and restriction in functioning brought by age.

Losses or decline in several areas call for a concentration of the limited resources into areas of behaviour of great importance for the individual. The selection presupposes a re-evaluation of goals, and can be reactive as well as proactive. That is, it may pertain to adjustment to limits or to overriding them by saving the resources for the most important tasks. A performer such as a singer or a musician may find it fruitful to select a more limited repertoire, performing only those pieces that were always performed well. Pianist Arthur Rubinstein has described how he selected the piano repertoire that he performed in the latter part of his career, and how he at that time abstained from performing very tricky pieces (Baltes and Baltes, 1990).

Optimisation in contrast involves ongoing effort or rehearsal to acquire or improve performance towards those selected goals. Optimisation is linked to behavioural plasticity and the ability of the individual to modify the environment both to create more favourable or desired outcomes for the self and to meet the continual challenges and changes being experienced. Examples of optimising outcomes can be understood at an age-graded level (e.g. maturation and the accumulation of experience), or at a history-graded level (e.g. improvements in healthcare and education) (Marsiske et al., 1995). Optimisation strategies can also be understood at physical, psychological and social levels. An example within the physical sector would be a person who is overweight, and whose health therefore is in danger. Optimisation in this case would be to keep to a strict diet or to exercise more or to avoid situations that elicit eating behaviour.

An example from the psychological sector would be persons who feel that their memory functions are disturbed. Optimisation would mean reducing stress if over-stimulated or possibly getting help with a masked depression that might cause these problems. An example of optimisation from the social field would be an older person who has considerable difficulties in maintaining functional autonomy in everyday living activities. Optimisation and functional autonomy would mean asking for more help from a spouse, getting home-help care from a providing agent, or, if living in a residential or care home, forming an alliance with the care-taking personnel and delegating the performance of household activities to them (see Baltes and Carstensen, 1999).

When some capacities are reduced or lost, the third principle of compensation will be used to aid adaptation. The principle of compensation occurs in the context of actual or anticipated losses, and involves the use of alternate means to reach a desired goal or to maintain functioning and keep performance at desired levels. The strategy of compensation reflects the recognition of constraints or challenges in the environment and the need for adults to respond to these constraints or losses by taking counter steps so that any potential impairment is lessened. Examples of compensatory mechanisms include the use of hearing aids, glasses or walking sticks. Similarly, a pianist such as the earlier mentioned Rubinstein, who still wants to perform at top level but has problems with the slowness brought on by age, has to find alternate ways of performing fast passages particularly at high levels. A compensatory mechanism for the pianist who is growing older would be to slow down his performance prior to such a passage, to give the impression that it was being played faster than was actually the case.

Another example of compensatory strategies is where a ballet dancer, who 'ages' very early in his or her profession, might turn to substitute activities within the same field. Even if a career as a performing artist is over as the ballet dancer approaches midlife, this can be compensated for by taking up a new career as a ballet teacher. Despite serious disability in physical performance the aging teacher can show the right movements by using the bars as a support, or by showing the more demanding ones on videotape. Verbal instruction and correcting the students' inaccurate movements by pointing out their mistakes is the main mode of instruction in many ballet situations.

SOC strategies have been examined in a growing range of contexts and with different age groups, including young adults (Lerner et al., 2001). SOC strategies have been found to be significantly related to health and to successful aging (Carmichael et al., 2015). For instance, in a study by Freund and Baltes (1998, 1999) with older adults (mean age 83 years, SD 6.8) as part of the Berlin Aging Study, the relationship between engagement in SOC strategies and outcome measures was examined. The SOC strategies were significantly correlated with measures of subjective well-being, positive emotions and absence of loneliness, even when a range of other rival variables were controlled for, for example extroversion, neuroticism, control beliefs and intelligence. Freund and Baltes (2002) conducted two further studies with German participants from younger, middle-aged and older groups. Self-reported use of SOC strategies was found to be associated with display of positive emotions, environmental mastery, purpose in life and self-acceptance.

More recently, SOC strategies have been found to be positively associated with health, well-being and quality of life. Specifically, a positive association was found between SOC strategies and beliefs in future job opportunities (Zacher and Frese, 2011), better job performance under high workload levels (Baethge et al., 2016) and reduced job and family stressors (Young et al., 2007). Additionally, Müller et al. (2016) sought to examine the use of SOC strategies in helping work capacity of older nurses; this sample group is particularly important given an aging workforce, a dramatic shortage of qualified nurses in industrial countries, and the need to retain staff in work at all ages and career stages. Their sample was a group of nurses from a university hospital in Germany, who completed a specific SOC-In-Nursing-Scale to measure use of SOC strategies in the context of their nursing work (n = 438; mean age 38.5; age range 21–63 years; 84 per cent female). Items for this nine-item scale were developed from interviews with another group of nurses (n = 19) and results indicated that this SOC scale did have good psychometric properties, and a three-factor model consistent with the three SOC strategies. Additionally, results indicated that these participants did benefit from use of SOC strategies to manage resources more effectively and to cope better. This was especially the case for the older nurses, as an effect for age was also found. However, in another study Müller et al. (2016) sought to develop a six-session SOC intervention which encouraged groups of nurses to develop a personal project based on SOC to help them cope effectively and efficiently in their work. A trend towards enhanced well-being and improved control however did not reach statistical significance, nor was it maintained at follow-up, indicating much work in this area of intervention is needed.

In another very interesting study Wurm and colleagues (Wurm et al., 2016) examined whether perceptions of aging would influence use of self-regulation strategies that included SOC. Participants were 309 older Germans with multiple illnesses (aged 65-plus years) surveyed at two measurement points over six months. Results indicated that a serious illness predicted increased use of SOC strategies, which in turn were related to improved scores on measures of life satisfaction and self-rated health. Additionally, this effect was moderated by perceptions of aging, such that beliefs that growing older were associated with physical losses led to lower use of SOC strategies. Much more research is needed examining SOC strategies and health, or work-based stress, in the context of attitudes and beliefs about growing older (see also chapter to follow for some discussion of research in this area).

A range of measures are available to measure SOC, including early measures by Baltes and colleagues that are still in use (Müller et al., 2016). Two scales, a twelve and a forty-eight-item measure of the SOC strategies, have a similar format: participants choose one of two responses that most resembles their strategy of adaptation. Internal reliability scores for the SOC-12 tend to be low. In a study with young professionals under 36 years, Wiese et al. (2000) found internal reliability scores for this measure to be only around .5. Internal reliability scores for the SOC-48 tend to be higher at .67 and above (see Freund and Baltes, 2000). However, Wurm et al. (2016) used the four-item version of the original scale developed by Reuter et al. (2010); items are rated on a four-point scale from 'completely disagree' to 'completely agree' and this scale was found to have excellent internal reliability

(Cronbach's alpha = .84). Separately, Müller et al. (2016) developed a nine-item SOC-in-Nursing Scale to understand how staff manage the physical demands of nursing work. The psychometric properties for this three-factor scale are good (e.g. internal reliability scores of .63 or higher). However, much more testing of these scales is needed to understand adaptation with diverse groups of participants including non-professionals and harder-to-reach groups such as those with disabilities, those who are frailer or more vulnerable, those experiencing recent changes (e.g. health problems or bereavement), those in same-sex relationships, or migrants transitioning into a new cultural group/country.

The model of selective optimisation with compensation focuses on the personal meaning the individual ascribes to different arenas of action in late life. 'Successful aging' is thus defined by personal goal attainment and the development of individualised strategies to accomplish favoured tasks and behaviour. Whether an individual ages successfully or not cannot be predicted in a generalised fashion, but is dependent on the striving of the individual and the domains of functioning he or she considers it important to keep intact in late life. Agreeing with Jung and Erikson, Baltes and Carstensen (1996) suggest that finding meaning is the major developmental task of old age. Meaning is a multifaceted concept, however, and may refer to reaching a cognitive congruence between values, goals and actions in the retrospective recollections and interpretations of life. An element of self-discovery may enhance personal meaning in late life.

The possibility of defining successful aging by the flexible and multi-criteria approach that this model holds seems to be one of its most fruitful aspects. According to the model, success can be defined by different agents (individual–society) different criteria (subjective–objective) and different norms (ideal functional). Internal or external supportive strategies may be developed to support the individual when a wide range of activity or a high level of performance is needed to reach a preferred goal.

This model is also informative about the strategies adults use to achieve more favourable outcomes for the self into later life even under increasing constraints. By restricting the range of options and selecting only those experiences or activities which are most important or enjoyable for the self, adults can gain a lot of enjoyment and pleasure into advanced old age. This is also likely to result in better health and an associated higher quality of life. In contrast, through the notion of compensatory mechanisms, the above model is also sufficiently complex to recognise the losses and limitations that can also occur into later life and the strategies that need to be taken to overcome them. There is evidence that the use of the above strategies can be functional in maintaining or promoting successful aging; that is, in maximising positive or desired outcomes for the self (e.g. self-esteem, life satisfaction) and minimising or avoiding negative outcomes (e.g. loneliness).

A potential problem with this model is its lack of detail about either the nature of the processes involved, or the contexts within which these are likely to take place. Although goals may need to be reduced with age, the mechanisms involved or conditions needed to achieve this reduction are not yet sufficiently well understood. For instance, it is not yet clear why some people might be more successful than others in using these strategies. Perhaps adults most likely to engage in the above strategies are the ones who are currently experiencing the least amount of stress and threat in their lives. An alternative explanation is that adults who do not engage in the above strategies have lower levels of knowledge about the nature of old age and the opportunities this time of life can offer for continued growth and development. Given their potential importance for older people's health and psychosocial functioning, more research exploring these issues is urgently needed. Such work is now proceeding in various countries both in Europe and North America.

Future research in this area could include studies exploring adaptation and possible use of strategies of selection, optimisation and compensation in adults who have experienced particular problems, for example adaptation following falls or a hip replacement. The development of questionnaire measures of selection, optimisation and compensation has made possible their inclusion in a variety of studies from coping with cognitive decline to financial preparation for later life.

Shifting between assimilation and accommodation

In related but independent work to that just described, Jochen Brandtstädter and colleagues at the University of Trier in Germany (Brandtstädter, 2009; Brandtstädter and Renner, 1990; Brandtstädter and Greve, 1994; Brandtstädter and Rothermund, 1994; Brandtstädter et al., 1998) have attempted to explain the ways in which developmental losses or self-discrepancies with age can be reduced by two interrelated processes, assimilation and accommodation. Their dual-process model is based on the assumption that later life has many biological, social, and psychological challenges and losses that pose 'considerable strain on the individual's construction of self and personal continuity' (Brandtstädter and Greve, 1994, p. 52). Their theory also draws on the work of Markus and Wurf (1987) on representation of possible selves in the future and on protective strategies to enhance and maintain the self.

Assimilative coping refers to strategies where individuals attempt to change the environment in ways congruent with their own goals and expectations. Strategies of assimilation can include behavioural changes. Brandtstädter views the processes of selection, optimisation and compensation as well as socio-emotional selectivity theory (see next section) subpatterns of assimilation, because these strategies enable individuals to engage in their preferred activities at a high level of functioning. In addition, they help individuals to 'realize, maintain, and stabilize established self-definitions' (Brandtstädter et al., 1997, p. 108).

However, when threats or losses with age become too demanding and too difficult to maintain, Brandtstädter argues that it may be necessary for the individual to move towards processes of accommodation. Accommodative coping refers to strategies of readjusting goals or aspirations downwards in the light of constraints and limitations within the environment or the self, for example as a result of physical ill health or reductions in mobility. Examples of accommodative strategies include reappraisal of experiences or the attribution of positive meaning to new goals and experiences, and the making of self-enhancing comparisons (Brandtstädter and Greve, 1994).

There are a number of measures available for researchers interested in this topic. Brandtstädter and colleagues have developed two scales to measure processes of assimilation and accommodation: the Tenacious Goal Pursuit (TCP) and Flexible Goal Adjustment (FGA) scales. Each scale has ten items that are rated on a five-point Likert scale. In cross-sectional study with nearly 4,000 participants, Brandtstädter and Greve (1994) report a linear relationship with age for both the TCP (r = .19, p < .001) and FGA (r = −.22, p < .001). They found that older adults are increasingly likely to engage in accommodative processes, whereas younger adults are more likely to engage in strategies of assimilation. In addition, both scales were positively correlated with measures of optimisation, life-satisfaction and absence of depression. These measures remain in wide use, and researchers report good psychometric properties (see Kranz et al., 2010). Versey (2015) also reports on a very useful Lowering Aspirations measure from the Midlife in the United States Survey (MIDUS); this is a five-item subscale, and data from over 7,000 English-speaking adults aged 25–74 years at baseline (1995–6) shows it to have good psychometric properties.

According to Brandtstädter this more flexible process of accommodation assists adjustment when people are faced with stressful or challenging events. It necessitates disengagement from unrealistic aspirations to focus instead on attainable goals. Revising personal goals downwards therefore reduces both the threat of the stressful event and the person's perceived vulnerability to distress during that stressful event or encounter. This definition of flexible coping has been adapted by many others (Tobin and Raymundo, 2010; Janse et al., 2016) and found to be associated with improved well-being and greater resilience when confronted with challenges involving limited control or the potential for significant losses. For instance, Kranz et al. (2010) examined the relationship between chronic pain acceptance and affective well-being as measured by positive and negative affect, and accommodative flexibility as measured by pain acceptance. Participants were 150 chronic pain patients seeking treatment in (n = 150, 63 per cent female aged 18–65 years) presenting to a multidisciplinary German Pain Centre with a variety of pain complaints, from back pain to headaches. Results indicated that accommodative flexibility (readiness to adjust goals to situational constraints) facilitated well-being and activity engagement, particularly when average pain intensity was high. This study provides valuable insights into processes towards improved health and well-being, however a cross-sectional design is not enough to establish causality.

One longitudinal study examining this dual-process model is by Bailly et al. (2016) who sought to examine the influences and changes in coping profiles over a five-year period, and the impact on well-being defined as life satisfaction, depression and health evaluation. According to this model by Brandtstädter and colleagues, when goal pursuit exceeds available resources, it is necessary to change from the tenacity to the flexibility mode to regain a sense of well-being and integrity, despite functioning declines and challenges. Participants were recruited from a longitudinal study on adjustment to retirement, with data collected at three time points. In examining attrition rates, no significant differences were found between participants who completed the baseline assessment and those who had dropped out before 2012. Tenacious Goal Pursuit (TCP) and Flexible Goal Adjustment (FGA) were measured using a French version of these scales developed by Brandtstädter and colleagues. Three coping profiles were found: Profile 1 (35 per cent of the sample) was characterised by participants with high flexibility and tenacity scores, Profile 2 represented 50 per cent of the sample with moderate flexibility and low tenacity scores, and Profile 3 (15 per cent of the sample) was the least common, and characterised by low flexibility and moderate tenacity scores. The researchers found Profile 1 to be the most adaptive in terms of well-being; that is, high flexibility and tenacity were most associated with successful aging.

However, the study was biased towards those living independently, in good health and with high socio-economic status. Additionally, although stability was found over time, the study period of five years may not be long enough to demonstrate and understand change, particularly in the context of declines and challenge. Nevertheless, the study does provide evidence to support both flexibility and tenacity as being important for well-being. It also demonstrates that these interact to predict well-being rather than both working independently.

Recently, Kato (2012) sought to refine the flexible goal adjustment process further by arguing for an additional component; that is, recognition that a strategy no longer works (evaluation coping) in order to implement an alternative downward strategy (i.e. adaptive coping). He also developed an associated measure to facilitate research in this area called the Coping Flexibility Scale. He reports data demonstrating the independence of these two processes, though both are linked to psychological well-being. He also provides data in five studies, from around 4,400 Japanese college students and employees to test the hypothesis that flexible coping produces more adaptive outcomes. Studies 1–3 provided good evidence for the psychometric properties of this scale, while Studies 4 and 5 demonstrated that more flexible coping was indeed associated with improved well-being, including reduced depression, anxiety and distress. Additionally, these effects remained even when controlling for other measures and coping strategies. Further evidence for the role of accommodation and flexibility in psychological adjustment comes from Cheng et al. (2014), particularly in cultures that favour individualism.

Brandtstädter's theory makes important contributions to our understanding of the nature of later life, particularly in his analysis of the processes of accommodation as the self comes to experience more serious threats, constraints and limitations to continuity of functioning. However, much more research on his ideas are needed, and on the ways people decide on goals, and adjust these, particularly when there is a problem or when things are not going so well. This is especially the case when many people, if not most, are goal-directed, and those goals can contribute not just to our well-being but an increased probability of survival (Windsor et al., 2016).

We will come back to this theory again in Chapter 6 when we focus on adaptation in advanced old age. Like the theory of selective optimisation with compensation, it assumes that individuals play an active role in their own development and experiences until late in life, and that they are not just the passive recipients of circumstances.

Despite its strengths, Brandtstädter's model also has some limitations, not least in explaining the mechanisms involved in his strategies. Brandtstädter et al. (1997), for instance, argues that one of the key factors in the development of strategies of assimilation and accommodation is flexibility in adjusting goals and expectations in the light of the context in which individuals find themselves. However, researchers need to be more precise about the mechanisms involved, and why some people may be more successful in using these strategies than others. Specifically, it is not enough to propose that these strategies develop over time and generally occur outside conscious awareness. There are times when persons do not make optimal responses, when for example resistance rather than accommodation may be the most appropriate response for the type of constraints or limitations being experienced within the environment. More research is needed to understand better how these strategies come to be selected, their relationship to experienced change in the environment, and consequences for their functioning.

Research also needs to be undertaken examining these strategies within a range of contexts, for example with older adults of lower and higher socio-economic status, in various psychological conditions, and especially of different degrees of frailty or poor health. Typically these harder-to-reach groups are not recruited (for one exception, see Janse et al., 2016). Exploring differences in strategies of adaptation among adults in urban and rural areas would also be interesting. People in rural areas may have qualitatively different lifestyles and different means of accessing services. Researchers must take more account of the life experiences of older adults and the ways these experiences are represented psychologically. More interdiscipline, undertaken together with sociologists, anthropologists and geographers, would be valuable.

Future studies also need to find ways of interlinking different theoretical approaches. We have already mentioned the possible interrelationship between the concepts of assimilation and accommodation and the theory of selective optimisation with compensation. Another even more closely related framework is the theory of control and its model of developmental optimisation in primary and secondary control (Heckhausen and Schulz, 1995; Schulz and Heckhausen, 1996; Heckhausen, 1999; Schulz and Heckhausen, 1999; Watt et al., 2015). This theory is based on the assumption of the existence of a fundamental motivation for primary control; that is, producing effects in the environment contingent on one's own behaviour. The concept of secondary control refers to the person's internal world and maintaining resources needed to be able to exert primary control. Individuals vary in their ability to regulate their control strategies and this impacts on their mental health and affective well-being (Heckhausen et al., 2001). Assimilation is similar to primary control in that it refers to efforts on the part of the person to influence the situation. However, the primary function of the former is consistency of goals, and hence sense of identity, over time, rather than control over the environment. We will return again, when discussing care for frailer older adults in Chapter 6, to the related concept of autonomy.

Relationships and future-time perspective

Adaptation also occurs within a social context, and relationships can profoundly influence the type, occurrence and relative success of adaptive strategies. Socio-emotional selectivity theory (see also Chapter 2) claims that reductions in social contact across adulthood arise from changes in the salience of specific social goals; that is, a preference for present emotion-based relationships rather than relationships based on knowledge acquisition (Carstensen, 1991; Carstensen et al., 1999). Information acquisition and the regulation of emotion are two principle classes of goals that are achieved through social contact. The essential premise of this theory is that the relative importance of these goals changes as a function of perceived time. When time is perceived as largely open-ended, future-oriented goals such as information acquisition are of paramount importance. When time is perceived as limited, adults adapt by prioritising present-oriented emotion-based relationships. Age is associated with preferences for emotionally satisfying contact over other types such as information-rich contact.

Grühn et al. (2015) examined the predictive value of future-time perspective in explaining emotional functioning with 2,504 adults aged 17–87 years across nine studies. Future-time perspective was assessed with a ten-item measure with each item scored from 'strongly disagree' (1) to 'strongly agree' (7). They also asked participants how frequently they had thought about three time frames during the past week: the past, the present and the future. Subjective health measures included measures for each of depression, life satisfaction and general physical health. Emotional functioning was assessed using measures of empathy-dispositional positive emotions, and attitudes towards emotions, as well as perspective taking. Results indicated that future-time perspective was predicted by age, and by subjective health; that is, older people plus those with poorer health reported a more limited future-time perspective by comparison with others. Additionally, and contrary to the socioemotional selectivity theory, those with a more limited future-time perspective, did less well in terms of emotional functioning, even when the effects of subjective health were statistically controlled. Those with a more limited future-time perspective also reported thinking more about the past than about the present or the future.

Certainly further research is needed, and a range of measures are available to researchers in this field. For instance, future-time perspective can also be assessed by a three-item measure (Lang and Carstensen, 2002) which is still in use (John and Lang, 2015) and has good internal reliability scores. In contrast, Brothers et al. (2014) recognised that future-time perspective was being assessed using unidimensional measurements. They sought therefore to develop a brief multidimensional questionnaire for assessing future-time perspective, and to examine age differences on these assessments. Their participants were 625 young, midlife and older community-based adults aged between 18 and 93 years. The result was a three-factor scale measuring three dimensions: future as open, future as limited, and future as ambiguous. The scale has good psychometric properties, including good internal reliability, and significant associations with age in the expected directions. For instance, the 'Future as Open' subscale was inversely related to age, while the 'Future as Limited' subscale was positively associated with age. This measure however needs to assessed further in other contexts and with other sample groups, including adults in residential settings.

Ferraro and Wilkinson (2015) took a different approach to measure future health expectations, ten years ahead. Their participants were a national sample of 1,266 Americans aged 50–76 years in 1995 who were followed up again ten years later as part of the National Survey of Midlife Development in the United Status (MIDUS) (Brim et al., 2004). Around 16 per cent of the sample had died at follow-up. Participants were asked to rate their current (worst and best) health on a ten-point scale. They were also asked to rate their past and future self-rated health: 'looking back/ahead ten years, how would you rate/expect to rate your health?' The researchers also asked about somatic symptoms to assess preclinical morbidity risk. Consistent with other studies, self-rated health was a predictor of mortality, but expected health rating was also an independent predictor; that is, those with more negative expectations of future health were less likely to survive. In fact the authors report that this study is the first to use past, present and future health ratings to predict mortality.

Further research is needed using the same future-oriented health question, and exploring or examining the consequences on people's day-to-day lives, including their attitudes towards aging, lifestyle choices, levels of generativity or the quality and type of relationships they have with others. Such research could have much theoretical and applied value, not least in developing health-promotional interventions. Additionally, particularly when time is perceived to be limited (and to go fast – see John and Lang, 2015), the opposite of stress or anxiety is calmness, yet there is very little research on this 'ideal affect', its origins and consequences (for an exception, see Jiang et al., 2016).

More research is also needed taking a gender perspective to aging and later life. For instance, the difference in life expectancy between the sexes in many Western countries is around five years (in some countries the difference is bigger, such as Finland, where it is eight years). This means that older women often live alone, while most older men are married. It also means that women are primary caregivers to a greater extent than men, even if many men nowadays also act as caregivers. It is not clear what role gender plays in socio-emotional selectivity theory, or indeed other variables such as chronological age, geographical location or socio-economic status. Nor has much connection been made between selectivity in social relationships with age and consequences for health and well-being.

The dynamic maturational model of attachment

As a final example of theory in the field of aging and adaptation we look at the potential contribution of a major theory designed to explain behaviour earlier in the lifespan. Attachment theory as developed by the British psychiatrist John Bowlby (1969, 1973, 1980, 1988) draws attention to development and operation of the primary human motivation for safety and protection. Drawing on a range of evidence as diverse as psychoanalysis, ethology and cognitive psychology, Bowlby hypothesised that a biologically rooted, universal need was present in all human beings to attain or retain proximity to other preferred individuals. Bowlby argued that this propensity to form strong emotional bonds with particular individuals was desirable, and had protective value throughout the life course, from 'the cradle to the grave' (Bowlby, 1979, p. 129). Particularly under conditions of threat or danger, this need for closeness with others is hypothesised to manifest itself in certain behaviours used functionally to increase the probability of attaining or retaining proximity to the preferred individual. Bowlby also developed the construct of internal representational models to explain the continued importance of early attachment experiences in later health, development and behaviour. Specifically, Bowlby argued that individuals had a number of representational models linked to specific relationships and different memory systems. These representational models, Bowlby argued, would guide behaviour and development under different conditions.

A major contribution of Mary Ainsworth to attachment theory has been to recognise individual differences in patterns of attachment (Ainsworth, 1989). To assess individual patterns of attachment Ainsworth developed the 'Strange Situation' (Ainsworth et al., 1978). This assessment involves a videotaped laboratory situation when the child is left either alone or in the company of an adult unknown to him or her. Usually on about two occasions the mother or other attachment figure will depart when a stimulus such as a knock has been signalled by the researchers. For a very young child being left in a strange environment, alone or with a stranger, is an anxiety-provoking experience. The Strange Situation procedure above has shown that there is a range of individual differences in patterns of attachment. Children with the so-called Type B relationships welcome their mothers' return and are happy to return to play after a brief reunion with their mothers. Children with the Type A pattern of attachment tend to ignore the departure and return of their mothers, while children with a Type C pattern of attachment are those who are highly anxious and fearful when their mothers depart, and are ambivalent at their return.

Although researchers in attachment can view Type A and C patterns of attachment in terms of pathology (e.g. the inability of the child to regulate his/her emotions), Patricia Crittenden views these responses differently. In her dynamic maturational model of attachment the Types A and C patterns of attachment are not necessarily viewed in terms of pathology, but as appropriate and successful strategies to manage particular difficulties and problems being experienced. Specifically, critical to survival is the ability to identify the probability, extent and nature of danger soon enough to take protective action while having appropriate strategies in place either to protect the self and others, or to reduce the risk and extent of the danger.

Crittenden draws on diverse areas of evidence from cognitive psychology to evolutionary biology and child development to examine and document these strategies (Crittenden, 2015; Crittenden and Landini, 2011; Crittenden and Claussen, 2000; Crittenden et al., 2014). Within the Crittenden model, childhood patterns of attachment are likely to persist into adulthood, where they remain functional; that is, so long as they continue to enable individuals to feel a sense of control, predictability and safety in their environments. Crittenden (1997) argues that early experiences of danger can retain their impact on later development and functioning, given the immaturity of the central nervous system along with a tendency to overestimate the probability of danger. Within the strange situation therefore, each pattern of attachment is seen to reflect sophisticated and adaptive responses to particular kinds of danger and threat. Crittenden has also developed and extended the value and use of attachment to encompass any issue or experience where the self is under threat (Crittenden, 1995, 1997, 1998, 2015).

However, for Crittenden, early childhood experiences do not always predict experiences in relationships as adults. To the contrary, through a process of maturation, mental capacities develop greatly through adolescence and adulthood. Young children have a limited capacity to identify impending danger and do not have wide repertoires of available protective responses. By adolescence, individuals can process information in increasingly complex ways.

The most common method for assessing patterns of attachment in adulthood is the Adult Attachment Interview (AAI). This interview was first developed by Mary Main and colleagues (Main et al., 1985), but then developed and extended by Crittenden (1999) who added a range of new categories and classifications. The AAI is a structured interview which sets out to examine semantic, episodic and working (integrative) memory systems. These memory systems are addressed systematically through the interview, so that comparisons can be made between them. Each memory system can be evaluated independently, but discrepancies between memory systems provide the clearest guide to the speaker's mental functioning. Semantic memory is probed by requesting five adjectives to describe the relationships with each parent. Episodic memory is probed (1) by asking for early memories to support each adjective and (2) through probing of specific sorts of incidents, for example being hurt, rejected or separated from parents.

In addition, although the AAI is often referred to as one instrument, it has several components, including a particular set of questions and a specific way of analysing data. It is possible to substitute one component of this interview for another, for example using the questions as originally developed but changing the data analysis strategy, or substituting the questions on attachment to those in a different field, but retaining the method of discourse analysis based on comparisons between different memory systems.

Within Crittenden's system adults can be classified into A, B or C patterns of attachment; they can also be categorised in more refined and detailed ways.

For instance, individuals classified as dismissing can be coded as idealising (A1), derogating (A2), compulsively caregiving (A3) or compulsively compliant (A4). Adults can also use some of these strategies in particular instances, for example be idealising with reference to one parent, and compulsively compliant with the other parent. Further categories of the Type A classification are available for clinical populations (see Crittenden, 2002). Similar levels of detail are available for the Types B and C patterns of attachment (see Crittenden 1995, 2001, 2002).

Adults classified as Type A dismissing have transcripts in which negative affect such as anxiety and fear is omitted. The mechanism through which this is done will vary by subcomponent, for example idealising or derogating. Within Crittenden's framework, Type A individuals will try to distract themselves from negative affective states by not thinking about the stressor or by blocking the stressor from vision. In the context of aging, a Type A response may be one in which individuals react in a falsely positive and optimistic way, without necessarily having the evidence and means to support such positive views. Such adults may also learn from an early

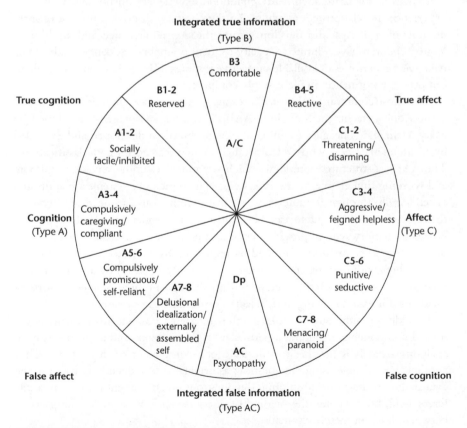

FIGURE 4.2 Crittenden's dynamic maturational model of attachment.

Source: Reproduced with permission from Patricia M. Crittenden.

age to inhibit their own negative feeling states (to avoid anger) and to organise themselves around 'if/then' contingencies, for example if I exercise and maintain a good diet then my old age will be fine. Nevertheless, although such strategies can be functional, the individual can still feel anxiety, which can be exacerbated because he or she feels unable to communicate this negative affect to others.

For the adult classified as Type C within the Crittenden system, a different strategy of adaptation is seen. Inconsistent responses from caregivers or attachment figures as a child along with continued inconsistency and unpredictability from close others as an adult means that the person with a Type C attachment cannot trust temporal (if/then) information, and instead adaptation occurs around intense affective displays; that is, anger, fear and the desire for comfort. Adults using the Type C strategy know that the probability of help or attention from others in the environment increases with heightened displays of negative affect. The purposeful heightening of affective display occurs because this produces results where a milder display of affect will fail (Crittenden, 1998). The problem is that when habituation occurs (others get so used to a certain level of provocative behaviours that they then ignore it), the individual needs to escalate into ever-increasing self-endangering behaviours to get the needed attention or support. The specific strategy of negative affect entails the alternation of affective displays around anger, fear and the desire for comfort (C1–4), such that one feeling state is exaggerated above others and/or then alternated. Further C patterns are available for clinical groups (C5–8, see model).

The above two main strategies of adaptation arise because of problems and challenges being experienced in the environment. Where such challenges are not so evident, adults do not need to develop strategies of adaptation, and in such cases, can cope with challenges using a balanced integration of both cognition and affect; that is, a Type B pattern of relationships.

Although there is little empirical work on Crittenden's model to date with older people, this model is a promising one and there are books and journal papers with other age groups to make research in this area very exciting (Crittenden, 2015; Crittenden and Landini, 2011; Crittenden et al., 2014). Her contribution to attachment has been to develop the use of attachment to encompass any issue or experience where the self is under threat. Specifically, rather than solely or primarily being about separation and loss, attachment theory is relevant for understanding any experience where the self is threatened, including threats around own prospective old age. Crittenden also developed earlier classificatory systems to reflect the increased number of strategies adults are using in response to a wider array of potential threats. The potential contribution Crittenden makes to the gerontological field lies in the application of this model to understanding the ways adults experience and respond to challenges they associate with their own old age.

The benefits and strengths of this model lie in its complexity and detail. In contrast to earlier views of the representational self as being unitary and integrated, Crittenden joins other researchers who assume a much more complex model of the self. For instance, Markus and Wurf (1987) describe how researchers have moved away from a static and fixed model of the self and towards an understanding of the self-structure as an 'active . . . multidimensional, multifaceted dynamic structure that is systematically impacted in all aspects of social information processing' (p. 301). Crittenden and Claussen (2000) also make reference to the self as a process that is continually adapting and changing to meet ongoing challenges. Also, the method of assessment lies in a series of comparisons between memory systems, which is outside the conscious awareness or control of most individuals.

Consequently, this model addresses criticisms put forward by Biggs (1999) among others, warning against the use of self-report assessments. It does, however, necessitate detailed and complex training. The complexity of the training is not necessarily a bad thing. Researchers always need to become increasingly detailed and refined in their observations of behaviour and experiences, and it should not be surprising that the achievement of such sophisticated insights does necessitate detailed training. We will describe further the value of this conceptual framework in describing research on attitudes to aging in the next chapter. Although offering very rich insights, analysis of the AAI is time consuming and complex. Areas for future research include developing and testing new self-report measures. This would save on time, and increase the use of this model in a wider array of settings.

In this chapter we set out to review a select number of strategies relevant to understanding adaptation and management of the self into later life. There are a large number of other theories which have been found useful in understanding adaptation and management of the self into later life, including self-regulation (Carver and Scheier, 1998; for a brief review of theories on self-regulation of development in adulthood and aging see Heckhausen, 2005). It is understandable why adaptation has become such a popular topic for researchers. Understanding the skills and strategies many older adults use to successfully regulate threats with own prospective old age is information which can be used to help adults who are adapting less well to an experience which is expected to become almost universal in the course of this century. Furthermore, given that many positive attributes associated with aging may arise only as a consequence of facing anxieties about one's future, research exploring the regulation of threats is clearly central to many other areas in the developmental psychology of aging that were discussed in Chapter 2. In Chapter 5 we will consider in more detail three current research themes that help us understand better the experience of aging.

5

CURRENT RESEARCH THEMES ON AGING AND ADAPTATION

In the previous chapter we saw how contemporary theory on adaptation to aging in later life has rejected the view that old age is intrinsically a difficult time of life. Older people by and large adjust well to the changes that occur, find ways of maintaining their principal goals and meeting their needs for competence, control and relationship. In subsequent chapters we will focus on the problems and challenges of advanced old age, but even in circumstances of frailty, most older people impress by their ability to cope. Why is this so? In some ways the resilience of the old in the face of decline and death is paradoxical. They appear happier than they should be, happier than younger people would be if faced with the same physical and social losses (Diener et al., 1999). In this chapter we discuss empirical research relating to three burgeoning themes in the study of aging and adaptation, which will help us to understand this paradox.

The first theme concerns adults' attitudes towards aging and old age and the role that such evaluations can play in influencing well-being. Researchers have found that participants with more negative attitudes towards their own old age have not only reported greater anxiety about aging, but also lowered subjective well-being when followed up longitudinally, and even reductions in the will to live. This is not a minor issue. A substantial number of adults in Western societies do have serious concerns about their own future old age and about what this time of life will mean for them. Research exploring the nature and origins of those with positive attitudes could be applied in helping adults with less positive attitudes.

The second theme is the role of personal relationships in adjustment to aging. Relationships are one of the most significant sources of meaning and enjoyment in later life. They have the potential to impact on a wide range of human experiences and behaviours, including emotional well-being, recovery following physical illness and mortality rates. We consider four areas of research within the relationship literature: loneliness and the absence of suitable relationships, informal caregiving in relationships, spousal relationships and particularly the factors that might influence adjustment following bereavement, and finally the developing area of research on grandparenthood.

The third theme is the study of personal meaning and spirituality. Stress and adaptation cannot be studied without attention to the subjective interpretation of life events. This was well recognised by the pioneer stress researcher Richard Lazarus:

> Throughout life people struggle to make sense of what happens to them and to provide themselves with a sense of order and continuity. This struggle is centered in divergent personal beliefs and commitments, shapes cognitive appraisals of stressful transactions and coping, and therefore has profound consequences for morale, social and work functioning, and somatic health.
>
> *(Lazarus and DeLongis, 1983, p. 246)*

Of the various sources of existential meaning (i.e. the meaning that justifies a person's existence in his or her own mind), the most widespread are those provided by religious and spiritual beliefs. Yet religion and spirituality have been relatively neglected subjects of research on aging. That situation has now changed as gerontologists, particularly in the United States, have recognised the power of spiritual belief and practice in sustaining older people's lives.

Attitudes to aging

With more people living longer than ever before, there is an increased urgency to identify the factors likely to influence health, autonomy and well-being in later years. These factors can include adults' attitudes towards their own aging and future old age. Attitudes can be understood as multi-dimensional constructs, reflecting 'a psychological tendency that is expressed by evaluating a particular entity, object or experience with some degree of favour or disfavour' (Eagly and Chaiken, 1993, p. 1). Attitudes can be divided further into beliefs (which include perceptions or expectations), feelings (which include anxiety about aging) and behaviours; these subdivisions mean that researchers can be increasingly refined about the nature of adults' attitudes, and the ways specific attitudinal components relate to other variables and outcomes.

Research on attitudes to aging is important given their impact on later development, health, healthcare usage, and even mortality. People with negative attitudes about aging do less well in terms of their physical and emotional health (Bryant et al., 2012). They are also more likely than others to feel a lack of control, predictability and safety about their futures; yet these attributes are central to the occurrence of health and the absence of pathology. They are also less likely to recognise or appreciate the many positive attributes and experiences that can occur in later life, such as increased experience and wisdom. The inability to appreciate the experience and insights that adults gain over many decades of life can have serious consequences for relationships and family functioning, particularly given the vital role that older adults can play in the lives of their children and grandchildren

(Gutmann, 1987, 1997). Adults with more negative attitudes may also be less moti-vated to prepare financially for later life, or to engage in healthy lifestyle choices in terms of exercise and diet behaviours. The latter is especially serious given the role that health behaviours can play on a range of factors, including later functional limitations, healthcare use, admissions to hospitals or nursing homes, and mortality rates (Levy et al., 2002; Kotter-Gruhm et al., 2009). Yet as discussed in this section, many research questions remain for new researchers to this field.

Ageist attitudes towards older adults

Aging is defined as negative stereotyping, attitudes or behaviours towards older adults due to chronological age, and this can show itself at individual, organisational and societal levels (Butler, 1980, 1995). On an individual level, aging can include being patronising, or assuming that older adults are set in their ways, and unable to change their behaviours or learn new things. At institutional or organisational level, aging can involve discrimination, segregation or inequality in terms of hous-ing, job status or enforced retirement, driving and access to healthcare. It can also be perpetuated covertly through communication styles (Lagace et al., 2012). At societal level, older people are often not visible in the day-to-day life of communi-ties, which is a form of 'ageism by invisibility' (McGuire et al., 2008). However, although increasing numbers of people will experience symptoms associated with frailty given an aging population, the goal of aging well, or being in good health, is realistic for most people. This is due to high-quality research into the potential of aging and later life, along with effective interventions to promote well-being and compress morbidity into fewer years (see also Chapter 4 for strategies of adaptation).

Nevertheless, negative and ageist attitudes towards later life or older people can be widespread and problematic. In a survey of adults aged 60-plus years, nearly 80 per cent of respondents reported experiencing aging as not being taken seri-ously, being told a joke or sent a birthday card that pokes fun at older people, or having others assume they had memory or physical impairments due to their age (Palmore, 2001). Additionally, healthcare staff have a responsibility to help older people manage or prevent functional decline; while many professionals hold positive attitudes towards older people (Tufan et al., 2015), this is not always the case (Kada and Booth, 2015), with patients sometimes left feeling passive, infe-rior, unmotivated and depressed. Additionally, there remains a paucity of research on aging by comparison with other types of prejudice such as sexism and racism (North and Fiske, 2012a).

While most of the studies in this area have been carried out on Western societies and in long-term care facilities with older people who become permanently and irreversibly frail, fewer studies have examined ageist and negative attitudes where the weakness is temporary, such as treatment and recovery following bone fracture. In an interview-based study in Taiwan, Huang and colleagues (2013) addressed this gap in information to explore felt experiences and responses to perceived aging following a hip fracture. Five male and six female older people were interviewed to explore their experiences and responses to aging post discharge in home visits at one, three, six and twelve months. Participants were asked if they had experienced any uncomfortable attitudes or language from others that were different from previous interactions (before their fractures), and to describe the situation, their responses and the consequences. Interviews were augmented by contextual information including location, body language and willingness or reluctance to express ideas. Data were analysed using the analytic tool NVIVO to group words into categories, informed in part by the literature.

Results indicated three types of perceived aging: *positive aging* (over-protection were participants were seen to be fragile, weak and dependent), *isolation* due to physical restrictions (being excluded from activities with family or friends), *and neglect* (feeling that their thoughts or needs were not being considered). In terms of over-protection, participants reported either being given too much assistance or having family deride their slowness or clumsiness. However, many participants reported feeling that they would recover soon so that their coping response was either to ignore or tolerate negative ageist attitudes. Nevertheless, they reported that over-protection, and being compelled to accept arrangements made by their families, reduced their autonomy and power, especially in the early weeks post discharge. Additionally, over the period of a year in this longitudinal study, participants gradually recovered, and they strove to improve their independence in order to overcome aging.

A longitudinal study over one year allows more detailed insights into changes in experiences over time. In this case, immediately post discharge participants reported over-protection and reduced autonomy, although over time the challenge changed towards neglect and isolation due to physical restriction. This study has several limitations however which can offer new areas of enquiry to emerging researchers. For instance, as noted by the authors, further research is needed to explore the origins of aging, and whether this is due to the hip fracture in this case, chronological age, disability or a consequence of all three. Additionally, the majority of participants in this study had good relationships with their families, so it would be interesting to explore whether those with more challenging family dynamics would hold similar accepting and non-malevolent attitudes towards aging. The use of surveys could also shed light on the factors that influence attitudes towards experienced aging. Such factors could include demographic and economic factors (males can be more ageist than females, see Boswell, 2012; Rupp et al., 2005; Türgay et al., 2015); psychological factors including anxiety about aging (see Allan et al., 2014) or coping skills; social factors including intergenerational relationships (see North and Fiske, 2012b); and resilience which can include the availability of resources.

In terms of understanding and managing attitudes, further research is needed to determine whether the amount of contact with older adults influences or combats ageist attitudes. In the case of university students, some researchers have found no relationship between quantity of contact and ageist attitudes (see Boswell, 2012), while others found that increased contact was related to more positive attitudes towards older adults (see Chen et al., 2011; Van Dussen and Weaver, 2009). An assumption underpinning this line of research is that knowledge about aging and older adults can influence attitudes and behaviours, including quality of care given by professionals to older adults.

Several studies have examined the impact of an aging game with older adults to determine whether experiential knowledge about age-related challenges improves attitudes and motivation (Henry et al., 2011). One such study uses the Geriatric Medication Game™ to see whether this simulation could help students understand and empathise more with older people and thus improve their attitudes towards older adults (Chen et al., 2015). The game addresses and attempts to simulate challenges associated with later life. It encourages students to 'become' or to role play later life by performing certain challenges (e.g. reciting their medication list) while experiencing physical, psychological and financial problems; these include simulating balance, mobility or hearing problems, or wearing goggles to simulate vision losses. Using a pretest–posttest design, students were assessed before and after the three-hour simulation, and statistically significant improvements were found on scores of empathy. Improvements on seven of the thirteen questions related to attitudes and healthcare understanding found post intervention, leading the researchers to conclude that simulation activities can improve empathy towards older patients.

It would be interesting to repeat the study above, with other students who did not already report high levels of empathy pre-intervention. Additionally, it is also possible that negative attitudes towards older adults are less about their knowledge or amount of contact with older people, and more about their own situations, including their health and well-being. For instance, ageist or negative attitudes towards older adults can occur, or be exacerbated, by that individual's own emotional states, which include levels of depression and anxiety, or by the social context including the quality of social or family support available.

There are many scales available to measure aging including Kogan's Attitudes towards Older People Scale (Kogan, 1961, or the Revised Kogan's Scale, Hilt and Lipschultz, 1999) which is still in wide use (e.g. Booth and Kada, 2015; Kada and Booth, 2015). Other measures can be seen in Box 5.1. All of these measures have evidence to support reliability and validity; however, all of them need further testing with a wide range of sample groups.

BOX 5.1 EXAMPLES OF SCALES TO MEASURE NEGATIVE OR AGEIST ATTITUDES

Palmore's Ageism Survey which measures the frequency of occurrence of ageism (Palmore, 2001). It includes twenty items examining the occurrence of ageism and includes examples of negative stereotypes and attitudes, personal and institutional ageism. This measure continues to be in wide use (see McGuire et al., 2008).

(continued)

(continued)

The Fraboni Scale of Ageism (FSA) developed by Fraboni and colleagues (1990), revised by Rupp et al. (2005) and widely used today (see Allan et al., 2014). The Rupp et al. version includes twenty-three statements which can be divided into three subscales:

- *Stereotypes* (e.g. 'old people complain more than other people do');
- *Separation* (e.g. 'I sometimes avoid eye contact with older people when I see them');
- *Affective Attitudes* (e.g. 'old people should be encouraged to speak out politically').

The Knowledge about Older Patients Quiz (KOP-Q) for nurses (Dikken et al., 2015) was developed from interviews with professionals and older adults, and a review of literature; early data indicates that this fifty-two-item measure has good psychometric properties.

Care is needed in the development or choice of survey and interview protocols to avoid language, labels and assumptions that might inadvertently be negative towards older adults, or that might stereotype them as being mentally or physically frail. For instance, terms like 'elderly' or 'old people' and 'getting old' can have negative connotations, and more suitable alternatives could include words like 'older adults', 'seniors' and 'growing older'. Researchers might also think about words that describe this population or group more specifically, for example 'people over sixty-five' or '*octogenarians*'. New researchers to this area might consider retesting some of the current measures to examine the psychometric impact of different phrases and in different contexts, for example 'old people are . . . ' versus 'older adults are . . . '. This may be important if negative phrasing could unintentionally influence research participants to respond more negatively than might otherwise be the case.

Older adults have contributed to contemporary society with many decades of service, yet negative attitudes towards this population are ubiquitous, and potentially very damaging for health professionals and older adults alike. New researchers to this area could consider testing or revising existing attitudinal measures, and with diverse sample groups that may differ by culture, socio-economic status or occupation. Another line of enquiry would be to consider interventions towards changing attitudes; perhaps knowledge or informational interventions, and/or compassion and empathy-based interventions. Additionally, there is comparatively little research on attitudes towards the positive and potentials of later life, rather than their constraints. In any new research projects older adults need to be included as partners and to be consulted first for their views through interviews, focus groups or with full representation as consultants on the management or executive committee of research projects.

Attitudes and beliefs about own aging

Attitudes towards own aging can develop over many decades and be informed by societal views and stereotypes about aging (Levy, 2009). This is of concern because negative labels, images and attitudes about later life are widespread, and can include assumptions that older people are senile, lonely, ill, demented or disabled. People can be socialised towards these labels and act or feel accordingly, and as if these labels or images were true (see Bari, 2015; Harris, 2005). Learning therefore may help explain the powerful influence attitudes to aging can have on adults' later health, well-being and behaviour. For instance, over time those with more negative attitudes towards aging and growing older are more prone to morbidity and mortality (Levy et al., 2002, 2009) and less likely to report good mental and physical health; the latter includes lower levels of satisfaction with life, and higher levels of anxiety and depression (Bryant et al., 2012; Coleman et al., 1993; Levy et al., 2002b, 2014; Wurm and Benyamini, 2014). However, positive self-evaluations about aging may have some disadvantages – see Wolff et al. (2015).

One of the first researchers to examine perceptions and beliefs about adults' own aging was Carol Ryff (1991). Ryff sought to compare actual and ideal self-ratings over the adult years, and whether any discrepancies would diminish with age. She based her research within the social psychological framework of possible selves, defined as evaluations about what people can become, what they would like to become and what they are fearful of becoming (Markus and Nurius, 1986). Community-based participants completed self-report scales measuring six dimensions of psychological health: life satisfaction, autonomy, personal growth, self-acceptance, environmental mastery and positive relations with others. Participants completed the scales under four conditions: in terms of (1) the present, (2) the person they would most like to be (i.e. their ideal selves), (3) what they were like in the past, and (4) what they felt they would be like in the future. Young and midlife age groups rated present and future functioning higher than the past, foreseeing improvements in most domains. For older adults, past ratings were similar to present evaluations, indicating stability in functioning; however, future assessments had both stability on some aspects of functioning such as self-acceptance, but declines in others. Ryff also found that older adults had the lowest discrepancies between their actual and ideal selves. These results are consistent with the view that development continues into the latter part of the life course towards greater acceptance of the self, even with greater awareness of flaws and limitations.

A strength and a limitation of Ryff's work is the way she measured positive health in different contexts. It contrasts nicely with other studies which have defined and measured attitudes solely or primarily in terms of illness or deficit;

that is, varying degrees of deviations and malfunctioning in individuals (e.g. Groves and Pennell, 1995; Hopton and Hunt, 1996; Prosser and McArdle, 1996). However, health is just one part of growing older, as are relationships; by measuring attitudes in this way it is not possible to examine the relative strength of association between health, or relationships, and attitudes to aging. This is due to the overlap in construct or meaning between these measures. Additionally, a cross-sectional design makes it difficult to assess changes over time, and whether attitudes to aging influences health, or whether health status influences the ways in which adults evaluate the experience of aging and growing older. The latter are important questions in understanding the nature of attitudes to aging, and their consequences for later functioning and development. Longitudinal research follows or tracks participants over time, and this design is particularly effective in providing evidence or data towards causality (e.g. see Table 5.1).

A recent longitudinal study in Ireland sought to examine the association between negative attitudes or self-perceptions of aging and persistent depression and anxiety at two-year follow-up (Freeman et al., 2016). Data from two waves of The Irish Longitudinal Study of Ageing (TILDA) were used. Participants were community-based Irish adults aged 50-plus years (n = 6,095). The Brief Ageing Perceptions Questionnaire (B-APQ, Sexton et al., 2014) was used to measure attitudes to aging, while depression and anxiety were measured respectively by the twenty-item Centre for Epidemiologic Studies Depression Scale (Radloff, 1977) and the anxiety subscale of the Hospital Anxiety and Depression Scale (Zigmond and Snaith, 1983). Consistent with other studies (e.g. Wurm and Benyamini, 2014; Levy et al., 2014) this study showed that more negative perceptions at baseline were predictive of both onset and persistence of depression and anxiety at two-year follow-up. These associations remained even when adjusting for other

TABLE 5.1 Examples of recent longitudinal studies on aging

- Survey of Health, Ageing and Retirement in Europe (SHARE): www.share-project.org/
- The Australian Longitudinal Study of Ageing (ALSA): www.flinders.edu.au/sabs/fcas/alsa/
- The Baltimore Longitudinal Study of Aging: www.blsa.nih.gov/
- The Berlin Aging Studies (BASE): www.base-berlin.mpg.de/en
- The Brazilian Longitudinal Study of Ageing and Well-being (ELSI-Brasil): elsi.cpqrr.fiocruz.br/en/
- The Canadian Longitudinal Study on Aging: https://www.clsa-elcv.ca/
- The Irish Longitudinal Study of Ageing (TILDA): see www.tilda.tcd.ie/
- The English Longitudinal Study of Ageing (ELSA): www.elsa-project.ac.uk/
- The Japanese Study of Aging and Retirement (JSTAR): www.rieti.go.jp/en/projects/jstar/
- The Longitudinal Aging Study Amsterdam (LASA): http://lasa-vu.nl
- The University of Michigan Health and Retirement Study (HRS): hrsonline.isr.umich.edu/

possible confounds or explanations, including demographic factors, and number of medical conditions. Additionally, no significant interactions were found by age group, suggesting that the relationship between negative perceptions of aging and mental health was consistent across age groups.

Although negative attitudes have been found to predict adverse outcomes among older individuals, Levy and colleagues sought to examine whether this influence extended to brain changes associated with Alzheimer's disease (Levy et al., 2016). They examined data from participants without dementia, who were taking part in the Baltimore Longitudinal Study of Aging. They had age stereotypes recorded decades before yearly magnetic resonance images and brain autopsies were performed. Findings indicated that there was a relationship between age stereotypes and biological markers. Specifically, those with more negative age stereotypes decades earlier had significantly more hippocampal-volume loss and greater accumulation of neurofibrillary tangles and amyloid plaques. These findings add momentum to the need to understand and manage negative attitudes and age stereotypes, even in the context of stressors and changes associated with growing older (see Bengtson and Settersten, in press; Cesari et al., 2013).

Despite some exceptions (see Freeman et al., 2016), many researchers have found that women can hold more negative attitudes to growing older by comparison to men (e.g. Koukouli et al., 2014). However, there is surprisingly little specific research examining attitudes to aging and women's issues. One exception is a very interesting study from Brown et al. (2015) examining women's attitudes to aging and how these might influence the experience of menopause as well as overall well-being at midlife. They hypothesise that cultural representations of older women are predominantly negative, so that women who hold negative attitudes about growing older can be more likely to have difficulties adapting to the menopause, and do less well on measures of subjective well-being. Participants were a subset of women recruited from the Australian electoral roll, and grouped into those who were aged 40–60 years (the midlife group, n = 517) and those aged 60-plus years (the older cohort, n = 259). Attitudes to aging were measured by the Attitudes to Ageing Questionnaire (AAQ, Laidlaw et al., 2007). Participants were placed into one of three groups based on their menstruation status: premenopausal (regular monthly cycles), perimenopausal (persistent changes in consecutive cycles) or post menopausal (at least twelve months of amenorrhea). The twenty-item PANAS was used to measure subjective well-being; this scale has two ten-item subscales measuring frequency of positive and negative affect over the previous week (Watson and Clark, 1988). Results indicated that psychosocial loss (but strangely, not attitudes to physical change) strongly predicted experience at menopause, and subjective well-being; that is, those who held negative attitudes towards psychosocial loss did less well in terms of negative affect, they held more negative beliefs about menopause, and struggled more with its symptoms. Thus the researchers argue that psychological aspects of aging are a valid target for intervention towards improvements in well-being.

There are many psychometrically acceptable scales available measuring attitudes, beliefs and expectations for own aging (see Box 5.2), though all of these need further testing across a range of sample groups and conditions. Measures with a larger number of items or subscales can offer more insights to new researchers due to the contributions of each subscale. However, where space is limited in questionnaire packs, or where participants may become fatigued, researchers can choose specific subscales most relevant to them or the general measures with fewer items. Choice of measure will also be determined by other factors, including the research questions being addressed, and the measure that can contribute most to those questions.

BOX 5.2 SCALES TO MEASURE ATTITUDES, BELIEFS AND EXPECTATIONS ABOUT AGING

The Attitudes to Ageing Questionnaire (AAQ, Laidlaw et al., 2007; Brown et al., 2015)

This is a twenty-four-item scale measuring three facets of aging: psychological loss (e.g. 'old age is a time of loneliness'), physical change (e.g. it is important to exercise at any age'), and psychological growth (e.g. 'wisdom comes with age'). Each item gets rated on a five-point scale from 1, 'not at all', to 5, 'extremely true'.

The Aging Perceptions Questionnaire (APQ, Barker et al., 2007)

This scale measures self-perceptions of aging along eight distinct domains or subscales, including timeline, consequences positive, consequences negative, control positive, control negative, and emotional representations.

The Brief Ageing Perceptions Questionnaire (B-APQ, Sexton et al., 2014; Freeman et al., 2016)

This is a seventeen-item scale and items are summed, so that higher scores equate to more negative self-perceptions.

Negative beliefs and attitudes towards growing older can have serious consequences on many aspects of day-to-day life, with more negative attitudes being associated with potentially less good health and well-being and poorer quality of life. Further research is needed examining the relationships between attitudes to own aging and other factors, including coping strategies, self-compassion or other affective evaluations about aging (see next section). New researchers to this field, however, need to be cautious about the phrasing and focus of their research. For instance, researchers have found that attitudes can be more negative when the target person is a 'representative' older person rather than a specific individual. Similarly, research findings on attitudes can be more negative when measures focus on the physical characteristics of older adults, or their economic welfare, rather than on personality traits or positive qualities of growing older.

Anxiety about aging and later life

While many studies have taken a purely cognitive framework to study attitudes (e.g. beliefs, knowledge, expectations), others have taken a more affective stance (e.g. anxiety, fear). Anxiety about aging is defined as an emotional response to anticipated physical, mental and personal losses during the aging process (Lasher and Faulkender, 1993). Anxiety about aging can comprise a wide range of distressing symptoms, including fearfulness, worry, restlessness and irritability, as well as physiological symptoms such as breathlessness and a racing heart. Over time, these symptoms can have high costs, emotionally, physically and in terms of relationships. Additionally, in a twelve-year follow-up study of older men, anxiety and somatic concerns significantly predicted an increased mortality risk, even when controlling for other lifestyle, and psychosocial measures (Tolmunen et al., 2014). Although people today are living longer and healthier lives than any previous generation, levels of anxiety and fear about aging are prevalent, and people can approach old age with significant dread. This may especially be the case for women who can face a triple jeopardy of discrimination and anxiety based on age, changes in physical appearance (or 'lookism'), while also being more likely than men to be disadvantaged economically if prioritising family and care responsibilities.

Anxiety about aging is not the same as other types of anxiety such as generalised worrying, but it is a component of attitudes to aging, and it can have significant adverse consequences at a work or cultural level. For instance, several studies found that nurses have higher anxiety about aging compared to other health professionals (see Wells et al., 2004). Anderson and Wiscott (2003) found that around 22 per cent of their sample had high personal anxiety about aging. Anxiety about aging is associated with more psychological distress in the present and the future. Several researchers have found associations between anxiety about aging and ageism (see Boswell, 2012). For instance, early researchers in this field found that university students anxious about aging held more negative attitudes towards the average person at age 70, and future rated themselves more negatively at age 70 by comparison with other students lower in anxiety about aging (Harris and Dollinger, 2001). However, there remains comparatively little research examining anxiety about aging, particularly among harder-to-reach groups which includes those with learning disabilities (for an exception see Newberry et al., 2015).

Greek researchers wanted to examine prevalence of anxiety about aging and whether this would be influenced by experience with older adults affected by a debilitating illness (Koukouli et al., 2013). This research was motivated by an awareness of an aging population, and the need to motivate and support professionals in their work with older adults. Three groups were recruited: professionals working in primary care; students of nursing and social work; and community residents. To measure anxiety about aging, participants were given the Anxiety about Aging Scale (Lasher and Faulkender, 1993) which has four subscales of five items each: fear of older people; psychological concerns about aging; anxiety about changes in physical appearance; and anxiety about expected sources of loss in old age, such as independence. Participants were also asked if they had any professional (the professionals) or personal experience (the students, and the community adults) of older people with either Alzheimer's disease (AD) or dementia. Students reported significantly more anxiety about aging, and this was attributed to their misconceptions and less accurate knowledge about the aging process.

Additionally, in the Koukouli et al. study, students who had personal experience or knowledge of an older person with dementia (e.g. relatives) reported lower overall aging anxiety compared with those who had no such experience. This finding is similar to that of other researchers who found a negative and inverse association between anxiety about aging and knowledge (e.g. Boswell, 2012b; Allan and Johnson, 2009). However, higher levels of anxiety about aging were reported by professionals who had experience of dementia (Koukouli et al., 2013). The researchers assume that the latter is a consequence not of a knowledge deficit, but of difficulties coping effectively with the associated stress. Further research is needed to examine this hypothesis directly, and perhaps consider alternative explanations, including economic resources, or social networks and relationships in terms of being able to access support if needed.

Many researchers have sought to develop interventions to reduce levels of anxiety about aging, but with mixed success. Some researchers have sought to change evaluations about aging through experimental conditions, for example by activating positive aging stereotypes (by using words such as 'wise', 'sage' and 'alert' (Abrams et al., 2008). Another novel intervention found that imagined contact with an older person can decrease anxiety about aging and produce more positive expectations, when direct contact is unavailable (Prior and Sargent-Cox, 2014). Participants were 201 undergraduate students who were randomly assigned to one of three conditions: (1) imagined contact with a 75-year-old male, (2) imagined contact with a 75-year-old female, or (3) a control group. Relative to the control group, results showed that imagined contact with either an older adult, male or female, was associated with less anxiety and more positive expectations of aging for male, but not female, participants. Interventions with an imagined or actual social contact could prove very effective given the role of relationships on anxiety and well-being (see Ivan et al., 2015).

There are scales available to measure anxiety about aging, although these need further testing with diverse sample groups, and new ones need to be developed. For instance, an early Anxiety about Aging Scale by Lasher and Faulkender (1993) is still in wide use (see Allan et al., 2014; Koukouli et al., 2013; Prior and Sargent-Coz, 2014; Sargent-Cox et al., 2014); this is a twenty-item self-report scale with four subscales assessing fear of older people, concerns about psychological changes associated with aging, anxiety about physical appearance changes, and anxiety about expected losses in old age, such as independence. A shorter measure is the six-item Aging Anxiety Scale (Yan et al., 2011). Items are rated from 1 (strongly disagree) to 5 (strongly agree). For both measures, higher scores indicate higher levels of anxiety about aging.

Anxiety can manifest itself in a wide range of ways and be associated with significant costs in terms of health, well-being, quality of life and even mortality. Further studies examining different affective components (e.g. anxiety versus fear about aging) could contribute towards our understanding of interventions, particularly if other possible explanations of anxiety were also assessed and statistically controlled, for example demographic factors (including gender and education), biographical factors (such as experiences with grandparents), knowledge resources/deficits (about the realities of aging), and measures of current well-being such as confidence or coping strategies. Another interesting line of research might examine whether anxiety about aging is best explained by the notion of aging in general, or certain subcomponents of aging, for example physical (such as health, or appearance changes), social (role and relationships changes), psychological (e.g. changes in identity) or a combination of factors. Drawing on concepts from positive psychology, post-traumatic growth and terror management theories (Pyszczynski et al., 2015), future research may also explore and examine the contexts and psychological mechanisms in which anxiety about aging may lead to further development, growth and resilience. Insights to these questions could contribute to improved quality of life, health and well-being for many more people.

The supportive role of personal relationships

Warm relationships with others are an important part of most people's lives and crucial to successful aging. In addition to the meaning and joy they can give to people, relationships are important because they serve a protective function. The direct protective role of close family relationships is evident across a range of psychological and physical experiences in later life; these include occasions when actual physical risks occur such as recovery following a fall, or when potential risks to the representational self are higher, such as transitions around retirement or moving into a care home. Relationships also serve a protective function socially, in terms of shared friendships and sources of meaning, particularly in long-term relationships that can last several decades. This protective value of relationships also occurs at a cultural level in terms of the opportunities made available for help and support.

Just as older adults need support from younger generations, younger adults also benefit from the skills and experience that older people can develop over several decades of life. This point is made strongly by Gutmann (1987) who draws on ethnographic, cross-cultural and anthropological data to argue that as a consequence of maturation and experience, older adults have their own unique strengths and talents which should be used, particularly in helping, supporting and teaching the next generation. Gutmann takes this perspective, particularly in the light of the 'parental emergency' (1987, p. 7); that is, the difficulties and problems involved in raising emotionally healthy children without the support of extended family and friends. In this way, Erikson's notion of generativity is being echoed; that is, the need many adults have to care for, guide and support the next generation (Erikson et al., 1986). Yet, although many older people are providers of care, services and financial support to young and midlife adults, these actions have so far received surprising little research. (Further discussion on the expertise adults develop over time and the ways older adults can care for and guide younger generations is made in Chapters 2 and 3, in the sections on wisdom and Eriksonian generativity.)

In later life however, relationships are lost, constrained or impaired. Personal work roles and relationships that the individual had and enjoyed may no longer be salient such as when children are grown up and leave home. Similarly, adult children may divorce so that older people can lose links with younger family members (Drew and Smith, 1999). Furthermore, given compulsory retirement, one's work friends and acquaintances may have to be surrendered and adults in later life are more likely to experience the loss of parents, spouses and/or other close relationships through bereavement.

Early researchers typically associated changes in relationships with unfavourable conditions including economic disadvantage and poor health. For instance, in outlining their disengagement theory Cumming and Henry (1961) believed that reductions in the frequency and nature of relationships with others was a consequence of the aging process including increases in health problems, decreases in mobility and energy, and ultimately the death of the self. Declines in relationships were similarly believed to occur as a consequence of the loss of contemporaries and reduced opportunities for social contact (Munnichs, 1964), and declines in cognitive functioning (Craik and Bryd, 1982).

Yet although relationships can change and become lost in later life, negative social images and stereotypes have been revised by many current researchers in this field. Some social losses and threats into later life which assume crises in mid- and later life (e.g. 'empty nest syndrome') have little empirical evidence to support them (Antonucci et al., 2001). Indeed, a contrasting view is that problems and challenges occur throughout the life course and not just in later life. In addition, even when challenges and losses in relationships occur in later years, negative stereotypes need to be revised to take into account both the ways expectations and interests change over time, and also the resilience and creativity of older people in managing their own experiences. The research discussed next offers insights into the nature of those losses and challenges in relationships, the adept way older people often socially manage changes with time, and the positive consequences that can occur over time in relationships.

Loneliness: the absence of suitable social relationships

Relationships are core to health and well-being in adulthood (Uchino et al., 2012; Whitley et al., 2016; Zhang et al., 2016), and the absence of meaningful relationships can contribute to higher levels of loneliness. Loneliness can have direct negative consequences on a range of health and well-being domains, including depression (Bodner and Bergman, 2016) and suicidal ideation (van Wijngaarden et al., 2015; Stickley and Koyanagi, 2016), sleep problems (Aanes et al., 2011; Kurina et al., 2011), cardiovascular disease (Ong et al., 2012), diabetes and stroke

(Whisman, 2010), and even an increased risk of Alzheimer's disease (Wilson et al., 2007). Loneliness has also been found to be associated with health-risk behaviours, including reduced activity, smoking and alcohol use (Shankar et al., 2011). Much more research is needed on this very prevalent condition, with around 10 per cent reporting severe loneliness, and 30–40 per cent reporting occasional loneliness (Victor and Bowling, 2012; Ferreira-Alves et al., 2014).

Loneliness can be defined as a subjective or felt experience arising from perceived deficiencies in social contacts, or a gap between desired and actual relationships. This is different to 'aloneness' which represents an objective absence of social ties, or 'social isolation' which reflects an objective state in which a person prefers to live alone or avoid social contact. Some researchers also differentiate between emotional loneliness (the lack of others with whom the person can connect or for an emotional attachment), and social loneliness (where an acceptable social network is lacking). For many people loneliness is transient, temporary and passing. For others, loneliness is a highly distressing condition that is chronic or prolonged. While temporary and chronic loneliness have an adverse effect on health and well-being, those effects can be more pronounced for those experiencing chronic loneliness.

Much of the research to date has examined loneliness solely as a psychological or felt inner experience, despite evidence that loneliness takes place within a wider social context. To examine the latter, Ayalon (2016) surveyed vulnerable older people aged 70-plus years (n = 388) in receipt of paid care, another of their family members (n = 686), and each care receiver's paid caregiver (n = 523). Each person interviewed reported his or her level of loneliness using the three-item Revised UCLA Loneliness Scale with responses on a simplified three-point Likert type scale from 'never' to 'very frequently'; scale items asked how often they felt a lack of companionships, felt left out or felt isolated from others. Additional measures included subjective health status (using a single-item question, with higher ratings representing better subjective health), and well-being using the five-item WHO-5 in which each of the three groups rated five items addressing positive mood, vitality and general interests on a six-point scale with higher scores indicating better well-being. Participants were also asked to rate on a ten-point scale their perceived control in three areas: health status, financial status and everyday life. Consistent with other research, higher levels of loneliness were associated with less favourable quality of life and well-being indicators. Additionally, two types of loneliness profile were identified: a larger group characterised by low levels of loneliness among all three members, and a smaller group that was characterised by relatively high levels of loneliness among all three members. While most research focuses on loneliness as an individual felt experience, it is not yet clear if these findings will be replicated with other groups and triads.

The authors note that their study is cross-sectional so that issues of cause-and-effect cannot be established. Several possible explanations for these findings arise. Although the mechanisms are still unclear, it is possible that feelings of loneliness do spread and get picked up by others, particularly vulnerable spouses or family members. Alternatively, this clustering effect of loneliness could also be a consequence of 'a common fate' (p. 209), suggesting that all members of the caregiving unit have similar experiences, for instance a challenging living environment, which in turn make them more prone to loneliness. A third possible explanation is that members within each unit were similar to begin with, even selecting paid care workers with similar levels of loneliness to their own. Clearly further research is needed.

There is a consistent finding that social networks and relationships can be vital resources in reducing levels of loneliness and promoting emotional health and quality of life (Cacioppo et al., 2010). For instance, The Irish Longitudinal Study on Ageing (TILDA) is a large-scale, nationally representative, longitudinal study of aging in Ireland. TILDA collects information on all aspects of health, economic and social circumstances from people aged 50 and over in a series of data-collection waves once every two years. It is one of the most comprehensive research studies of its kind in terms of the range of physical, mental health and cognitive measures collected. TILDA researchers measured social participants in terms of intimate social relationships, formal relationships outside work, active and social leisure, passive and solitary leisure. Findings indicated that those over 65 years who were 'most integrated' in terms of social networks, reported better mental health compared to those who were 'most isolated' (Santini et al., 2016).

However, few studies have examined the benefits involved in encouraging social participation among older adults already lonely or depressed. One exception is that from Cruwys et al. (2013), who used population data from the English Longitudinal Study of Ageing (ELSA) to investigate the effect of group memberships on depression symptoms over time among those with and without baseline symptoms of depression. They found that the number of groups people belong to was inversely related to levels of depression, and, that the benefits of social participation were stronger for those who were already depressed; the latter was examined in analyses that statistically controlled for other explanations such as initial depression, demographic factors (e.g. age, gender, SES), subjective health, and relationships status. Specifically, depressed isolated older people who joined one group reduced their risk of depression relapse by 24 per cent; if they joined three groups their risk of relapse was reduced by 63 per cent. They also found that the number of groups a person had joined was both protective against depression for those who were non-depressed, and curative of depression among those who had depressive symptoms. One possible explanation considered by the authors is that social connectivity with others should not be considered in terms of interpersonal bonds of affiliation. Instead, they draw on social psychological theory to regard social connectedness as having psychological outcomes whereby people see themselves as 'part of something bigger', thereby defining themselves socially rather than solely in terms of personal identity (p. 184). Further qualitative research however is needed to explore the meanings and identities that people associate with group membership. Such findings could contribute theoretically, and in applied ways, to the promotion of more social participation and involvement.

Additionally, the benefits of social networks and relationships on well-being and health may not yet be fully applied or maximised by clinicians, health professionals or policy makers. As noted by Cruwys et al. (2013) medical doctors rarely question patients about social group memberships and do not typically encourage them to join more groups. However, psychologists and cognitive behavioural therapists are more likely to encourage efforts to increase social support among those who are depressed, and indeed this can be one of the first interventions towards improving health and well-being.

Research findings from social and behavioural gerontology offer exciting insights into the ways that older adults can contribute proactively to the quality, quantity and function of their social relationships and networks. Such findings can have transferrable value in understanding and managing loneliness. For instance, information acquisition and the regulation of emotion are two types of goals that are achieved through social contact. According to socio-emotional selectivity theory the relative importance of these goals changes as a function of perceived time (Carstensen, 1991; Carstensen et al., 1999). When time is perceived as largely open-ended, future-oriented goals such as information acquisition are of paramount importance. When time is perceived as limited, adults adapt by prioritising present-oriented emotion-based support relationships. (For more information on this theory, see Chapters 2, 3 and 4.)

However, it is not yet clear why adults who are lonely have difficulties in connecting with others, or joining social groups. Possible barriers can be physical (e.g. no transport to attend social groups), especially in rural areas. Social barriers can include not having information about events or activities for older people, not knowing others at these events, and managing and reducing any perceived stigmas associated with older people's groups. Psychological barriers contributing to loneliness can include low confidence, social anxiety or intense shyness, and feeling like they do not matter to others. Flett et al. (2016) found that feeling they did not matter to others was linked to loneliness, as was social anxiety, and past experiences of maltreatment. Mattering is the sense that others are interested in us, and care about what happens to us. This sense of mattering was seen by Flett et al. to be a component of self-esteem, and they wanted to understand the predictors of this sense, and its consequences. University students (n = 232) completed a range of surveys, which included measures of childhood maltreatment and social anxiety or social phobia measured by the seventeen-item SPIN scale (Connor et al., 2000). Low mattering was associated with loneliness and social anxiety, and these findings remained when controlling for other factors, including neuroticism and extraversion. Further research may find similar results with older adults.

Whatever the barrier, many regions and cities are attempting to be age friendly, or places that are supportive of the diverse and changing needs of older people (Buffel and Phillipson, 2016; Steels, 2015). The World Health Organization (WHO) promotes age-friendly environments as a way to address the challenges and needs associated with a growing older population which includes the need for social inclusion, connectivity and social participation, and a reduction in levels of isolation and loneliness. Therefore older people can remain in place as they grow older, knowing their needs will be addressed and met. A human-rights approach can also help address the social, structural and community health and well-being barriers faced by older adults (Baer et al., 2016).

Efforts to reduce levels of loneliness and promote social participation instead are needed given the continuing protective benefits of relationships even into advanced old age. For instance, Gerstorf et al. (2016) found that social engagement and goals can offset or postpone any losses or declines in functioning. They examined pre-death measures of social orientation and engagement to longitudinal data from deceased participants who had taken part in the nationwide German Socio-Economic Panel Study. Participants had been asked how often they had taken part in a range of social and communities activities, with responses ranging from at least once a week to never; the last social participation rating before death was used in analyses. Data were analysed for 2,910 participants who had taken part in the study, but had then died. All analyses were statistically controlled for factors associated with poorer health and increased mortality risk, including age, gender and lower levels of education. The outcome measures were mortality status and year of death. To measure social goals, participants had been asked to rate the importance of social goals like helping others and being involved in social and political activities, while family goals were assessed by two items asking how important it was to have a good marriage, and a good relationship with children. Results indicated that social participation was related to individual differences in later-life well-being, with more social participation and more valuing of goals each being uniquely associated with well-being one year prior to death, and less steep terminal decline. Significant interaction effects were found (see Chapters 6 and 7 for further research on well-being in advanced old age).

The above study has very exciting implications for increasing the number of modifiable factors that can contribute to well-being and quality of life. The authors were able to use advanced statistical modelling to examine many parallel associations at one time. Their results highlight the need to continue to encourage and facilitate social activities, despite challenges such as poor physical health, or changes in social status such as widowhood. The authors note that further research is needed to determine the specific mechanisms by which social participation facilitates improved well-being. It may be that the benefits are direct, in terms of enjoyment, or indirect though improvements in self-esteem and a sense of control.

Further research can examine the links between loneliness and other facets of social engagement, goals and participation; these can also be examined with many different types of relationships and networks. In the context of social cognitive theory, individuals create working models or representations (e.g. attitudes, beliefs, expectations) about themselves through social interactions, and these judgements and beliefs then influence behaviours (Bandura, 2001) and feelings (Cacioppo et al., 2006). An examination of these factors, alongside earlier experiences in relationships, can also facilitate a better understanding of the psychological as well as the social antecedents of loneliness. Creative solutions and interventions will also need to be identified, refined and tested, so that more older people feel they matter, and the higher health risk associated with loneliness is managed appropriately.

Caregiving in relationships

The care and support received within close relationships can be significant contributors to health, well-being and quality of life in later years. Living with a spouse or partner for instance, is often associated with a reduced risk of morbidity and mortality, particularly for men (Molloy et al., 2009; Kilpi et al., 2015). This protective effect for men is attributed to the more necessary role of intimate relationships for social, emotional and practical support; this contrasts with the wider range of social relationships that is more typical of women.

Additional benefits include a shorter delay in seeking care after experiencing symptoms, and ongoing support to manage chronic conditions (Kilpi et al., 2015; Teerawichitchainan et al., 2016). Spousal and intergenerational relationships can also influence lifestyle choices. For instance, Cobb et al. (2016) followed 3,261 spousal pairs from a large US-based study on atherosclerosis to examine the association between an individual's level of activity in exercise or sport and any corresponding changes in partners' activities. Significant associations were found: increases by one partner in terms of sport or exercise activities were associated with increases by the other partner, and these findings were evident for both older men and women. Although further research is needed to understand these mechanisms, these findings suggest that health interventions should consider targeting couples rather than solely individuals, or families, particularly those that share the same lifestyles and environments (see also Deek et al., 2016; Di Castelnuovo et al., 2009).

In contrast, living alone can be a choice for a growing group of people. Those living alone include those who never married, those who are widowed or divorced, those with children living away, and the one-in-five older people in the UK who never had children. While living alone was traditionally associated with increased vulnerability, including greater risk for loneliness (Lim and Kua, 2011), those living alone can be healthier, more socially active, more educated and more affluent by comparison with previous generations and their married/cohabiting counterparts.

However, those living alone can be at a disadvantage when care is needed. This is because spouses are often involved in decisions about care, and indeed family relationships can be a vital resource and support towards adaptation and recovery, particularly following surgery. For instance, Turner et al. (2016) found that living alone was associated with a 9 per cent increase in in-hospital stay and an increased probability of re-admission either to hospital or to costlier care facilities. Additionally, the proportion of households with single-occupancy is increasing, making care or discharge supports an increasingly urgent challenge. Creative solutions warranting further research and study include peer networks, befriender interventions or the use of telecare and telehealth.

Looking after a spouse or a parent with a chronic illness is associated with increased emotional and physical health problems (Dunkle et al., 2014). For instance, Saito et al. (2015) found that serious spousal illness or hospitalisation had a detrimental effect on self-rated health among older carers, particularly among those whose children lived 30-plus minutes away (however, see also Rosso et al., 2015). This means that creative solutions to care for those living alone could also have transferable value to other groups.

There are many studies examining the support given to older family members, particularly practical or financial support, but fewer studies are available examining supports to older parents from situations of providing ordinary support, to support involving increased dependency. This limitation was addressed by Kim et al. (2016) who used two waves of data to examine the impact increasing disability has on everyday supports, relationship quality and psychological well-being (see Box 5.3). Participants were community-based adults (n = 380) taking part of the Family Exchanges Study (Fingerman et al., 2009); they completed surveys in two waves of data collection five years apart. Measures included parental disability, the frequency with which participants provided help with activities of daily living with ratings from 1 (less than once a year or not at all) to 8 (daily). To measure relationship quality participants were asked to rate four qualities (loving and caring, feeling understood, criticising and demanding) from 1 (not at all) to 5 (a great deal). Two dimensions of psychological well-being were also assessed: depression and life satisfaction.

BOX 5.3 SCALES TO MEASURE QUALITY OF SUPPORT IN CAREGIVING RELATIONSHIPS

Caregiver experiences

- Fourteen-item *Perceived Stress Scale* (Cohen et al., 1983) remains in wide use (see Lyons et al., 2015); possible scores range from 0 to 56, with higher scores indicating more stress.
- To measure *ADL care provided*, participants can be asked directly how often they provide help to another with activities of daily living from 1 (less than once a year or not at all) to 8 (daily)
- To measure *carer supports*, Kim et al. (2016) asked participants to list any others who help a family member with activities of daily living; these can be categorised into three groups: family members, friends or neighbours, and paid help.
- *Relationship quality* with the person receiving care can be assessed with four items (Birditt et al., 2012); participants can rate four relationship qualities (loving and caring; feeling understood; criticising; demanding) on a five-point scale from 0 (not at all) to 5 (a great deal).
- Depression is often assessed using the short-form of the Centre for Epidemiologic Studies Depression (CES-D-10) Scale (Andresen et al., 1994) – see Mausbach et al. (2014).

Care receiver experiences

- To measure levels of disability among those receiving care, items from the *Community Disability Scale* (Rovner et al., 1996) are still in wide use (Kim et al., 2016); participants are asked whether a family needs help in a range of contexts such as personal care, housework or transport, and items are summed to get a measure of disability.

Results indicated that parental disability did increase over the five years; the proportion of parents with disabilities increased from 22 per cent at baseline, to 55 per cent five years later. Offspring support also increased between baseline and follow-up, and this increase remained significant even when other sources of help were statistically controlled. Increasing parental disability however did not impact adversely on offspring's levels of depression or life satisfaction, but this finding may be explained by the still relatively low levels of disability among the parental sample. Nevertheless, it is interesting to find that increasing disability led to more tangible or practical supports, but not non-tangible support (listening, emotional support); the one exception was for advice, which did increase over time. Additionally, increasing disability among parents was associated with impairments to relationship quality.

Caregiving can take a physical and emotional toll on the health and well-being of family members, especially those who do not have other sources of support. The increase in health problems among informal caregivers is often attributed to their caregiving responsibilities that can result in a reduction or cessation of social and recreational interests. For instance, a recent meta-analysis found that activity restriction, regardless of marital status, was associated with an increase in depression in a variety of contexts and relationships (see Mausbach et al., 2011). Pearlin and colleagues' (1990) stress-process model of family caregiver burden is still in wide use and describes four key areas that contribute to caregiver distress: background and context (which includes socio-economic status); primary stressors (e.g. level of help required by the care receiver); secondary role strains (e.g. level of conflict with family); and secondary intrapsychic strains (e.g. diminished sense of control). According to the model, an increase in primary stress will lead to a corresponding increase in secondary role strain. Therefore with a wider family network of support the caregiver can spend less time managing the primary stressors, and more time engaging in social and leisure activities, which should promote better well-being. To test this theory, Mausbach et al. (2014) carried out a five-year longitudinal study of 126 spouses giving care to spouses with Alzheimer's disease. Although their study requires replication, increases in leisure and social activities following support (placing spouses into long-term care) helped explain variance in depressive symptoms.

Other interventionists have focused on self-efficacy as the moderator of psychological well-being among family caregivers (e.g. Zhang et al., 2013). For instance,

Tang and Chan (2015) carried out a literature review to examine interventions used to enhance self-efficacy, particularly in the context of care receivers with any type of dementia. Self-efficacy is defined as the belief that one can successfully carry out a given task or behaviour, and this belief can become impaired with caregiving responsibilities. Based on fourteen studies that met their criteria for inclusion, Tang and Chan found evidence that self-efficacy scores could be improved by psychosocial interventions. These adapted a range of theoretical frameworks, including cognitive behavioural therapy, social learning theory, role transition model, behavioural therapy, and mindfulness-based cognitive therapy (MBCT). The types of interventions included skill-building psychoeducation, information-based psychoeducation and mood management; all of these demonstrated improvements in self-efficacy. However, with millions of caregivers, much more research in these areas is needed.

While a vast literature has documented the physical, emotional and health costs involved in providing care to a family member with a long-term illness, much less is known about the positive aspects of caregiving, or the factors that might protect spousal caregivers' health and well-being. The latter can include relationship quality, feelings of accomplishment, self-efficacy and support network. In an exciting study, Monin et al. (2015) examined the role of compassionate love among individuals with Alzheimer's disease and their spousal caregivers, and whether this was associated with caregiver burden, more positive caregiving appraisals and less depressive symptomatology. Taken from Sprecher and Fehr (2005), compassionate love is defined as thoughts, feelings and behaviours that are focused on concern, tenderness and an orientation towards supporting, helping and understanding the other, especially when the other is perceived to be suffering or in need.

Fifty-eight individuals with Alzheimer's disease aged 50-plus years (with a Mini-Mental State Examination of 16 or higher to ensure reliable reporting), and their spousal caregivers took part in interviews. The twenty-one-item 'close other' version of the compassionate love scale (Sprecher and Fehr, 2005) was used to assess both groups' attitudes towards the other. Caregivers also completed the twelve-item Zarit Burden Interview (Bédard et al., 2001), the ten-item Center for Epidemiological Studies Depression scale (Irwin et al., 1999), and a thirteen-item list of physical conditions, such as arthritis, high blood pressure (responses were rated on a binary yes/no scale). Caregivers were also asked whether their spouse needed assistance ('yes' or 'no') on six activities of daily living (e.g. bathing, grooming) and eight instrumental activities of daily living (e.g. housework or cooking) (Katz et al., 1963). Results showed a positive relationship in ratings of compassionate love between participants with Alzheimer's disease and their spouses. Additionally, by comparison with their counterparts, caregivers who felt more compassionate love for their spouses reported less perceived burden, more positive appraisals of caregiving and lower ratings of depression. In contrast, care-receiver compassionate love was also associated with less caregiver burden, more positive appraisals, but not caregiver depressive symptoms. Consistent with other studies, greater burden was also associated with more depressive symptoms.

The pattern of findings from the Monin et al. study is consistent with other studies showing that compassion is associated with more positive attitudes towards aging (Brown et al., 2015), increased positive emotions and greater well-being (Crocker and Canevello, 2008; Allen and Leary, 2013). The study is limited in terms of its small sample size, and the larger proportion of female caregivers who may benefit more from compassionate love compared to male caregivers. Further research can attempt to replicate findings, and ideally extend these findings in other contexts, or with other sample groups.

This study also has exciting implications for new lines of enquiry. For instance, further research may show that compassion as measured by these authors, or others (e.g. see a twenty-six-item self-compassion scale by Neff, 2003), has protective health or social benefits across other domains of functioning, or types of caregiving relationships, for example care relationships with those transitioning from hospital to home, or those with temporary care needs such as recovery from surgery. Feelings of compassion may also be useful in predicting or improving health and well-being, including resiliency, self-esteem and self-efficacy. Compassionate love may also help identify care receivers at risk of abuse, as further research may show that a lack of compassion or gratification in the caregiver role may fuel feelings of anger or burden. Future research may also examine compassion in other contexts, including self-efficacy, self-esteem or relationship functioning more generally. Additionally, data on the longer-term consequences of self- and other compassionate love could have theoretical and applied value, for example by combining this line of enquiry with elements of the more widely used stress–process model of caregiver burden (Pearlin et al., 1990), or by assessing any relationships between self-compassion and self-care which include the adoption of healthier lifestyles.

Research with spouses and couples has a range of methodological and ethical challenges (Forbat and Henderson, 2003; Norlyk et al., 2016). Interviewing couples together can generate information, insights and memories that would not be available through individual interviews. However, interviewing both spouses separately can allow each person to describe his/her experiences and feelings without any concerns about being judged by the other. This is especially the case in relationships where one interviewee may defer to the other, or be reluctant to contradict another view or memory. Additionally, interviewing individuals separately or together can alter power balances and challenge roles or identities, especially in cases of vulnerability such as illness or caregiving (Ussher et al., 2011). To address and minimise any negative consequences researchers need to consider the ethical aspects of interviewing couples separately or together and this includes managing the unexpected presence of a partner, even when doing individual interviews. When interviewing couples separately, jointly or with the unexpected presence of a partner, Norlyk et al. (2016) highlight the need to be aware of methodological and ethical challenges, which can include consideration for the impact of partner presence on the quality and nature of the data being collected.

Factors influencing well-being after bereavement

Relationships can play a significant role in adult health and psychosocial functioning and the loss of such relationships through bereavement has the potential to impact adversely and seriously on many aspects of health, well-being and quality of life. Distress post bereavement can include depression, anxiety and complicated grief characterised by grief symptoms and intense yearning for the person who is deceased. Those bereaved are also more likely than others to experience disability and to have health problems, including limitations in activities of daily living, hypertension and stroke. Additionally, widowhood is associated with unhealthy behaviour changes such as increases in smoking and drinking behaviours (Stahl and Schulz, 2014). Widowed persons have higher odds of dying by comparison with their married counterparts, and neither good health nor material circumstances protect bereaved individuals from this increased mortality risk (Shah et al., 2012).

Bereavement is one of the most prominent and consistent risk factors for depression (Cole and Dendukuri, 2003). In a study of factors that might bias reporting of major depression among older adults, Buchan et al. (2015) found that older adults who were bereaved were statistically more likely than others to have many depressive symptoms, including being more likely than others to have suicidal ideation or thoughts about their own deaths. They drew upon data from a nationally representative household sample of adults aged 50–85 years taking part in the Australian National Survey of Mental Health and Well-being (n = 629). Of interest were the contributions of four factors that could explain symptoms of depression and/or anhedonia: physical ill-health, recent bereavement (within five years), depression onset or length, and recall biases. Although physical health predicted the severity of depression, multivariate analyses indicated that depressive symptoms were not predicted by episode recency or episode length. However, those who were bereaved were more likely than others to report thoughts about suicide, and these findings remained even when statistically controlling for other likely explanations, such as depression severity. Further qualitative research is needed to understand these findings, and the detail, nature and base for these types of thoughts being endorsed, such as helplessness, self-harm or self-loathing.

Although the experience of death and bereavement can occur at any time through the life course, the death of a spouse is a stressful experience more likely to occur in later life, and to be an experience most salient and most distressing for older women given gender differences in longevity. Yet there are some discrepancies in the literature about whether men or women are most at risk for health problems following bereavement. Some researchers believe that women do less well than men following the death of a spouse (Li et al., 2013); this may be a consequence of greater psychological distress (including depression and anxiety), physical morbidity (poorer physical functioning and loss of physical strength) and social morbidity (less social support compared to male spousal caregivers). Other researchers, however, have found that men become more distressed following the loss of their spouses. Lee et al. (2001) drew on data from the 1987–8 National Survey of Families and Households to select a subsample of respondents aged 65 and older who were married or widowed. These researchers found that gender was significant in explaining the variance in depression, with older men adapting significantly less well than their female counterparts.

Studies of individual differences in bereavement have indicated a range of outcome profiles. Using complex statistical analysis, Galatzer-Levy and Bonanno (2012) identified empirically driven trajectories of outcomes following bereavement: *resilience* (characterised by little or no depression), *chronic grief* (characterised by depression), *pre-existing chronic depression* (ongoing high pre- through post bereavement) and *depressed-improved* outcomes (high pre-loss depression that improves after the bereavement). Financial strain predicted depression in all groups. These researchers also found that health status only contributed to variability in the *Resilient* and *Depressed-Improved* groups.

Others have also sought to identify experiences that can influence well-being following spousal loss. These can include the suddenness of the bereavement (Carr et al., 2001), the level of depression associated with caregiving (Kim et al., 2013) and contextual or situational factors, including the nature and intensity of any illness before the death. The passage of time can reduce the distress and sense of loss that can occur with bereavement. Although under researched, existential issues may also influence well-being following spousal loss. Existential issues can include experiences such as optimism, purpose in life, religious involvement and spirituality (see next section for more information on the latter two).

Caregiving during illness can also offer opportunities to adjust to an impending bereavement; this is also termed 'forewarning', 'anticipated grief' or preparedness, but the effects on adjustment remain unclear. Anticipatory grief was first described by American psychiatrist Eric Lindemann during the Second World War when he observed the wives of soldiers rejecting their returning husbands after the war; drawing on Freud's grief work, he assumed that these wives had begun to grieve and relinquish emotional bonds before the loss as a way to aid adaptation. More recent researchers have drawn on a range of theoretical frameworks for their work, including the cognitive stress, appraisal and coping theory (Lazarus and Folkman, 1984), attachment theory (Bowlby, 1980) or the integrative risk factor framework (Strobe and Schut, 1999). The latter comprises groups of factors that can impact bereavement outcomes, including (1) the nature of the stressor (e.g. type of death), (2) intrapersonal factors (e.g. previous depression), (3) interpersonal factors (e.g. family dynamics or social support), and (4) appraisal and coping strategies. Certainly, losses during the illness trajectory can lead to grief and distress (Kim et al., 2013); these can include general deterioration and loss/uncertainty around future plans. In a meta-analysis examining issues relating to anticipatory grief and preparedness for death, Nielsen et al. (2016) found that poor bereavement outcomes were associated with high levels of grief or low levels of preparedness during caregiving; that is, the assumption that grief work before the loss would alleviate bereavement outcomes was not supported.

Close personal relationships can also be an important resource and support during stressful events and transitions, including bereavement. While a lot of research examines perceptions of support (support that people believe is available should this be needed), less is known about enacted support (i.e. support provided during a difficult time, such as bereavement). Enacted support includes questions about the relationship type, quality or duration, and also any contextual factors that might facilitate, or impede, support during challenging times. Findings about the links between stress and enacted support are contradictory. According to the stress mobilisation hypothesis, greater distress is associated with greater enacted support (e.g. Iida et al., 2010). However, enacted support can decrease when the support is ongoing, as in caregiving or dealing with chronic illnesses.

The Support Provision Process Model was the framework adapted by Birditt et al. (2012) to understand the associations between stress, relationship quality and enacted support. According to this model, enacted support will vary by many factors, including individual stress levels, the quality of their relationships, and other recipient and provider characteristics. They examined whether enacted support (emotional and instrumental) varied by relationship quality and stress appraisals. Participants were community-based adults who had experienced three or more stressful events in the previous year and their identified support ties. Enacted support was measured with a series of items examining support received; the same items were reused but rephrased to support givers to ascertain the type and quality of support provided. To assess relationship closeness participants were asked to place the people who were close and important to them into three concentric circles (Kahn and Antonucci, 1980): the first circle represents those with whom they feel closest, the middle and outer circles represent relationships that are still close, but less so. Circle number was used to rate the level of closeness between participants and their supporters from 'inner closest' to 'outer, close' so that higher numbers represent less closeness. To measure stress, participants rated the most stressful life event in the past year on a five-point scale. Consistent with the model, enacted support did vary by stressor and relationship factors, with higher quality of relationships enacting greater levels of support, irrespective of high or low stress appraisals. In contrast, those with lower-quality relationships only enacted greater emotional support when their stress levels were higher. The authors theorise that such individuals rely on their lower-quality relationships for support when under extreme stress rather than in all conditions.

The study above was limited to participants experiencing high levels of stress, and further research is needed to determine if these findings apply to those experiencing fewer life-stress events, or specific life events such as bereavement. Additionally, as noted by the authors, those providing support were identified by participants as helpful supporters, and it is not clear whether these findings apply across a range of social support partners. Further survey and interview-based studies should examine and explore in more detail some of the complexities in perceptions, for example subjective evaluations about relationship quality, or relationship satisfaction, especially where there are other confounds such as ongoing difficulties following bereavement. Nevertheless, in understanding enacted support, this study is very useful in emphasising the need to consider the wider context of the relationship and the stressor. This need also warrants increasing sophistication in how survey and interview data get analysed so that multiple variables or factors get considered or analysed together.

Alongside analytical challenges there are many methodological challenges which researchers need to consider. These include biases in retrospective recall, as participants may believe they should respond with distress and anxiety congruent with social expectations following the loss of a spouse or other close relationship. Ideally, one could address this by designing large prospective studies whereby participants are assessed before as well as after the bereavement. An alternative and more modest way to address possible biases in recall may be to have independent coders comment on participants' attitudes or else to have a control sample. Having independent raters comment on participants' attitudes or relationships prior to the bereavement could be feasible. Having a control group is more difficult, but such a group could have many benefits. It would mean that the researcher could compare well-being of bereaved spouses with others perhaps of similar age and background who have experienced a different stressor. In this way, a control group might shed light on the experiences, health and coping strategies unique to participants experiencing spousal loss by comparison with other stressors and challenges.

Future studies should examine other factors influencing well-being before or after bereavement, including situational or contextual factors; the latter can include the suddenness of the death, or the amount of financial/social/practical resources available to manage the loss. Further research is needed exploring the above issues with other sample populations, including less typical groups such as those involved in same-sex relationships or among single adults mourning other lost relationships. In examining the relationship between bereavement and subsequent well-being, researchers also need to control for the type of relationship being examined; this is because variables found to be important in influencing well-being following the death of a spouse may not be so important following the death of a close friend or more distant family member. More research is needed examining the influence of culture on bereavement. Culture can have its effect in terms of variations in expectations, shared meanings, socio-economic resources, geography or history. Researchers need not assume differences will occur between different cultural groups, but instead need to include a measure of the cultural variable that interests them.

Grandparenting relationships

Grandparenting relationships can be very important for both grandparents and their grandchildren (e.g. Smith and Drew, 2004; Bengtson, 2001), and indeed this relationship may even have increased in importance in recent years. Specifically, increasing longevity along with decreased fertility means that there are fewer grandchildren per grandparent compared to previous generations. Additionally, contemporary grandparents are more affluent, and in better health compared to their parents and grandparents, and they can have more free time. These differences can impact positively on the quality and quantity of time that grandparents have with their grandchildren, and in lives that overlap for a longer period of time (Bengtson, 2001; Di Gessa et al., 2016; Geurts and van Tilburg, 2015). As with any family relationship, however, intergenerational conflicts and ambivalence can also occur. As discussed in this section, these conflicts can be very challenging for grandparents and grandchildren alike. Yet there is comparatively little research exploring and examining grandparent – as well as great-grandparent–grandchild relationships and their consequences on identity, health, and quality of life. Even fewer studies have been carried out examining intergenerational relationships with adult grandchildren as adults. Although there is some evidence that contact decreases when grandchildren are older (Geurts et al., 2009), adult grandchildren can contribute significant emotional and practical supports to their grandparents (Fruhauf et al., 2006; Moorman and Stokes, 2016).

Many decades of research and theory, particularly from Europe and North America, have shown that relationships with grandchildren are typically very positive and rewarding, and that grandparents have a vital role to play in the development and well-being of their grandchildren (Bengtson and Robertson, 1985; Drew and Smith, 1999; Smith, 1991, 1994). Intergenerational relationships can also be very important for grandparents (Carstensen, 1991), adding meaning to life, and contributing significantly to grandparents' well-being, identity and ongoing development (Erikson et al., 1986). By comparison with parents who may be working, grandparents can have more time to engage with grandchildren, and are often very willing to pass on family traditions and values. Grandparents can also offer informational, practical or financial support, including childcare (Hank and Buber, 2009) and provide a stabilising support to grandchildren, and great-grandchildren (Bengtson, 2001). This is especially the case during times of transition or adversity.

In an early classic US study, Neugarten and Weinstein (1964) identified five major styles of grandparenting from interviews with seventy sets of grandparents. The 'formal' style describes grandparents following prescribed roles with definite differences in parenting and grandparenting responsibilities. Other styles include the 'fun seeker' (seeing grandchildren as fun and a source of satisfaction), 'surrogate' (involving parental or caregiving responsibilities), 'reservoir of family wisdom' (dispensing skills and information) and 'distant' (with infrequent contact). In contrast, more recent studies have focused on the quality and type of caregiving carried out (Craig and Jenkins, 2016; Eli et al., 2016), or the health benefits and social costs of caring for grandchildren, particularly for grandmothers (Di Gessa et al., 2016; Heyslip et al., 2015; Tsai, 2016).

Demographic factors can influence the relationship between grandparents and their grandchildren, and both the quality and frequency of contact. The age and health of the grandparents for instance can impact on the frequency of contact with grandchildren, with less contact occurring for grandparents in older age groups, or in poorer health. Grandparents with a large number of grandchildren may prioritise some of these relationships over others. In cases of geographical separation, contact may be maintained by electronic means, including social media and Skype. However, it is not yet clear what impact the mode of contact has on the quality and frequency of contact between grandchildren and their grandparents. Additionally, grandparents may have other demands on their time, and researchers have found that recent cohorts of grandparents can spend less time with their grandchildren by comparison with earlier generations of grandparents (Lyyra et al., 2010; Silverstein and Long, 1998).

The grandparent–parent relationship can also influence the nature and frequency of contact between grandparents and their grandchildren, particularly in cases of parental divorce or separation. Indeed, the ability of grandparents to interact and engage with their grandchildren can be constrained or lost by family rifts and feuds, and more general life transitions and changes for the middle generation, such as illness or divorce (Drew and Silverstein, 2007). This is especially the case for paternal grandparents, who can be at higher risk of losing contact with grandchildren by comparison with maternal grandparents. This can be due to a number of factors, including situations were mothers move out of a given area with their children, or where non-custodial fathers lose contact with their children. The latter is especially the case for fathers who are not married, as they may not have automatic legal rights of access to their children, and can even struggle to be listed as a parent on a child's birth certificate. The rights of grandparents in these contexts will vary by jurisdiction. For instance, in cases of parental death or divorce it may be possible in the United States for grandparents to sue for visitation rights with grandchildren. However, in the UK grandparents have no legal rights of contact, although the 1989 Children Act allows them to apply to have contact. Court applications however can be costly, time consuming and stressful, and mediation may offer a more reasonable alternative.

The loss of contact with grandchildren, and the associated loss of the grandparenting role, can have a significant and adverse effect on health, well-being and identity for both grandparents and their grandchildren (Drew and Smith, 1999). Negative consequences can include bereavement-type chronic grief, helplessness, lowered life satisfaction and mental health problems, including depression, anxiety and symptoms of post-traumatic stress disorder. Hope for a reunion can exacerbate or prolong feelings of intense distress and loss, as can rumination over a child or children who are physically absent, but preying on the minds of their grandparents. Additionally, while support may be available initially, this can wane over time.

Using data from the Longitudinal Study of Generations in Southern California, Drew and Silverstein (2007) examined emotional well-being among grandparents who had lost contact with grandchildren for a number of reasons, including parental separation, divorce, family feud or a sudden event such as relocation. A comparison group who had not lost contact with grandchildren were also recruited. The final sample included 442 grandparents with an average age of

71.5 years, who were tracked over fifteen years with follow-up surveys every three years from 1985 to 2000. Findings indicated that those grandparents who had lost contact with grandchildren did less well initially and reported more depressive symptoms compared to other grandparents. This was especially the case for sudden losses, rather than where grandparents may have had more time to prepare, such as in cases of divorce or family feud. After three years however, depression levels returned to their previous levels. There are few studies examining grandparent–grandchild relationships over time, and so this study is exciting in examining short- and long-term consequences of losing contact with grandchildren. It also compares grandparents who had lost contact with grandchildren with peers who had not lost contact, and such an approach is really useful in establishing and testing differences.

Even within the context of a normal family life, the role of grandparents in the lives of their grandchildren is not clear. Several studies have shown that grandparents do have a direct influence on their grandchildren's educational attainment (Chan and Bolivier, 2013; Modin et al., 2013), particularly in the context of the resources they bring to the grandparent–grandchild relationship. Other researchers however have found no such influence. Inconsistencies in findings can be attributed to a range of factors, including overlaps in measurement of resources between grandparents and parents. Bol et al. (2016) sought to address this limitation by asking extensively about the resources available from both grandparents and parents; while controlling for overlaps they then found no direct grandparent effects on educational attainment of grandchildren. These findings may be unique to the Netherlands, or to the fact that these grandparents did not play a strong role in the way their grandchildren were being raised.

Further research could explore or examine psychological and developmental routes through which grandparents can influence the lives of their grandchildren. Such factors can include communication around identity, support and confidence levels. Further studies might also explore grandparents' ideas about their roles, and the level of involvement they have or would like to have in raising grandchildren. The latter can include attitudes and anxieties around 'non-interference' and the factors that might influence or predict such anxieties, including the quality of relationship, and the quality of communication between parents and grandparents. Many grandparents may choose limited involvement with grandchildren in order to pursue their own interests and activities. Understanding the views and attitudes of grandparents could make significant contributions to our understanding of the grandparenting role and the consequences that different perspectives have on health, well-being and development for both grandparents and grandchildren. Further research using surveys, interviews, or both, is also needed examining generative inclinations towards the next generation among a growing number of older people who have remained childless, or those who have no access to their own grandchildren, for example those who may have a vicarious grandparenting-type interest in the welfare of younger people, including grandnieces and grand-nephews.

Meaning, spirituality and religion

As previous chapters have illustrated, many studies on aging since the 1960s have sought to identify the key factors underlying aging well, whether continued activity or a turn to disengagement, maintenance of positive self-perception and continued control over one's life situation. In recent years more consideration has begun to be given to issues of meaning and spiritual development (Wong and Fry, 1998; Reker and Chamberlain, 2000; Marcoen, 2005; Krause, 2009).

The study of perceived meaning in life is a diffuse area. It includes issues of perception of purpose, value and commitment applied to one's own life as well as to the society in which one lives. The time perspectives may be limited (e.g. the goals of one's present actions) or very broad (e.g. the meaning of life in this universe). Humans are naturally inclined to ask questions about purposes and ends of human action and to apply these questions also to the world around them. It is an area of study which addresses a different dimension of experience to those commonly spoken about but of fundamental importance. As people age, questions about meaning appear to become more insistent, in part perhaps because of increased free time and isolation. In Western societies at least, older people appear to find it more difficult to perceive purpose in their lives or to have a sense of continuing development (Ryff, 1995)

Victor Frankl (1964) was one of the first psychologists to stress the importance of the study of existential meaning (i.e. what gives meaning to continuing to live). He had witnessed the holocaust of European Jews from close hand and on the basis of his personal experience and subsequent studies with victims he argued that any trauma could be survived so long as some meaning could be found in the situation. His comments have obvious relevance to aging and the experience of loss and impending death which are intrinsic to it.

Some of the major sources of meaning in life are provided by religious systems of thought, which provide an ultimate perspective on life's final goals and purposes, against which present failures and disappointments can be set. They offer hope for eventual resolution of difficulties, and consequent peace of mind. Religion has also been the traditional provider of meaning to aging. It allows older people to experience their lives as meaningful despite lowering quality of life. Life's tribulations can be reinterpreted in a positive light, new meanings created to replace meanings that have succumbed to societal change and life events. Particularly when the capacity to exercise other forms of control diminishes, religion provides elderly people with continued control over meaning (McFadden, 1996b; Coleman, 2010). Some of the theorists we have cited in earlier chapters, such as Jung and Erikson, have acknowledged its importance. 'No matter what the world thinks about religious experience, the one who has it possesses the great treasure . . . that provides him with some of life's meaning and beauty' (Jung, 1938, p. 113).

As that quotation implies, modern psychology has tended to give minimal or unsympathetic consideration to the benefits of religion (Pargament, 2002b). In this it reflects the loss of Christian influence on Western civilisation during the latter part of the twentieth century. There has been a search for alternative sources of meaning, often still spiritual in character but outside the boundaries of traditional faith (Heelas and Woodhead, 2005; Lynch, 2007). But as a consequence we now experience a greater separation between the more religiously socialised present older generations and their less religious children and grandchildren. Other cultures by contrast, in Africa, Asia and South America, have remained much more religious. As a result meaning, spirituality and religion constitute an area of research on aging where one feels strongly the absence of comparable scientific studies in non-Western societies.

In this section we first examine attempts by researchers to conceptualise and define the terms personal meaning, spirituality and religion. Conceptual clarification is an important research task which is often neglected in the rush to operationalise and measure. The changing relationship between religion and spirituality in Western thought has made this especially necessary in this area of study. In the succeeding sections we will examine studies investigating age, gender and racial differences in meaning and spirituality, followed by those examining the role of spiritual and religious beliefs and practices in coping with later-life stresses.

Conceptual issues in the study of meaning and spirituality

For most of the time the meaningfulness of our lives is not something we consider. Our goals and their value are implied in our actions. Such harmony of action and intention is captured in Csikszentmihalyi's (1990) discussion of 'flow' as the key to peak experience, where there is total congruence between the activity and ability of the person, and the impact on the environment around. Meaning is central to this experience. The person is achieving his or her purpose, what he or she feels called to be.

When life becomes problematic, the meaning of our activities ceases to be implicit and the values and commitments that characterise our actions become the object of examination and evaluation. Marcoen has made a useful distinction between the surface or provisional meanings that reflect immediate goals, and the ultimate meanings, the wider values, hopes and concerns which give meaning to our present goals (Marcoen, 1993). Often loss of meaning relates to a perception of dissociation between the implied meanings of our present actions and our underlying aspirations. As we develop a personal meaning system through adult life there are likely to be clashes with the values conveyed by society. Later life provides fresh incentives, as a result of greater experience, freedom from outside pressures, and disillusion with previously accepted values, to develop our sense of meaning further.

The importance of the study of the personal meaning system for research on aging was first signalled by Gary Reker and Paul Wong in Birren and Bengtson's volume *Emergent Theories of Aging* (Reker and Wong, 1988). They reviewed different approaches to assessing personal meaning, including their own measurement scales which constituted a major contribution to advancing the subject. These are based on operationalisation of Frankl's concepts, including life purpose, existential vacuum, life control, death acceptance, will to meaning, goal seeking and future meaning.

A noteworthy element of these scales is their freedom from religious language. It is therefore possible for someone who is not religious but who has developed strong commitments and values to score highly. Nor do all people who practise a religion necessarily possess a highly developed meaning system.

Spirituality by contrast is a much more difficult concept to study. Previously it was closely intertwined with religion, but with increased autonomy in choice of belief systems as well as more critique of the functioning of religious institutions spirituality has acquired a greater independence of usage (Heelas and Woodhead, 2005). Certain understandings of the term 'spirituality' no longer imply belief in a transcendent power such as is characteristic of most religious traditions. Some have gone so far as to equate spirituality more with personal meaning than with religion. Thus it has been conceptualised as 'the motivational and emotional foundation of the lifelong quest for meaning' (McFadden, 1996b, p. 164). However, it is doubtful that a shared definition of spirituality can be constructed on this basis. The concept will necessarily be used differently by those who ground their experiences in a non-material reality, whether defined as transcendent or immanent (e.g. sensing God's presence within creation), and by those who wish to accept them simply as psychological experiences to which humans are inclined.

Zinnbauer et al. (1999) have criticised the tendency to separate religion from spirituality, and especially to evaluate the latter as superior to the former. Religion they have argued is by definition concerned with spiritual matters, and treating it merely in terms of formal group membership, as some researchers are inclined to do, misses its dynamic operation in the lives of individuals. Similarly treating spirituality solely as a personal matter loses the social context in which it arises and is nurtured. A concept they argue which is important to both religion and spirituality is that of the 'sacred', which typically refers to an experience of deep value whose source lies outside the world as we ordinarily experience it. Therefore they prefer a definition of both religion and spirituality which brings out this interrelationship, spirituality being a 'search for the sacred', whereas religion involves a 'search for significance in ways related to the sacred'.

Such a definition of spirituality is reflected in the work of most researchers in the field of aging. Thus Wink and Dillon (2002) in assessing signs of spirituality on the basis of interview material drew on Atchley's (1997) definition of spirituality as 'engagement in a personal quest toward an understanding of the ultimate ground of all being that involves an integration of both inner and outer life experiences through systematic practice'. Coleman and colleagues in their study of adjustment to loss of spouse in later life (2007) stressed the close relationship of religion and spirituality, and their distinctness from perceived meaning in life. Spirituality was defined as concerned with higher levels of meaning, value and purpose in life, usually associated with belief in a power or force beyond the material world. Perceiving meaning in life on the other hand does not depend on belief in a transcendent power. Thus one can justifiably distinguish philosophical beliefs, which exclude any such reliance, from religious and spiritual beliefs. The term 'existential meaning' is perhaps the most useful generic term to refer to the perceived purpose of one's own life, whether provided by religious and/ or spiritual beliefs and/or philosophical, community, family or other principles, values and goals.

A further reason for choosing such a definition of spirituality in current research with older people in most Western societies is that they tend to have retained the closely connected understandings of religion and spirituality into which they were socialised when young. The consequences for later life of the current shift, which has taken place especially in Western Europe, but also in North America, from a predominance of traditional Christian religious to novel spiritual understandings of life, often drawing on Eastern traditions such as belief in reincarnation, will become more evident with the aging of the post-Second World War 'baby boom' generation (Coleman, 2011).

Religion, as Pargament and colleagues' definition indicates, is a much more complex concept. This point deserves reflection, because often the opposite is assumed; that is, that religion is simply the practice of a particular faith. In reality religion is much more than this. It is a resource which can be used in different ways to provide not only meaning to life but also other benefits. It does this not only through language but also through the practice of rituals and use of symbols. But these same means can be used for secular as well as spiritual purposes. Religion can be misused, and it can harm people.

Research on religion and aging has also been limited by its focus on a relatively restricted number of dimensions of practice, typically attendance at communal worship and the practice of prayer in private. The role that religious ritual plays in older people's lives has been particularly neglected (Coleman et al., 2013; Traphagan, 2004). Future study also needs to link more directly with general theorising about the psychological and social functions of religion. For example, Sedikides and Gebauer (2013) provide a thorough analysis of evidence for the various potential benefits religion provides to the self: enhancing not only self-esteem but also personal and compensatory control, reducing uncertainty, and providing secure attachment figures together with a sense of belonging and meaning. All of these various human needs are accentuated in the course of aging, and one might therefore on these grounds alone expect some degree of increased religious expression and practice in older people's lives. Research hypotheses in the field of religion and aging need to be similarly specific in conceptualisation.

A good example is provided by Hayward and Krause's (2013) recent study on age-related increase in sense of God-mediated control (i.e. relying more on God's help to achieve one's aims in life), a significant aspect of Judaeo-Christian belief, but one that has been neglected within studies of adjustment to aging. As we have seen in the previous chapter (and will discuss again in Part III of this book), maintenance of a sense of control and the ability when needed to change strategies of control are central aspects of contemporary theorising about adjustment to aging (Rowe and Kahn, 1998; Baltes and Smith, 2003; Brandtstädter, 2006). In their own study Hayward and Krause hypothesised that as persons aged, loss of personal control would be compensated for by a stronger belief in God-mediated control.

They analysed data from the first four waves of a large US national longitudinal survey of both Black and White older adults of varying ages, and found results largely supportive of their hypothesis. Increases in a sense of God-mediated control clearly compensated for the loss of personal control with age in the Black sample. A similar relationship was found in the White sample, but only among those with a high religious commitment. In those of low religious commitment the sense of God-mediated control in fact decreased with age. Why should there be this difference? As the authors conclude, it seems that the central position of the church in African-American culture (Taylor et al., 2004) makes religious ideas salient even for those with relatively weak ties to their church community. They also acknowledge that older White adults may have more access to alternative secular resources to compensate for declining personal control.

Variation in secular, spiritual and religious world views

As we stressed in the last chapter, studying variation in aging has become as or more important than identifying common changes with age. This is certainly true of differences with age in secular, spiritual and religious world views. In fact the traditional expectation that persons become more religious with age is not supported by the evidence. Certainly, the greater religiosity of older people compared with younger adults is evident from numerous surveys conducted in the United States, and several European societies since the 1970s (Moberg, 2001, 2005; Voas and Doebler, 2011). Older people attend religious services more and express firmer belief in a personal God to whom one can turn for assistance.

However, the evidence points most strongly to cohort rather than developmental changes underpinning the observed age differences in religious participation in Western countries. Only three substantial longitudinal studies on attitudes to religion involving older people have been conducted, all three in California (McCullough et al., 2005; Dillon and Wink, 2007; Bengtson et al., 2015). They reflect historical changes between birth cohorts in declining religious identification, but do not report significant and consistent changes in religious faith and practice within cohorts. Rather, religious commitments appear to be established by early adulthood and to remain fairly stable thereafter. A longitudinal study of a British pre-First World War birth cohort in fact showed a significant decline in the numbers of participants attributing importance to religious faith in their later years (Coleman et al., 2004).

The generational differences appear to be the result of major societal shifts in attitudes to religion characteristic of Western societies since at least the 1960s. Altogether the UK and Western European evidence suggests that age differences in religious attitudes can be explained in terms of intergenerational decline, with each successive generation being less successful in transmitting religious faith and practice to succeeding generations (Crockett and Voas, 2006). US data analysis also shows historical decline in religious affiliation and attendance at worship, although, compared with the UK, to a much lesser degree and only beginning in the post-Second World War years (Putnam and Campbell, 2010). However, as a result it seems very unlikely that current cohorts of young or middle-aged people in both Europe and North America will show the same levels of religious engagement when they grow old as current older people display.

The more appropriate developmental question is likely to be whether people become more spiritual with age. As we saw in Chapter 2, a number of developmental theories of aging address this question, especially gerotranscendence theory (Tornstam, 2005). The general literature would suggest that issues of meaning and spirituality become more salient as people age. US studies indicate older people incur more problems with perception of purpose in life (Ryff, 1995), and it would appear to become more important for older people to have answers or at least strategies for dealing with questions about life's meaning. Longitudinal evidence remains limited in scope but suggests that non-organisational religious activities such as prayer and religious reading increase in later life, as if in compensation for decreased public religious activity (McFadden, 1996b). Analysis of the Berkeley study of adult life, a study of a 1920s birth cohort, found that spirituality defined in terms both of interest in spiritual questions and engagement in spiritual practices did increase over the lifespan (Wink and Dillon, 2002; Dillon and Wink, 2007). This analysis also found an association between experience of negative life events and subsequent spiritual development.

Much more significant than any association with age is that between religion and gender, at least in Western societies (Davie and Vincent, 1998). Women practitioners greatly outnumber men. They also rate their own religious activities as more meaningful to them, and are more likely to turn to religion as a way of coping with life's difficulties. Explanations for this phenomenon include women's greater socialisation to expression of emotion, and their greater caregiving role and consequent need for support within this role (McFadden, 1996a). These observations have major implications for aging. Religious organisations can expect to minister to growing numbers of older women in the population, but they should also reflect on what more could be done to minister to the spiritual needs of men. Theory with some evidence to support it suggests some gender cross-over effect with age, with men becoming more receptive to belief in advanced age, and women more sceptical (Gutmann, 1987; Henry, 1988; Coleman et al., 2004).

Other important influences to consider include culture and ethnicity. One can only draw confident conclusions about the role of religion and spirituality in older people's lives within the societies and communities studied. Few if any major psychological studies appear to have been conducted on the significance of religion for the increasing numbers of older people within the developing world. Comparative study of religion also remains rare, with few notable examples (Mehta, 1997; Berger et al., 2008; Coleman et al., 2013). Most studies have been conducted on those with a Christian socialisation, and relatively little on aging within the other great religious traditions. Moreover research is required which compares not only those of differing strength of spiritual belief but also those with considered non-religious and non-spiritual world views, such as atheistic humanists (Wilkinson and Coleman, 2010).

Perhaps the most significant comparative studies of religion have been conducted with migrant populations both in North America and Europe. They indicate important differences. In Britain, for example, two-thirds of older Afro-Caribbeans attend church regularly, a far higher proportion than the host community, and the importance of the local faith community is emphasised in studies of other ethnic groups (Davie and Vincent, 1998). In the United States major studies have been conducted with different racial groups. These have confirmed the higher levels of both organisational and non-organisational religious activity, including religious coping, among older Blacks compared with older White Americans even when other sociodemographic variables are controlled for (Taylor et al., 2004; Taylor et al., 2007a, 2007b). As explanation for these differences Taylor and colleagues (2007b) draw attention to the role of religion in integrating individuals and families within a community as well as compensating for social disadvantage.

Recent research on religion, well-being and coping in later life

Studies on older people provide both the largest and most coherent body of evidence about the effects of religion on well-being and health (Koenig et al., 2012). Recent studies have continued to find large benefits for religious participation: attendance at services associated with increased longevity and lower rates of depression (Hill et al., 2005; Norton et al., 2008); private religious practice with higher quality of life and recovery from depressive illness (Idler et al., 2009; Payman and Ryburn, 2010); strength of spiritual belief with increased psychological well-being (Kirby et al., 2004); and daily spiritual experience with protection against stress and promotion of a positive mood (Whitehead and Bergeman, 2012).

Associations of course do not prove causal connections and some at least of these associations, for example between church attendance and physical health, likely involve influences of health upon religious practice rather than vice versa. It is also true that most of these findings have come from research conducted on Christian samples in the United States, which remains more religious than most other Western societies.

Nevertheless, the sheer weight of evidence lends support to Pargament's view that the challenges of aging provide a key and generally positive test of the value of religious belief and practice (Pargament et al., 1995). Religious faith, spiritual belief and philosophy of life are clearly important resources people bring to aging. The major lack in the literature is the absence of studies on the beneficial or other effects of non-religious and non-spiritual perspectives on life's meaning (McFadden, 1996b; Wilkinson and Coleman, 2010) (see Box 5.4). It is likely that people continue or adopt religious practices in part at least because of the benefit they perceive they obtain from them. Therefore the only fair comparison is with people who claim benefits from other forms of belief, not from those who find little benefit in religious practice.

BOX 5.4 COMPARING THE COPING BENEFITS TO OLDER PEOPLE OF ATHEISTIC AND RELIGIOUS BELIEFS

Although research examining the health benefits of religious belief to people as they age is a relatively well-developed field of study, most studies have concentrated on comparisons between those of strong and weak beliefs. Comparison with those holding strong atheistical or other non-religious world views have been neglected so far. In a study attempting to address this subject Wilkinson and Coleman (2010) interviewed two matched groups of older people, one holding strong religious beliefs and the other strong atheistical beliefs. They compared pairs who had recently faced similar types of challenge: painful non-spousal bereavement; bereavement of spouse; the likelihood that their health would deteriorate in the near future; severe physical decline; expectation of their own imminent death. All the religious participants were Christian or Jewish and the atheists selected from the local branch of the British Humanist Association.

Interviews and their analyses were conducted employing the eight principles of positive aging proposed by Richard Lazarus, a pioneer in research on the psychology of stress and coping, in his posthumously published book *Coping with Aging* (Lazarus and Lazarus, 2006):

- to be clear about the realities of one's situation;
- to accept those realities and view them in the best light possible;
- to be able to cope effectively with those realities;
- to be able to compensate for losses and deficits;
- to be actively engaged in purposeful striving;
- to be wisely selective about what one takes on;
- to maintain close ties to others;
- to retain positive self-regard despite losses and deficits.

The analyses showed that all the study participants – regardless of their beliefs – were coping well, and suggested that a strong atheistic belief system can fulfil the same role as a strong religious belief system in providing support, explanation, consolation and inspiration. The researchers concluded that the strength of people's beliefs and how these beliefs are used might have more influence on the efficacy of coping than the specific nature of the beliefs.

(Wilkinson and Coleman, 2010)

There is evidence from less religious societies such as the UK that spiritual belief is not necessarily associated with favourable health outcomes (King et al., 1999). This may reflect differences in degree of belief, with uncertain belief being associated with more negative outcomes (Krause, 1995b). A UK study on older people's adjustment to spousal loss showed higher levels of depression in those with low to moderate levels of strength of spiritual belief than in those with very strong or no beliefs (Coleman et al., 2007).

Linda George and colleagues' (2000) analysis of the possible explanations of the benefits of religion and spirituality upon health still appears valid. Besides the meaning-giving qualities of a spiritual belief system, they also identified positive influences on healthy behaviours and respect for the body, and the provision of social support from incorporation in a social network of other believers. In those studies they reviewed which looked at all of these factors together, the sense of coherence provided by a religious and spiritual belief system, including the positive mental attitudes it engendered, appeared the most significant.

Kirkpatrick (2005) has suggested an interesting theoretical integration of the literature on religion and well-being in terms of attachment theory. Religion can be conceptualised as an attachment process, in which religious practice provides a sense of security, confirming that there is a caring presence in the person's life. As McFadden and Levin (1996) have pointed out, theistic religions are essentially relational. The child is typically introduced to God by parents, and God functions as an extension of the parental figures, usually for the better (more powerful, more forgiving, more understanding), but sometimes for the worse (more demanding, more judgemental, more punishing). Even those who appear the least religious seek safety and help in situations of extreme stress, such as warfare, in appeal and prayer to God. Consistent with attachment theory are Pargament et al.'s (1995) proposed explanations for how religious belief strengthens older people as they face decline through exchanging personal mastery for surrendering to God's will, through overcoming fear of dying in His presence, and through a sense of growing intimacy with Him. This may imply the need to change religious coping styles with age from active to more passive forms of coping. As described earlier, Hayward and Krause's (2013) recent study on age-related increase in the sense of God-mediated control addresses this topic.

The tangible social support provided within well-functioning religious communities can also be seen as an extension and confirmation of divine care. This helps explain why participation in community acts of worship remains particularly high among older people before physical frailty intervenes, and often continues afterwards despite the difficulties of accessing places of worship. The considerable investment of time and energy older people give to attending religious services is rewarded by the improvement to emotional balance that acts of public worship provide. In attachment theory terms, the religious building functions as a safe haven, providing a place of 'sanctuary'. Even passing the church building or anticipating entry may be sufficient to induce positive feelings. Also many aspects of private religious observance can be understood as an extension of belonging to a worshipping community.

The evidence on links between religiosity and well-being is sufficiently strong to justify more detailed studies of religion in action. Coping with stress is a prime example. Religious coping is commonly reported in US studies, and people experiencing high levels of stress report more favourable well-being if at the same time they indicate high levels of spiritual support. One relatively well-developed area of research on religious coping in later life has been the study of adaptation to bereavement, especially of spouse and children. The evidence for the benefits of a religious world view in bereavement situations are well established (Fry, 2001; Becker et al., 2007; Wortmann and Park, 2008). However, as Carr and Sharp's (2014) recent study has demonstrated, uncertain or negative views of an afterlife are associated with the greatest psychological disturbance. Pargament has also drawn attention to characteristics of maladaptive religious coping such as questioning the power and mercy of God (Pargament, 2002a).

Such research results show how important it is to study the actual content of beliefs that are being drawn on by the bereaved person. Most religions contain beliefs related to issues of death and practices that can be used in the expression of grief and mourning. Research by Spreadbury (Spreadbury and Coleman, 2011; Spreadbury, 2013) with religious older adults found that religious cognition such as belief in a life after death, life-after-death reunion and belief in a protective, omniscient and omnipresent God were used in ongoing coping and adjustment. Participants were able to make sense of their bereavement by interpreting it as part of a purpose or plan known to God and find benefit in beliefs that their spouse was in a life-after-death location free from suffering and had achieved their spiritual goal of reaching their desired afterlife.

Participants were also able to use religious rituals such as prayer and receiving Communion/Eucharist to facilitate continuing bond processes (Klass et al., 1996) with their deceased spouse. Through religious rituals participants felt they were able to continue or maintain a cognitive and emotional relationship with the deceased and feel a sense of psychological and emotional closeness, as well as rituals helping participants to regulate grief-related emotions. In addition, participants drew on favourite passages from the Bible to support sense-making processes and to sustain coping.

The three research themes we have addressed in this chapter all provide insight into the paradox of well-being and aging that we emphasised at the beginning of the previous chapter. The process of adaptation to aging is fostered by a growing acceptance of its products, including a wider and less egocentric perspective on life, and a realisation that at every stage (except perhaps the very last) the experience of aging exceeds expectations. As contemporary society hopefully develops a more positive attitude to the potential of age, we can reasonably expect these aspects of the experience of aging to be enhanced.

Social relationships remain crucial until the end of life. These are dynamic, interchanging and challenging. Although contemporary society offers older people more possibilities for new types of friendship, there is no evidence that the traditional reliance on the family has diminished. Despite major changes in the character of the modern family, the caregiving role of the family remains essential to well-being in later life. In addition, the role of grandparent (and great-grandparent) may be gaining greater salience.

Religion and culture are important sources of existential meaning which may grow in importance in later life. There is a striking contrast in this regard between North America and the more prosperous parts of Western Europe. In the latter, religion has a diminishing importance (Berger et al., 2008). It is a pertinent question for future research whether alternative sources of existential meaning, such as are provided by new spiritual movements, are able to match the traditional power of religious belonging in old age.

PART III

Development and adaptation in advanced old age

So here it is at last, the distinguished thing.

(Henry James, in Edel, 1985)

6

PERSPECTIVES ON LATE LIFE

'Real old age'

We now move deeper into the experience of aging, to what has now come to be referred to as the 'fourth age', a period of time when issues of disability and frailty begin to dominate the lives of older people. This is 'old age' proper, the time of life when people finally do ascribe the adjective 'old' to themselves. It is what many have been waiting for all along, expecting it with varying degrees of apprehension (see Chapter 5). As he incurred his first stroke, the Anglo-American novelist Henry James said that in the very act of falling 'he heard in the room a voice which was distinctly, it seemed, not his own, saying, "so here it is at last, the distinguished thing"' (Edel, 1985, p. 706). Thus opened for him the last stage of life, a time he had feared but in some sense also respected.

The fourth age can begin dramatically, with an event such as a major stroke, but it can also show a more gentle gradient of approach, as one becomes aware year by year, month by month that one's energies and capabilities are diminishing. Perhaps most people would prefer the latter, if only because it allows more time for adaptation. Many might also prefer a quick death, without awareness, 'to cease upon the midnight with no pain', although that too has its sorrowful aspect, in the lack of opportunity for farewells. We know relatively little about people's preferences in this regard. They remain for the most part unspoken. That is why Henry James's remark has such resonance. We know immediately what he is talking about, even though it has not been mentioned before, and maybe will not be mentioned again.

In fact Henry James, in the almost three months he remained alive after his stroke, went through many struggles. A second stroke produced some brain damage, and he was concerned not only that he had become mad but that people would notice the change. He seemed to one friend who knew him well to have lost 'his own unmistakeable identity'. He was unsure of his surroundings, thinking of himself at times in various places he had visited during his life in Europe and America. The diaries of friends and relatives record 'a kind of heroic struggle to retain his grasp on reality in the midst of death-in-life' (Edel, 1985, p. 709). This reflected that 'terror of consciousness' he had been attempting to describe in his unfinished novel *The Sense of the Past* that he had been working on in the evening before his first stroke. But there were also periods of peace as, looking out from the window of his apartment in Chelsea on the barges passing along the river Thames, he imagined that he himself was on a boat voyaging and visiting foreign cities.

The study of advanced old age has been especially neglected by developmental psychologists until relatively recently, remaining the preserve mainly of clinicians such as geriatricians and clinical psychologists. The opportunities of the 'third age', of continued employment and/or more time for freely chosen activities, aroused more interest than managing declining activities and energy levels and increasing problems in daily living. But as death, and particularly the quality of life of dying persons, has become a more ready topic for discussion in recent years, so more attention has been given to the period preceding death. Concerns about dementia in particular have greatly increased, making it in some Western societies the major health concern.

The increase in longevity of the human population is one of the major achievements of the modern world. Although very few people are reaching the upper limits of the human lifespan – regarded as being around 120 years – many more are reaching their eighties, nineties and one hundreds (Poon et al., 2005 – see also Box 2.1). The most extreme example is Japan, whose population's lifespan doubled in only fifty years from an average of 42 years in the Second World War to over 80 in the new millennium. Large increases in the proportion of populations aged above 80 years is expected up until the middle of the century, with almost a doubling from 2025 to 2050, 4.5 per cent to 8.8 per cent in Europe and 2.9 per cent to 5.7 per cent in the Americas (Peace et al., 2007).

The downside of this achievement is that advanced aging is characterised by markedly higher levels of disability and frailty. In the UK nearly a half (47 per cent) of those 75 years and over have been reported as having a limiting long-standing illness (UK Office for National Statistics, 2013). In those of 85 years and over the figure is much higher at more than two-thirds (69 per cent) (UK Department for Work and Pensions, 2009). A US study has shown that by age 80 one in two individuals indicated difficulties in mobility tasks, such as walking a quarter of a mile (Ostchega et al., 2000). Other features of this sector of the population which strongly distinguish them from the rest are the greater proportion of women, calculated as comprising 65 per cent of the world's population over the age of 80 (United Nations, 2002). The oldest old are disadvantaged in various ways, with much higher proportions living alone, subsisting on limited finance, and residing in institutions. Correspondingly greater levels of resilience are needed to cope with life's demands.

Because until recently the very old were a numerically insignificant part of the population, the issue of their declining health status had less impact on society.

People did not live long in poor health, and advanced age in particular was for most people who reached it a relatively short phase of life. A vital issue for twenty-first-century society is whether this period of terminal decline is increasing and along with it the need for enhanced resources to physically support elderly persons in their activities of daily living. Extra resources would not be required if the average age of needing assistance rose along with increased life expectation. Indeed, there has for many years been a hope among gerontologists that morbidity and disability could be compressed into a shorter and shorter period at the end of life, but there is no clear evidence that this is occurring. In fact some recent analyses of US data indicate the contrary that the period of life in which older persons experience both disease and limitations to their mobility has been expanding. As the authors of these analyses conclude, 'compression of morbidity [in the last years of life] may be as illusory as immortality. We do not appear to be moving to a world where we die without experiencing disease, functioning loss, and disability' (Crimmins and Beltrán-Sánchez, 2011, p. 83). Other analysts however are more hopeful that the onset of decline is shifting to later ages and that some degree of compression of disability is possible (Gerstorf et al., 2015).

The academic study of aging along with other social institutions has moved slowly to adapt to the new challenges of an aging population. For Paul Baltes, whose major contributions to the psychology of aging we have already referred to in Chapter 4, this represents a general cultural failure. As a consequence, human development is insufficiently supported in its last stages. Baltes's metaphor is that of an ill-designed building whose vulnerabilities become more manifest after a certain time. 'Neither biological nor cultural evolution has had sufficient opportunity to evolve a full and optimizing scaffolding (architecture) for the later phases of life' (Baltes, 1997, p. 367). The paradox is that 'historically speaking, old age is young'. A major investment of resources, social, material and technical, as well as improved understandings of older people's needs, is required to properly support human development and adaptability in its last stages. At the present time the pressures for improving support for an increasing elderly population are being felt acutely. The economic difficulties of the early twenty-first century have led to cutbacks in public funding which have diminished both the quantity and quality of care offered to frail older people in countries such as the UK. There are genuine fears for the future of late life.

Perhaps adequate support to old age will never be forthcoming, because the processes of human development and aging are fundamentally incomplete. As people through history have lamented, the advantages of age do not fully compensate for the losses of youthful vigour. The discrepancies between human wishes and human potentials widen, so that eventually death is a blessing, a release from decay. This is a theme found in many cultures. A nice literary example is found in Jonathan Swift's *Gulliver's Travels* of the Struldbruggs, a race condemned to live for ever with all the defects of old age, including susceptibility to disease and loss of memory. But the fact that we will eventually encounter failure does not mean that we should not seek to promote human development until the end of life.

Lack of attention to advanced old age has led to an imbalance in theories of aging. Our discussion in Chapter 4 indicated that a major focus of recent literature has been on the concept of 'successful aging' (Rowe and Kahn, 1998) as well as on the idea of the 'third age' with its connotations of continued learning and development (Laslett, 1989). Other positive concepts such as 'active aging' and 'productive aging' have also been adopted as slogans in recent years, finding particular favour with policy makers understandably concerned to postpone the age of retirement to minimise the future costs of paying adequate pensions to an aging population (Hamblin, 2013). But the nature of the criteria employed to describe positive states of being old, including avoidance of disease and disability, preservation of higher mental function, and engagement with life, means that sooner or later many people fail these tests. As Higgs and Gilleard (2015) have commented, the notion of the third age has required as its counterpart the additional negative concept of a 'fourth age' embodying 'the most feared and marginalised aspects of old age'. As Sheldon Tobin, a pioneer researcher in the psychology of late life, pointed out, we need to ask the question 'what comes after successful aging?' (Tobin, 1999, p. 31).

It is worth noting that already thirty years ago the cultural historian Tom Cole referred to the growing stigma surrounding the last stage of life, despite generally improving attitudes towards growing older:

> Today's 'enlightened' view of aging, which encourages older people to remain healthy, active, independent, etc. . . . harbours potentially pernicious effects . . . Unless the attack on ageism is amplified to address the existential challenges and tasks of physical decline and the end of life, we will perpetuate a profound failure of meaning.
>
> *(Cole, 1984, p. 335)*

Positive meanings also need to be found for this period of life, not only for the sake of the very old themselves but also because failure to do so will inevitably cast a shadow over the preceding years. As we noted in Chapter 2, Erik Erikson himself towards the end of his life questioned whether the eight psychosocial stages he had delineated were sufficient for the realities of present-day aging. His widow Joan Erikson welcomed the introduction of new concepts such as 'gerotranscendence' (Tornstam, 2005) which could fill a gap in our appreciation of old age that is increasingly keenly felt.

One reason for the neglect of late life is that it is difficult to study using standard quantitative and survey methods. Longitudinal studies of aging have typically given an over-optimistic view of the later stages of life because of selective drop out. Those willing to respond to long schedules in their late eighties and nineties tend to be the fit old, those with high self-esteem and low depression ratings, who perceive much continuity with their earlier lifestyles and activities. Despite these difficulties there have been some notable advances in recent years in collecting representative data on the very old.

In this chapter we will discuss what we know about psychological change in the later stages of aging for those living both in their own previous homes and in assisted-living settings. Development and adaptation are evident in persons' lives even in the trials of extreme old age. But imagination is required to appreciate what it is like to have lived long and to experience the loss of abilities, of close others, and of frames of reference for daily life. Sensitivity is also needed to the different ways older people do in fact respond to changes both in themselves and in their surroundings.

We begin by examining the defining characteristics, both physical and psychological, of advanced old age. We follow with a consideration of the beginnings of theory development in psychology on the subject of adaptation to becoming very old. We then focus on two subjects that have been the subject of particular concern, first how older people's lives are affected by their greater need for receiving care as they become physically weaker and frailer, and second the impact of increasing mental frailty on quality of life. Finally we draw a distinction between advanced age and the period of life immediately preceding death. In the following chapter we examine in more detail current research activity in the study of late life. We have selected three topics for more detailed presentation: maintenance of a positive self-attitude in late life; meeting psychological needs within care settings; and living well with dementia.

Characteristics of the very old

The current Western differentiation between two periods of aging is foreshadowed in the vivid but cynical description of stages of life provided by Shakespeare's character Jaques in *As You Like It*. Following the 'fifth age' of 'the justice . . . full of wise saws and moral instances', he distinguishes between the 'sixth age' of the 'lean and slippered pantaloon' and the seventh age of 'second childishness and mere oblivion, sans teeth, sans eyes, sans taste, sans everything'. But although such systematic change in people's character as they aged might have been common knowledge, it seems not to have been given much practical importance. Indeed, even as late as the 1970s policy makers at the Department of Health in London based planning for future health and service needs solely on projections on numbers above the UK male retirement age of 65 years. Only later was proper attention directed to the rising proportion of those beyond 80 and 90 years within an aging population.

Although levels of disability clearly increase with age, it is important to realise that disability is not the sole determining feature of advanced old age. Also younger people become disabled. Moreover disability is not necessarily a progressive characteristic of people's lives. Many of those who suffer severe injury when young and become disabled as a consequence can hope to live full lives within the limits set by their disability. Much more indicative as a concept applicable to late life is 'frailty', which has established itself as a major concept in the literature on aging over the last twenty years (Strawbridge et al., 1998; Rockwood et al., 2011). Disability is a much more limited concept, and does not necessarily indicate the person's need for care or supervision. He or she might have difficulty walking yet be functioning well on all other accounts. The greater usefulness of the concept of frailty to gerontology is that it encompasses 'increased vulnerability to stressors due to impairments in multiple systems, and increased risks of adverse outcomes such a disability, falls, hospitalization, and death' (Langlois et al., 2012, p. 400). The key point about frailty, unlike disability, is that it constitutes an unstable state with a risk of functional loss. As it threatens quality of life, regular monitoring is essential.

There is no consensus yet as to how frailty is most usefully operationalised (de Vries et al., 2011). However, most studies show a substantial rise in prevalence in the eighties. A recent analysis of four Swedish longitudinal data sets on the very old (Fauth et al., 2012) has indicated onset of difficulties in personal-care activities (bathing, dressing, toileting or feeding) to begin at an average age of 86 years. Such a dividing line for the fourth age also seems to be supported by older people themselves. A Finnish longitudinal qualitative study noted that by 85 years most participants felt that they had crossed the line into old age (Heikkinnen, 2000). Whereas at the age of 80 years most were not living an old-age existence, by 85 years the new life narratives were about change and decline, in particular bodily change. Walking had become a bit more awkward, feet heavy, and participants were troubled by a nagging sense of insecurity and of not having proper control over their lives. Days had to be structured more and more according to physical needs, which as a result had replaced their earlier interests. In short by the age of 85 years bodiliness had become a major concern.

Are the physical changes of later life accompanied by comparable psychological change? The evidence for cognitive decline is much stronger than for social and emotional aspects of psychological functioning. Although such studies are not the subject of this book, they provide important contextual material for studying adjustment to aging (Stuart-Hamilton, 2012; Rabbitt, 2015). Cognitive decline is a complex phenomenon, with changes tending to be more pronounced in some functions, especially memory and reaction time, rather than in others, such as verbal ability. However, the evidence from longitudinal studies is that by the age of 75 years most measures show some average decline, although there are some individuals who still show little or no decline in most functions even at the age of 80 years. An important question for researchers is whether cognitive decline can be influenced by mental and physical activity. Another interesting area of current debate is the relationship between 'normal' (i.e. age-related) cognitive decline and 'abnormal' changes associated with organic brain disease (dementia). Are they distinct processes, or are some types of dementia simply accelerated forms of normal aging? Current research evidence suggests that physiological changes in the brain may prefigure symptoms of dementia by many years.

A longitudinal study directed by Paul Baltes in Berlin was one of the first to provide detailed evidence on change for a large range of psychological indicators, emotional as well as cognitive, into advanced old age. By means of profile analysis Smith and Baltes (1999) compared very old Berliners (85 years and over) with younger older people (65 to 84 years) on intellectual functioning, self and personality characteristics, and social relationships. In general the very old reported significantly lower subjective well-being as well as poorer cognitive functioning. But the relationship was by no means clear cut. Some of the most disadvantaged groups indicated average levels of well-being. These included very old people who were markedly cognitively impaired and either had perceptions of high external control (i.e. believing that the actions of other people determine what happens to them) or high social aloneness (i.e. perceiving themselves as neither belonging to a social group nor having other people to rely on). Yet they appeared reasonably happy both with their life circumstances and with their own company. These findings already suggested caution in assuming that the social, physical and cognitive losses of late life inevitably result in lowered states of well-being. They also implied that processes of adaptation to loss were continuing to take place.

Initial reports from a second study conducted in comparable areas of Berlin twenty years after the first indicate that the more recent older generations studied (born 1913–44) perform to a higher level on an intelligence measure and also report higher morale, less negative affect and more positive affect than the earlier study samples (born 1890–1923) (Gerstorf et al., 2015). These differences remained even after controlling for number of years education and number of serious physical illnesses, although it is still possible that it is improved quality of education and medical care in the post First World War period that is responsible for this interesting historical change. Perhaps the most important implication of the study is its optimistic suggestion that cognitive deterioration as well as decline in perceived quality of life not only can be but actually have been postponed to more advanced ages.

Since the first Berlin study there have been a number of other investigations into psychological well-being in late life in various Western societies. As we saw in Chapter 3, studies in North America and Western Europe (but not Eastern Europe) suggest a peak in well-being in the earlier stages of aging with a decline thereafter. But this decline appears much less than one might expect given the circumstances of elderly people's lives. Both Danish and Swedish studies (Nybo et al., 2001; Haynie et al., 2001) support the view of the Berlin Aging Study that very old people adapt well to disability, and that they are in fact less depressed, anxious and dissatisfied with their health than one might expect when one takes the greater prevalence of disability and loss into account. In fact it seems that the discrepancy between self-rated health and objectively measured health status (the so-called 'aging/well-being' paradox already referred to in Chapter 4) reaches a maximum in the oldest old (Galenkamp et al., 2013). One of the most telling pieces of recent evidence on quality of later life is a recent report of an English Longitudinal Study of Ageing (Jivraj et al., 2014) which confirms that – *under similar circumstances* – older cohorts have equivalent or better subjective well-being using a broader measure comprising eudaimonic (self-assessed worth), evaluative (satisfaction with life situation) and affective dimensions of well-being than young cohorts. However, other studies indicate that, although other indicators of well-being and life satisfaction remain high, struggles with depression are a feature of late life (Wettstein et al., 2015) (see Box 6.1).

BOX 6.1 CONTRASTING ASPECTS OF PSYCHOLOGICAL WELL-BEING IN LATE LIFE

Advanced old age is marked by the contrasting characteristics of exceptional survivorship and fragility. A group of researchers from Heidelberg University in Germany attempted to capture the subtleties of psychological well-being in late life by assessing a broad range of characteristics intensively over time. They interviewed 124 participants (with a baseline age between 87 and 97 years) seven times over four years. They included measures within three broad categories of well-being: 'hedonic' well-being (life satisfaction, positive affect and negative affect); 'eudaimonic' (sense of autonomy, purpose in life, self-acceptance and environmental mastery); mental distress (depressive symptoms, anxious attitudes towards death and dying, and diseases phobia).

The majority of the sample expressed very high scores on most aspects of hedonic and eudaimonic well-being, such that the means for most measures were above the theoretical scale midpoint. They also expressed a high acceptance of death and dying, little fear of death, and a very low anxiety about the likelihood of disease. Somewhat less positive were the sample's expressions of positive affect, purpose in life, and fear of dying, on which the means were similar to norms established with younger populations. But standing alone as an indicator on which the sample scored more negatively were depressive symptoms. In fact the mean score was close to the cut-off point for indicating likelihood of clinical depression. This confirms clinical experience that depression is common in very old age, brought on especially by physical limitations and health constraints. Longitudinal analysis also showed slight but significant increases in depression over time, and declines in positive affect and sense of environmental mastery.

The authors suggest that the rise in depressive symptoms in late life may result from increasing interference with the ability to engage in everyday positive physical and social activities which constitute major sources of feelings of elation and pleasure. If these hindrances could be minimised, perhaps by more effective prosthetic and environmental aids, there would seem to be no reason why older people's mood should not be as positive as their general attitudes to and appreciation of life. Particularly striking was the sample participants' lack of anxiety about illness and death, threats that might be expected to be particularly salient to people of advanced age.

(Wettstein et al., 2015)

Two things appear clear from the present literature on life at an advanced age. In the first place as people grow older the variability of their experience continues to increase into late life (Poon et al., 2005). Not only are very old people affected by different life events, but they also differ greatly among themselves in resources which can help them cope with change. Attitudes to aging as we have seen in the previous chapter are important protective factors. Swedish studies (Femia et al., 2001) have demonstrated the role of subjective attitudes to health in influencing disability severity independently of impairment. Even in the nineties, measures of self-rated health, while still being sensitive to change in severity of chronic disease and disability (Galenkamp et al., 2013), have been shown to be predictive of survival in Danish and Finnish studies (Nybo et al., 2003; Vuorisalmi et al., 2012) and in Chinese studies (Peng et al., 2010).

Social integration also appears an important predictor of level of disability (Femia et al., 2001) as well as of avoidance of depression. Although there is a conceptual overlap between measures of loneliness and depression, which is difficult to avoid, there is substantial evidence that the experience of social belonging largely accounts for the prevalence of depressed mood (Golden et al., 2009). Engagement in social networks has also been shown to be associated with the prevention of and further progression of disability (de Leon and Rajan, 2014). Other factors suggested to provide protection include level of education (Yang and George, 2005) and strength of spiritual belief (Fry, 2000; Kirby et al., 2004).

The second and perhaps more important point is that processes of adaptation are still very much at work in late life. This is shown powerfully in the analysis of the Swedish longitudinal data sets already mentioned on those encountering difficulties with self-care activities in their eighties (Fauth et al., 2012). Depressive symptoms are raised slightly with the approach of disability, increase at onset and decline in the post-disability phase. In the following section of this chapter we will consider in more detail some of the recent theoretical thinking which attempts to explain how it is that the very old come to terms with the increasing limitations placed on their personal lives. This suggests that there is a change in the relative balance of different forms of adaptation which people employ as they become older, frailer and more limited in their activities.

It also needs to be recognised that circumstances can change dramatically in late life, with the experience of multiple losses in close combination, which are difficult if not impossible to adapt to. Such changes lead to sharp declines in well-being. For example, in one nine-year longitudinal study levels of well-being among 80-year-olds were reported to decline at three times the rate of a group of 60-year-olds studied over the same period of time (Zaninotto et al., 2009). Widowhood and the onset of significantly poorer health accounted for most of these changes. A further consideration is that accelerated decline in well-being in the very oldest cohorts may reflect entry into the terminal period of life. There appears to be a further important distinction to be drawn between advanced stages of aging and the very last phase of life leading directly to death which we will return to at the end of the chapter.

Adaptation to late life

The ability to maintain a positive view of self has long been thought central to adjustment to life changes, whether the transition to school, work, marriage or parenthood.

Because of the generally negative perspective on aging of much early gerontological research there was an expectation that self-esteem would lower as people became older as a consequence of physical, psychological and social changes in their lives. As we have seen in Chapter 4 this is not generally the case, at least not in contemporary Western societies where most of the research has been conducted.

The trajectory of self-esteem across the lifespan appears very different from that, for example, of a cognitive function such as memory. Global self-esteem, in Western populations at least (see Chapter 1), tends to show two periods of marked decline during the course of the lifespan, during adolescence and during late life (Robins et al., 2002) (see Figure 6.1). In between self-esteem consolidates, so that those in their sixties and older often show peak levels of self-esteem. However, there are two important qualifications to this generalisation. First, far from every very old person shows such decline. As we noted in the previous section inter-individual variation increases even further in late life. Second, as Robins et al. (2002) acknowledge, developmental theories of aging such as were discussed in Chapter 2 imply a 'diminished need for self-promotion and

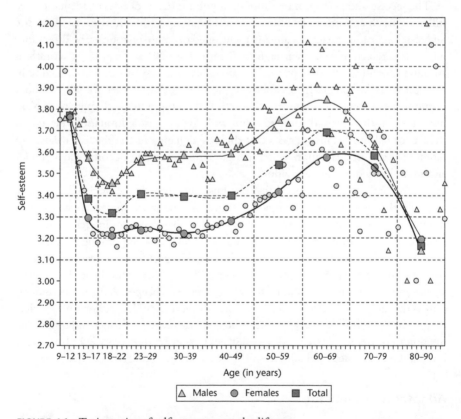

FIGURE 6.1   Trajectories of self-esteem over the lifespan.

Source: Robins et al. (2002, p. 428): image reprinted with permission, American Psychological Association.

self-aggrandizement which might artificially boost reports of self-esteem earlier in life' (Robins et al., 2002, p. 431). Thus decline in self-esteem at the end of life may not necessarily mean lowered emotional health, but simply a more modest, balanced and ultimately truthful view of the self.

Robert Atchley (1991) was one of the first to articulate a theoretical explanation for the age changes observed in self-esteem. The experiences of normal aging, he argued, tended to influence the self mostly for good until the onset of frailty. Older people had generally acquired in the course of a lifetime more robust self-concepts as well as more tested and stable sets of processes for managing the self. It was weakening health which usually did not occur until late in life that posed more serious challenges to self-esteem. As he pointed out, older people did not become by virtue of their age expert at dealing with problems of disability and frailty. The problems posed particularly by sudden change in physical capacities were immense: interrupted continuity in way of life; more need for more extreme coping methods; reduced capacity to use defences such as selective interaction; difficulty in identifying new possible selves; depersonalisation of the social environment; changes in reference groups; and lack of practise in skills in using feedback from others to fashion new self-conceptions.

However, in the last twenty-five years a more positive view of the aged self has developed. As Figure 6.1 also illustrates, late life may be characterised by an average lowering of self-esteem but it also shows continued increasing variation, some older persons remaining with very high self-esteem and others showing a drastic decline. If we understood better the differentiating factors, also at the level of personality characteristics, we might be able to help those who struggle more. Theoretical developments in this field have therefore paid more attention to the study of individual differences in adaptation to advanced age. In the remainder of this section we consider two possible relevant attitudinal factors, the ability to accommodate to change and self-transcendence.

Accommodation

Early work on the self in late life tended not to use representative samples, either the long-term survivors of longitudinal studies of aging who had the stamina, good will and morale to meet the investigators' demands, or else the minority of older people living in institutional settings who might have found it more difficult to refuse compliance. In recognition of these limitations recent research has taken more care to study and follow sensitively over time representative samples of the very old, including centenarians (Martin et al., 2000; Poon et al., 2005). One of the earliest such studies, conducted in San Francisco (Johnson and Barer, 1997), sought samples of the over 85s living both in the community and in assisted-living settings. Rather than burdening their participants with a long battery of questionnaires, they employed an anthropological-based approach to data collection, using informal observations and paying particular attention to the actual content of conversation.

Their study indicated that acceptance of change was normal among the very old people, as well as disengagement from potentially bothersome or stressful roles and relationships. Contrary to findings on the younger old, the oldest old appeared to gain benefit from giving up some control. Living in the present, one day at a time, was a favoured mode of life, and new emotional attachments were avoided. The sense of aloneness resulting from multiple bereavements was counterbalanced by the very old's special status as long-term survivors. Cultural differences were also evident in the way long life was evaluated. African Americans, for example, tended to see their long lives most positively, attributing to them religious and supernatural significance. But in both Black and White members of the sample change was accepted more readily than might be imagined, not only in the outside world but also in the self. People conveyed the sense of having lived beyond their old lives and selves.

The qualitative material collected in the course of this study provided a more in-depth understanding of the changed mentality of the very old. For example, it illustrated how they ignored bothersome events: 'I put a frame around my life and only see what I want to see'. The bonds of reciprocity were loosened: 'Life gets easier all the time because people don't expect much of me'. There was increased detachment both from the present ('More things are beyond my control, so I just roll with the waves') and the past ('I have no regrets about the past because I've just forgotten them') (Johnson and Barer, 1992, pp. 359–361).

Compatible with these observations is one of the first theories to emerge on late-life adjustment. As we described in Chapter 4, a major approach to understanding successful development during aging has been examining processes of maximising gains and minimising losses. Such processes, such as selection, optimisation and compensation, can help maintain role and function into late life, but a positive outcome becomes increasingly more difficult to achieve in late life. According to Jochen Brandtstädter it is then that accommodation comes into its own as a way of adjustment (Brandtstädter and Greve, 1994; Brandtstädter, 2006). To refer back to the illustration we gave in Chapter 4, how does an aging pianist, who may have adapted to aging changes experienced up to this point on the basis of selection, optimisation and compensation, know when he or she should cease playing in public? Concentrating on a limited repertoire and finding strategies to compensate for failing capacity may have been successful so far. But there may come a time when public performance will reveal an embarrassing lack of judgement in regard to one's continuing pianistic ability.

Brandtstädter's theory parallels Atchley's two-stage view of aging referred to earlier, but in addition provides a model of coping at more advanced ages. It views the self as a protective and dynamic system, comprising 'immunising' (e.g. denial, selective attention, and reinterpretation of evidence), 'assimilative' (e.g. self-correction and compensation, selection of enhancing environments, and self-verification) and 'accommodative' processes (e.g. rearrangement of priorities, devaluation of blocked goals, rescaling of self-evaluative criteria and construction of palliative meanings).

Immunising processes are well illustrated from earlier US studies on relocation of elderly people to institutions in the post-Second World War years. These demonstrated how powerful is the ability of some older people to manipulate perceived reality in self-threatening situations, for example to reinterpret circumstances in favourable ways and to intermingle evidence from the past and present (Lieberman and Tobin, 1983; Tobin, 1991). They present a picture of extreme and sometimes bizarre manoeuvres, of denial and illusion, which older people can use to preserve their previous sense of self. However, it would be misleading to overemphasise such processes. They are more likely to be characteristic of people in settings where they have had little or no time to adapt to change.

The most common response to challenge is assimilation, and this appears true of older as of younger people. Many older people fight long and hard to keep desired aspects of themselves alive through preventive, corrective and compensatory activities. Assimilation is a key element stressed in the Baltes and Baltes (1990) earlier model of successful aging, and research studies have supported an association between processes selection, optimisation and compensation with subjective well-being (Freund and Baltes, 1998; Gignac et al., 2000). But while assimilative processes rightly predominate in younger old age, Brandtstädter argues that they are subject to a law of diminishing returns. There comes a time when it is best to switch to the accommodative mode, to accept change, to disengage from blocked commitments and to adjust aspirations to what is feasible. This transition from assimilative to accommodative modes of coping may be marked by feelings of helplessness and depression, but accommodation itself should not be confounded with depression. According to Brandtstädter it is the failure to accommodate that more often marks depression. We will describe recent studies testing these hypotheses in the following chapter.

Brandtstädter's model is both positive and optimistic in that the accommodative processes of later old age are neither devalued nor seen as difficult to realise. This is consistent with previous theoretical positions on adaptation to aging, especially the changing value given to previously important life goals. Processes of (re) interpretation have been common to much theorising about the self in later life. While control over external events may be relinquished, control over the meaning given to experiences and events remains (Kaufman, 1987; Dittmann-Kohli, 1990). Research within both the stress and coping paradigm as well as control theory also support this model. The old-old are more likely to find ways of avoiding problems and accepting difficulties that they cannot avoid (Aldwin et al., 1996). A similar argument to Brandtstädter's is presented by Heckhausen (2005), that the increasing constraints with aging on the exercise of primary control are compensated by a heightened investment in secondary control strategies such as disengagement and positive reappraisal.

Nevertheless, Brandtstädter notes that societal pressure often works against such psychological adaptation in late life. Striving to maintain the goals of younger life is admired in our society and, as a result, may be conducive to enhancing self-esteem in the short run. In the long run of course death intervenes. Some people may never incur severe disability in their lives but die suddenly or after a short illness. Both assimilation and accommodation are valuable in the course of aging, and skill is required in judging when one or the other is appropriate. While the correct balance may seem difficult to define, most elderly people seem capable of finding an acceptable solution for themselves. The ability to discern which goals are of lasting importance and to accept which may have to be relinquished links with the concept of wisdom discussed in Chapter 2. We will return to this subject when presenting longitudinal case studies of adaptation to the problems of later life in the following chapter.

Self-transcendence

Not unrelated to this renewed interest in the value of disengagement to adaptation to the later stages of aging is the increasing emphasis on the importance of self-transcendence in late life. We have referred to the concept of 'gerotranscendence' (Tornstam, 2005) in Chapter 2 and to the growing research literature on spirituality and aging in Chapter 5. Research on religious involvement and spiritual belief in later life has indicated that stronger associations with well-being may be observed in those older people with greater levels of physical frailty (Fry, 2000; Kirby et al., 2004).

Also still relevant to understanding issues facing the self in late life is Alfred Adler's pioneering approach to those with feelings of inferiority and inadequacy which was mentioned already in Chapter 2 (Adler, 1927; see also Brink, 1979). Adler recognised that concerns about sense of worth, competence and efficacy are bound to resurface in later life as one loses physical power and social influence over others. His solution for both older and younger people was to look beyond self-assertion towards *Gemeinschaftsgefühl* (social interest), working with others for a common good that transcends self-interest. Of course self-transcendence is easier spoken about than achieved in an acquisitive and individualistic culture such as the US or UK.

One way of understanding the benefits of self-transcendence to aging is through the distinction which can be made between judgements of competence and judgements of value. It is possible for someone to accept declining competence while maintaining that life has not lost any of its meaning or value. A key concept in this context is 'commitment'. Even if a person feels their own contribution is minimal or non-existent, to feel committed to a cause, whether religious, ideological or political, or simply to one's family or community, gives reason for living, if only to continue to witness to that cause.

The gerontologist Edmund Sherman first coined the term 'psychophilosophy' to refer to a way of thinking about life and the self that actually influences one's daily experience (Sherman, 1981). He realised that such an attitude of mind is a major asset in coping with the inevitable losses and changes associated with aging. In his own old age he has written about the importance of 'contemplative aging' (Sherman, 2010) which he also sees as a way of transcending the many difficulties encountered in later life by making a transition to a state of being and belonging rather than having and doing. Although he notes that the contemplative style of later life he recommends may be more welcome to an introverted-stable personality type, he considers that more extraverted individuals would also benefit from the more mindful and meditative practices he describes. In the next chapter we will explore recent research on attitudes to the self in late life.

Coming to terms with living in care settings

This resiliency of late life was first demonstrated in the unlikely setting of institutions for elderly people. The general tenor of British as well as American social science research on old-age homes has been to focus on the negative features of institutional life (Goffman, 1961). Unlike neighbouring continental European countries Britain broke with the older more charitable tradition of religious-based care for the old and infirm as a result of the destruction of the monasteries at the time of the sixteenth-century Reformation. It was not until the latter part of the twentieth century, after the pioneering investigations of sociologists such as Peter Townsend (1962), that determined efforts were made to change the demeaning and stigmatising character of the 'Poor Law' and 'Work House' system by which local authorities provided care for older people who lacked other means of support.

It is important to bear in mind this historical and cultural context when interpreting the first studies into the psychology of late life carried out in US homes for elderly people. These studies focused in particular on maintenance of the self and the influence of subjective control. The institutionalised aged provided an easily available set of participants with whom psychological studies could be conducted, but the studies also reflected rising social concern in the United States about quality of life in these institutions (Vladeck, 1980). Environmental regimes were clinical, physical care poor and mortality rates high. In a culture that particularly prided itself on individual independence institutionalisation was a dreaded outcome at the end of life. Although quality of life in what are now called care and nursing homes, as well as assisted-living settings, has generally improved over the last thirty to forty years, the observations made at this earlier time still have useful lessons for understanding older people's behaviour in circumstances which threaten their sense of self.

Defending the self

In a set of detailed studies, Lieberman and Tobin (1983) examined how elderly people in the United States adapted to the stress of relocation to nursing homes. The studies demonstrated the remarkable stability of self-image that many older people maintained across these transitions, but this was often achieved by changing the basis on which the self was constructed. Rather than relying on incidents from their current interpersonal interactions to confirm their image of self, people in these situations of loss and change also gave many examples from their past lives as well as reiterating general statements of conviction about themselves and their lives. They even seemed prepared to forego present reality altogether and used evidence based on wishes and distortions to maintain self-consistency. Such behaviour might appear distorted, as when an elderly resident referred to a picture taken fifty years previously as if it were a picture of herself today. But perhaps it was important for this person to affirm the persistence of her identity. She was not the frail, impaired person you thought you saw but the continuation of a long series of life experiences and events, of which the last might have been of relatively little importance to her.

Other features noted about the very old by these researchers included a mythicising of the past, a dramatisation in which the important people and events became 'bigger and better'. The greater vividness, the recall of feelings of love and devotion from parents and others, created a sense of specialness. Kaufman (1987) also illustrated from her studies of frail older people how they were able to transform present experience in ways that conformed to the important themes of their lives. It was the theme for example of being the loved mother of a united family which provided the persistent sense of meaning even when the reality failed to match.

In other ways though, very old people appeared to show a truer awareness, particularly of their own feelings. Destructive and anti-social feelings were admitted without the embarrassment and defensive explanations that might have been elicited earlier in life. According to Tobin (1991) this was because even previously unwelcomed motives could be useful for self-definition in the face of the losses of old age. They affirmed who one was and had been. Coherence and wholeness could be and was achieved, Tobin argued, even by those 'whose reminiscence is, unfortunately, filled with vivid and, most likely, accurate memories of losses and deprivation' (p. 12). These studies of relocation to institutions showed that it was those who were prepared to be more assertive and combative in defining their own interests who survived longer. Passivity – including accepting how others defined one – led to earlier decline and death.

Lieberman and Tobin (1983) pointed to the analogies between maintenance of sense of self and of physical survival. It could be as desperate a matter. Many older people found it difficult to acknowledge change. For example, changing appearance could be hard for a woman to bear who had always prided herself on her appearance. The same applied to a man who had emphasised his physical strength which he now saw declining. Evidence of change, whether from mirrors, photographs, individual comparisons, were therefore resisted. Sometimes extreme strategies were used to maintain the old sense of self, which could appear strange and illogical to observers. Often these involved myths which exaggerated and dramatised certain personal qualities – myths of being in control of circumstances, myths of self-constancy which denied change, and the blurring of the boundaries between past and present.

Tobin (1999) elaborated further on the behaviours people used to maintain the self in advanced old age, including making the past vivid and distortion of both past and present. The material he cited provided an important learning exercise for staff working in care settings. Sometimes the distortion of past or present reality would become too extreme and diminish the possibility of successful adaptation, but generally a great deal of bending of reality was acceptable, and indeed in certain circumstances might seem almost essential to survival. For example, an elderly man who had always insisted that he would not accept relocation to an institution, but die first, in fact flourished in the home in which he was eventually placed. He had persuaded himself that he had been invited to live there in order to keep an eye on the other residents, to make sure that they behaved well and that their needs were properly catered for. Thus he had a role in the home, a reason for being there.

Lieberman and Tobin's research findings, although valuable for what they reveal about psychological survival in difficult circumstances, are a reflection of the demeaning quality of institutional care in the United States (and also in Britain) in the 1960s and later. A completely different perspective is provided by Scandinavian studies in more recent times which have attempted to apply Tornstam's theory of gerotranscendence (see Chapter 2) in educational initiatives with staff within elderly care settings (Wadensten, 2005, 2010). The results showed that a significant minority of them reported that the theory had positively affected their outlook on old age and on their own aging and that the effect was stronger among the better educated professional caregivers (e.g. the registered nurses). Almost every second interviewee reported that the theory gave them new understanding of the care receivers. The care receivers' need for solitude was recognised, as well as a clearer view of the difference between the value-systems of the caregivers and the caretakers, such as concerning the 'need' for activation which often the caregivers overemphasised. These insights helped in giving higher priority to the desires of the care recipients. The theory also functioned as a stress-releaser for guilt feelings among the staff for not being engaged enough in activating their clients (Tornstam, 1996b).

Maintaining sense of control

In a separate set of studies on US institutional care Langer and Rodin (Langer, 1983, 1989; Rodin et al., 1985) highlighted the importance of the experience of being in control of daily life. Control has become an important subject in general health psychology with clear evidence for the benefits on recovery and well-being for the patient having some control over the administration of treatment. However, it is interesting that the value of a subjective sense of control was first demonstrated in the field of elderly care. Those residents of nursing homes who felt – truly or falsely did not seem to matter so much – that they had a say over their daily activities fared better emotionally and cognitively than those who felt life was determined for them. The studies involved manipulating variables such as staff instructions and behaviour. Even taking minor responsibilities (e.g. for the care of a plant) was associated with more favourable outcomes.

Similar observations were made by other investigators in Europe (Baltes and Baltes, 1986). But in addition they noted that a major problem in residential care was the tendency of staff to 'prefer' elderly people who gave up self-control and thus became more easy to 'manage' (Baltes et al., 1991). This is because encouraging self-control and individual participation could often be more costly in staff time. Designing institutions or altering them in ways that facilitated independence, despite frailty, should have enhanced well-being. But there was a further countervailing factor at work. A pattern of 'dependency script' operated in institutions whereby dependent behaviour was the most likely to result in staff providing social contact and attention, which in learning theory terms functioned as 'rewards'.

In an intervention to alter this pattern of staff behaviour, Baltes et al. (1994) developed a training programme which involved confronting staff with their own videotaped interactions. They were told the aim was to improve their interactions and communications with all residents. To assess the results on residents, the researchers needed to develop careful assessment of the elderly people's behaviours. They differentiated between independent and dependent self-care behaviours, and among constructively engaged, destructively engaged and non-engaged behaviours. The intervention produced an increase in independence-supportive behaviours and a decrease in dependence supportive-behaviours in the experimental group of staff, who received the intervention, as opposed to a comparison group, who did not. Impressively the same study also demonstrated an increase in independent behaviours among residents after the intervention period.

This important line of research strongly suggested that it is possible to design institutional environments which are both stimulating and protective. To quote Margret Baltes:

> if staff behavior is tailored to the individual competence level of elderly residents – that is, providing security and support only when and where truly needed and otherwise supporting autonomy and stimulation – the elderly residents can compensate for deficits with the help of staff but maintain and even optimise remaining competencies.
>
> (Baltes et al., 1994, p. 186)

These and the other studies indicated that it was possible to move towards a more person-sensitive system of care for people in the fourth age, where individual differences in needs for autonomy and support could be better catered for.

Subsequent research has provided a more nuanced view of the contribution of control to well-being. There appears to be an optimum level of subjective control for a particular individual in a particular situation. In most environments we operate below optimum. But exceeding that level can also be counterproductive, provoking anxiety and consequent under-performance. This type of 'U'-shaped performance function can be seen in other areas of research on aging. For example, studies of social support show limits to the beneficial effects of assistance provided to older people. Social support beyond a certain level may actually exacerbate the noxious impact of stress (Krause, 1995a). Older adults may be able to increase their coping skills if they are encouraged to confront stressful situations without the undue involvement of others.

It is also apparent that in high-constraint environments which cannot be changed, elderly people with an external locus of control may actually appear better adjusted (O'Connor and Vallerand, 1994; see Chapter 7). Also Smith and Baltes (1997) have shown that high belief in being controlled by others can coexist with average levels of well-being in cognitively impaired elderly people. These findings illustrate the value of 'person–environment congruence' theory developed by Powell Lawton (Lawton, 1980; Parmelee and Lawton, 1990), where well-being is predicted to be a function of matching between environmental characteristics and a person's needs. In the following chapter we will illustrate recent studies on the significance of self-determination for elderly people residing in institutions that use this framework of analysis. Lack of autonomy and control remain very important issues in the transition to residential care (Reed et al., 2003). Modern societies need to find more effective ways of involving older people in decision making about their future.

Certainly as important as autonomy and control is a sense of belonging within care environments. Thus in principle another approach to good quality of life in residential settings would be to put less stress on individuality while emphasising the importance of community, shared tasks and the sense of 'team spirit' stressed by Alfred Adler (see previous section). It is significant that some of the most successful examples of community day centres recorded in the literature are of this kind. Hazan's classic ethnographic study of a Jewish day centre in North London described how it had evolved to meet the needs of its members by eschewing conversation about individual life outside the centre, while emphasising group activities within the care setting (Hazan, 1980). Although it is hard to imagine such an establishment functioning in this way nowadays, this centre clearly satisfied the psychological and social needs of most of its attenders, many of whom had been disappointed in their family, and welcomed the new 'family' they had entered. Jerrome's studies on day centres in Brighton, England, have also emphasised the benefits of identification with others achieved through repetitive ceremonies and assertion of strong in-group values (Jerrome, 1992). We will consider recent research on relationships in care settings, as well as research promoting a sense of control and independence, in the following chapter.

Dementia: the negation of development?

The onset of physical disability, suddenly as with a stroke, or more gradually with osteoarthritis, is one form of entrance to late life. A quite different pathway is through the various forms of dementia, diseases of the brain, of which Alzheimer's disease is the most common. Dementia has become in the last fifty years the major health concern of later life in modern Western society. It is also the most age related of all the disabling conditions, the rate of dementia increasing with age in a strikingly consistent manner reaching a prevalence of 20 per cent in the over eighties and 40 per cent in the over nineties. With many more people surviving into their eighties and nineties, the overall prevalence is increasing. Dementia is the major reason for entering nursing and care homes. But despite these facts dementia has until recently been a neglected condition, not only in terms of quality of provision but also of research into its nature, cause and treatment. Research effort is expanding but remains far below that of heart disease and cancer.

Dementia involves a qualitative change in mental performance resulting in impairment in ability to function independently (Gavett and Stern, 2012). Alzheimer's disease in particular has a long trajectory. Recent longitudinal analysis of case histories suggests that cognitive decline may begin many years before dementia is diagnosed and accelerates during the course of the disease with notable effects on well-being (Wilson et al., 2012, 2013). With greater publicity and openness about dementia, beginning notably with Ronald Reagan's admission that he was suffering from Alzheimer's disease after he ceased to be US president, there is now much greater curiosity about the condition. This has extended to the sufferer's own experience of becoming and being demented. Also family caregivers' accounts have become important material for books such as in John Bayley's writing about his wife, the philosopher Iris Murdoch (Bayley, 1998).

There is much in this field to challenge psychologists. Considerable imagination is required to appreciate the impact of crumbling powers of memory and identification upon the individual's feelings of security. A lifespan developmental approach too can be valuable in understanding an individual's behaviour and the cues to which he or she responds as a consequence of habits established earlier in life. There is also the possibility that a study of psychological factors, motivational and affective as well as cognitive, will eventually contribute in significant ways to a total picture of the aetiology and process of dementing illnesses. If this seems implausible, one should ask oneself why psychology should be relevant to understanding the origins of heart disease and cancer, and not a condition which affects the brain.

It might be thought that dementia is incompatible with considerations of development and adaptation, that in fact it is their very antithesis. But this view deserves challenging. Of course one would wish for there to be some cure for the neurological disease processes which seemingly underlie the condition. But this does not mean that other types of positive change, in attitudes and personality for example, may not occur in the presence of these losses and perhaps even because of them. For example, the experience of dementia may produce changes in relating to others, which may actually be perceived positively. As some spouses note, dementia may lead to an acknowledgement of dependency in a previously distant individual, which strengthens rather than weakens the marital bond. In what follows we will focus on the subjective experience of becoming demented, particularly the emotional responses the condition evokes.

Maintaining the self

It is insufficient to characterise dementia mainly in terms of cognitive failure. Its impact is more global, more threatening than this, and for many years has been described in terms of loss of 'personhood' or 'self' (Gilleard, 1984). Whereas the person who suffers from amnesia, for example as a result of brain trauma, still usually retains a sense of self and a grasp on reality, the onslaught the dementing person faces eventually takes away this basis. Perhaps the most disturbing aspect of the memory disabilities associated with dementia is the loss of the past. It would not strike at the core of the self if the memory losses concerned only new information. An older person could live reasonably well with the experience of the long years already built up. But dementia attacks the sense of self already achieved, as well as the possibility of building a new self.

Psychologists have been in the forefront of developing more constructive ways of keeping a dementing person's sense of self alive. Already by the later 1980s the British psychologist Tom Kitwood had begun to argue for a radical rethinking of our understanding of dementia, to give more attention to internal psychological factors, such as personal reactions to the stress of finding oneself mentally frail, as well as external social circumstances, including the quality of care (Kitwood, 1988). He realised that the degree of psychological disturbance caused by dementia is not related principally to the condition itself but to the way it is understood and responded to. It is still common to hear comments made about elderly people with dementia which imply a lack of sensitivity to their needs as human beings to be understood, respected and loved. People scoring low on cognitive tests tend to be excluded from consumer studies, yet with effort and imagination their reactions to the way they are treated can be gauged (Sutton, 2004). Issues in the developmental psychology of aging referred to in previous chapters, such as coming to terms with the past, with both personal losses and social change, apply just as much to persons with dementia.

For any person involved in dementia care it is important to try to appreciate the implications of being demented. This is not easy. It is hard to realise what it is like to suffer from relatively simple handicaps such as blindness and deafness, let alone a set of disabilities as complex as those resulting from dementia. What is it like to hear people talking but to be unable to make sense of what they are saying? Or to understand that someone is angry but not to be able to understand why? The lack of understanding shown by demented people and their difficulties in communicating their own needs require that those who try to help them should use their own powers of imagination and empathy to help bridge the gap in understanding. It is a proper concern of psychology not only to describe a person's behaviour patterns, but also to conceptualise the view (or lack of view) of the world which may underlie them.

Kitwood, along with others, has recognised that the key to improving dementia care is the concept of the 'person':

> the core of our position is that personhood should be viewed as essentially social: it refers to the human being in relation to others. But also, it carries essentially ethical connotations: to be a person is to have a certain status, to be worthy of respect.
>
> *(Kitwood and Bredin, 1992, p. 275)*

Relationship is central to this conception of personhood. This also has theological roots, which define a person in terms of relationship to other persons and ultimately to God (Coleman and Mills, 2001). Kitwood in fact referred to Martin Buber's 'I and Thou' (1923/1937), which contrasts two ways of being in the world, two ways of forming a relationship, the first being purely instrumental, the second involving commitment. To be a person is to be related to in the second sense, to be addressed as 'Thou'. At the other extreme is the 'I–It' mode of relating. Kitwood argued that modernity, as a product of Western reason and logic, had brought with it a distancing and objectification in human relationships (Kitwood, 1997).

The American psychologist Steven Sabat (Sabat and Harre, 1992; Sabat, 2001) has distinguished between different conceptions of selfhood which are affected by dementia. Whereas loss of 'social self' is greatly influenced by others' behaviour towards the person with dementia, 'personal self' is usually preserved until the late stages of dementia and is demonstrated by the use of first-person indexicals. When we refer to loss of self in dementia we refer principally to the social self and articulation of this self depends crucially on the two-way process of communication. The problem is also other people's failure to understand the increasingly fragmented and fragile cues the dementia sufferer expresses. As a result the social self can no longer be sustained.

Thus the fundamental cause of loss of social self is to be found in the character of the social interactions and the interpretations that follow in the wake of the difficulties in communication. 'The ultimate result of such a situation is the fencing off of the sufferer so that no adequate self can be constructed' (Sabat, 2001, p. 459). Others have also taken the research line of analysing speech and communication as a way of revealing the demented person's vulnerability to personal demotion. Small et al. (1998), for example, videotaped nursing staff and resident interactions, and analysed use of personal pronouns, proper nouns, interpersonal conflicts and discursive positioning. They observed decline in 'self' indexicals and discuss how changes to institutional policy could prevent this process occurring.

Dementia therefore poses a particularly difficult challenge to care services. There is the risk of loss of inter-subjective insight. Caregivers may no longer make the effort to understand what the other person is thinking or feeling, showing a disregard for the other that would be unthinkable in other professional or interpersonal circumstances. Mental infirmity – in a similar but far greater way than hearing impairment – disables the caregiver. It is a hindrance to getting on with the tasks one is required to do. This situation is made worse by the chronic 'busy-ness' of dementia care settings. The combination of pressure and insensitivity may lead to a loss of belief in the personhood of the person with dementia, together with all the rights and dignity which that term implies.

Kitwood referred to a 'malignant social psychology' that may surround the person with dementia (Kitwood, 1997). A habitual way of responding to a person's confusion, distress and discomfort may develop that demeans or confuses further. Examples of such behaviours are using tricks or lies to get persons to do what the

TABLE 6.1 Psychological needs of persons with dementia

ATTACHMENT
LOVE
COMFORT
IDENTITY
INCLUSION
OCCUPATION

Source: Kitwood (1997).

caregiver wants, doing things for them which they are actually able to do for themselves, so as to complete tasks more quickly, and accusing a person or throwing back in their face something they did or didn't do in order to try to make them 'see sense'. Caring for someone with dementia can be highly stressful, but in such circumstances it is important always to bear in mind the cared-for person's needs (see Table 6.1). Responding at the emotional level is the key to high-quality care of someone who is mentally frail. Thus this may mean careful explanation and reassurance to someone who is saddened by a sense of loss and the disturbance of their normal environment, and calmness and support with someone frustrated by their inability to change their circumstances.

These are not easy tasks and require training and support themselves. Even more demanding is the responsibility for maintaining 'personhood'. Ideally this requires a continued presence, seeking to understand the needs of the other and drawing out meaning from every communication. Kitwood has made an analogy with Winnicott's description of the 'good mother', one who makes sense of a child's gestures, who draws meaning from them wherever possible, and who does not dismiss or ignore them (Winnicott, 1965). In looking for and making meaning the mother promotes the child's development. The aging process leads ultimately towards dissolution, but that does not mean effort should not be made to preserve meaning where it can still be found. Care, even for the dying, is about life not death.

Attachment and dementia care

One developmental theory that has been applied successfully to dementia care is the theory of attachment (Bowlby, 1969, 1973, 1980) (see also Chapter 4). Research has confirmed Bowlby's view that the patterns of secure and insecure attachment he described in young children are acquired in early life rather than determined by one's genetic or biological make-up (O'Connor and Croft, 2001). These attachment patterns remain important at all stages of life, and have been studied for their influence on relationships and loss of relationships across the lifespan. The study of aging and attachment is a more recent development. We know that children provide the oldest old with one of the most significant buffers against loneliness (Long and Martin, 2000). But at present we can only speculate whether the striking variation that we see among older people in their response to loss – the ease or unease at which they are able to let people and things come and go from their lives – reflects early attachment styles.

Bére Miesen, a clinical psychogerontologist in the Netherlands, was the first to recognise the relevance of attachment theory to dementia care. He became increasingly aware that much of a dementing person's behaviour reflected feelings of insecurity as a consequence of diminishing cognitive capacities. Miesen took the initiative to contact Bowlby about the relationship of attachment to aging, and their resulting interview was subsequently published (Bowlby, 1986). For Miesen attachment theory became the key that unlocked much of the behaviour of demented people that caregivers typically find puzzling and disturbing (Miesen, 1992, 1998). Emphasising that we need to see situations through the eyes of the person who experiences them, Miesen has suggested that the experience of becoming demented is rather like entering Ainsworth's strange situation. Behaviours such as crying, clinging and calling out represent attachment behaviours in elderly people with dementia. The constant request and searching for parents, which becomes more common as the illness progresses, can be seen partly as a reflection of the greater clarity of the more distant past, but more helpfully as a search for security and comfort in an increasingly uncertain world, a response to feeling 'unsafe'. Seen this way it is much easier for caregivers to appreciate how elderly people eventually fall back on their deepest memories of security in attachment to their families, as the more recent past gradually fades from view.

Miesen developed an intriguing method for testing his theory. Bowlby had first identified the significance of childhood attachment behaviour in explaining the persisting distress experienced by infants when they were separated from their primary caregivers for long periods of time. As a consequence of this observation Mary Ainsworth developed the so-called 'strange situation' to study styles of attachment in young children (Ainsworth et al., 1971), and Miesen developed an analogous way of observing older persons. He had noticed that 'parent fixation', as he described it, was associated with certain types of behaviour on the nursing home ward during family visits. So he adapted Ainsworth's strange situation into what he described as a 'Standard Visiting Procedure' to analyse elderly people's behaviour in relation to their family before and after the latter left.

He observed that participants expressed themselves towards family members through different forms of attachment behaviour such as touching, crying and calling. Those with lower levels of cognitive functioning behaved differently, for example being more inclined to touch other people they knew. When family members left, those with higher cognitive functioning called after them. Lower cognitive functioning participants had apparently more difficulty keeping family members in mind and called more after their deceased parents. There was also a longitudinal element to Miesen's research. As dementia became more pronounced and participants could no longer recognise their caregivers, so they called more on their parents than they had done before. This strongly suggests that 'parent fixation' substitutes for attachment to caregivers after the latter are no longer recognisable.

Through his training programmes in the Netherlands Miesen has had a significant impact on practice. Care staff are encouraged to see what it means to feel unsafe and insecure, and so to appreciate what demented persons are looking for. Miesen shows how important it is for caregivers to understand their own previous experience of attachment. The goals of training are thus both psychoeducational and psychotherapeutic. Participants become familiar with both the demented person's emotional needs and their own characteristic responses, which are modified in the course of the training. This reflects an important new trend in research on attachment behaviour, which is to attempt to understand better the caring motivation which underlies the response to attachment behaviours in the infant (Bell and Richard, 2000). Similar training courses have been developed for care staff in the UK focusing on the carers' own emotions as well as developing skills in dealing with older people's feelings (Coleman and Jerrome, 1999).

The biological basis for caregiving of adults appears less strong than for child care. That makes analysis of motivation to care more rather than less important. We know that mental frailty makes older people more unpopular to professional caregivers and it is important to understand precisely why this is so (Cooper and Coleman, 2001). Even where caregivers are more enthusiastic, questions can arise about quality of care. One of the concerns commonly expressed about even good dementia care settings is that professional caregivers may adopt an approach to care which turns elderly persons into dependent babies or young children. This approach may make caring easier for the caregiver because they are drawing on a fundamental 'instinct'. However, although preferable to the impersonal approach to care, there is danger in this attitude to care. Some elderly persons may like to be cossetted – perhaps a reflection on their attachment needs – but many do not (see research on 'baby talk' in the following chapter). Despite the undoubted parallels between elderly and child care, their phenomenological worlds are completely different.

Attachment theory has provided a much-needed boost to a developmental perspective on aging, particularly in the last stage of life which so far has been considered rather unimaginatively. It is a particularly good example of the enriching value of theory, providing new perspectives on phenomena thought to be well understood but in fact often simply observed without much understanding. We will consider current research examining some further new constructive psychological perspectives on dementia in the following chapter.

The terminal phase of life

There has been a renewed interest in recent years in studying the terminal phase of life. Increasingly it is the very old who die and it is necessary for all those involved in caring for and accompanying frail persons in the last years and months of their lives to have an understanding of the psychological factors that promote better quality of life at its end.

The concept of 'terminal decline' or 'terminal drop' has a long history in gerontology but was originally formulated exclusively in relation to cognitive change.

It proposed that that 'time to death' might be a better indicator of lowered mental acuity than actual chronological age (Kleemeier, 1962; Siegler, 1975). The process of cognitive decline before death does not occur uniformly across individuals but there is consistent evidence for a faster rate of change occurring between approximately seven and eight years before death (Bäckman and MacDonald, 2006; Piccinin et al., 2011). Most experience a period of slight decline followed by a much sharper decline (Muniz-Terrera et al., 2013). Various factors appear to influence the pace of change. To the investigators' surprise, more-educated individuals experienced a more rapid decline before and slower decline after the change point. An older age at death is associated with a slower rate of change before the onset of terminal decline and a faster rate afterwards.

However, it is now realised that terminal decline is much more than cognitive deterioration and involves changes in affect and life satisfaction as well as cognition. In Chapter 3 we stressed how the body of evidence on emotional functioning across the lifespan is broadly favourable to older people. But as Gerstorf et al. (2010) highlighted in the title they gave to an influential article on late-life decline in well-being, 'something is seriously wrong at the end of life'. In this publication they brought together evidence from longitudinal studies of aging conducted in the United States, the UK and Germany to show that although well-being was relatively stable over time it declined rapidly with impending death. The implication is that the resources that older people usually rely on to support them through the losses of later life often eventually fail them towards the end. In particular the character of physical decline in the period preceding death appears to become too difficult to cope with. The modes of self-regulation referred to earlier in the chapter cease to operate as before.

In his original statement of this thesis of terminal decline in well-being Gerstorf located the prototypical transition to this terminal phase at approximately four years prior to death on the basis of data from the German Socio-Economic Panel Study 1984–2005 (Gerstorf et al., 2008). Including the US Health and Retirement Study 1994–2004 and the British Household Panel Study 1991–2005 led to a more precise indication that decline begins between three and five years from death. It is important to note that these studies also confirmed what had been suggested from earlier research that there is considerable stability in older people's well-being over a long period of time even at advanced ages. But this stability does eventually break down in often striking ways with a precipitous decline in well-being. Perhaps the closest parallel is with the impact of bereavement (see Chapter 5) which triggers sharply lowered well-being. As Gerstorf et al. comment in their conclusions these findings imply that 'mortality-related mechanisms or other progressive processes leading towards death (e.g. deteriorating health) overwhelm the regulatory or motivational mechanisms that usually keep well-being stable and become the prime drivers of late-life decline in well-being' (Gerstorf et al., 2010, p. 483). The phenomenon of terminal decline seems to be unrelated to age, with those dying earlier in middle age showing the same negative effects of impending death.

A number of other recent studies in different parts of the world have also indicated that distance to death is more predictive of declines in life satisfaction and affect than chronological age (Carmel et al., 2013; Vogel et al., 2013; Infurna et al., 2014). The report of the Amsterdam Longitudinal Study is particularly significant because of its length (fifteen years) and resulting high mortality rate (Vogel et al., 2013). The authors demonstrate that time to death accounts better than chronological age for negative trajectories of both positive and negative affect. Both accelerate as death approaches, suggesting that the various different processes of biological decline may also stimulate change in the emotional systems of the brain. The study's findings suggest an earlier onset of decline in positive affect, at about 5.6 years prior to death, compared with 3.7 years for negative affect, figures that are comparable with Gerstorf and colleagues' results. The Dutch study observed earlier interference with social and leisure interests whereas self-care-related problems emerged later. Gender differences were also noted as women tended to carry over higher levels of negative affect from the pre-terminal phase and thus showed less steep decline.

Now that the phenomenon of terminal decline in well-being has been charted it is important, as Gerstorf notes, to devote research resources to identifying factors that might limit it. There is evidence for considerable variation in the amount of decline shown, and clearly individual factors play a large role. Some of these have already been suggested by research studies. Findings from the German Socio-Economic Panel Study (SOEP) (Infurna et al., 2014) indicated that individuals who were able to maintain independence while living at home were best able to preserve their life satisfaction at the end of life. The importance of continued engagement with social networks for quality of late life has also been demonstrated from the German SOEP study (Gerstorf et al., 2016), as well as from the English Longitudinal Study of Ageing (Zaninotto et al., 2009). In addition, an Israeli study (Carmel et al., 2013) has shown that a commitment to continued living seems to act as a buffer against the detrimental effects of being close to death and thus helps to preserve sense of satisfaction with life until its very end. As the authors note there is an 'instinctual reaction to grasp life tightly in a way that even overrides considerations regarding the quality and worthiness of living' (p. 1122). Shmotkin (2005, 2011) has also suggested that it may be more adaptive for subjective well-being to be at least partially disconnected from perceived threats of dysfunction at the end of life.

There is clearly much to learn also from literature in the field of palliative medicine on adjustment to advancing and end-stage illness. For example, Knight and Emanuel (2007) describe a model of meaning-making with end-of-life losses which itself draws on concepts from lifespan psychology concepts, delineating processes of comprehension (realising and affectively processing loss) followed by creative adaptation (transcending of previous views of oneself) and reintegration (understanding oneself in a new way). In the following chapter we will examine in more detail recent research studies which explore factors that promote positive self-evaluation and well-being at the end of life.

7

CURRENT RESEARCH ON DEVELOPMENT AND ADAPTATION IN LATE LIFE

As in Chapters 3 and 5 we have selected three topics from which to illustrate current research on the psychology of development and adaptation in advanced old age. Self-regulation has been a major theme in the psychogerontological literature since the 1960s, but relatively little research has been carried out with the very old, apart from those living in institutional care, until recently. Our first section therefore describes current investigation into how self-management may change in representative samples of people over the age of 80 years. Opportunities for these analyses have arisen as a result of the continuation of longitudinal studies into late life, but there is also more theoretical and practical interest in drawing comparisons across different stages of aging.

As we saw in the last chapter the psychology of institutional care was one of the first research fields to be developed in the study of aging. Our examination of recent research in this area examines some of the new literature on psychological factors affecting quality of life in assisted-living and care settings. It considers research that has followed the pioneering studies of Langer and Rodin on the importance to healthy functioning and well-being of having a sense of autonomy and control (Langer, 1983; Rodin, 1986) described in the last chapter. But it also focuses on recent studies on the equally important human need for relatedness and belonging emphasised in Deci and Ryan's influential model of human motivation (Deci and Ryan, 2000).

Our third topic also deals with issues relating to the provision of support services in old age, but specifically directed to the needs of those with dementia. It examines some of the latest research which builds on the newer perspectives on dementia already referred to in the previous chapter. In particular it considers the importance of coming to terms with a diagnosis of dementia and how the process of adaptation can be fostered by group support and counselling. It also considers research findings on the importance of gearing care practice more precisely to assessment of individual needs and interests. With an ever-increasing proportion of the population developing some degree of mental infirmity before death, we need to ensure that each person can continue to live with dignity.

All three topics have been chosen because they have clear developmental implications: regulating one's sense of self through the vicissitudes of late life, achieving an appropriate balance in catering for different psychological needs within care settings, and maintaining individual identity in the presence of mental frailty. The quality of late life, as at all stages of life, depends on sensitive support from those around the person.

Continuity of the self in late life

The study of the self has a long history in gerontology. As stressed in the last chapter the early concern with preventing decline of self-esteem with aging was replaced by a growing appreciation of the continued robust development of the self with increasing maturity. It was realised that too much emphasis had been given to threats to the self with age and not enough to the expansion of self-conceptions in the second half of life (George, 1998). Nevertheless, maintenance of the self has returned to become again a key subject in the study of advanced old age. How are the very old to retain a positive outlook when biological decline becomes an increasingly troublesome element in daily life and when loss of close others removes major sources of attachment, identity and belonging?

An important distinction in the concept of the self drawn by William James, an early pioneer in the study of psychology (James, 1890), is that between awareness of the perceiving self, the 'I', and the perceived self, the 'me'. Most psychological studies, also of age changes, have concentrated on the latter, the objective self. This corresponds to the 'self-concept'; that is, individuals' descriptions of themselves. The subjective or phenomenological self which does the perceiving, interpreting or evaluating, has been far less studied, and hardly at all in studies of aging. Yet it may be of great importance to a sense of maintained identity. Does the perceiving self come to play a more important role in sustaining the person as changes in the observed self take their toll? As Sherman (2010) notes, the 'I' can be seen as the transcendental aspect of the self, the centre of awareness that with increasing separation from what it observes helps the person to become less 'self-centred' with age.

One of the first attempts to examine both the objective and subjective sense of self in the very old was conducted in the latter part of a longitudinal study on persons living in the San Francisco area of the United States by Troll and Skaff (1997). The participants then had an average age of 89 years and were interviewed on two occasions, thirty months apart. The analysis drew not on fixed answers to test items but on analysis of the person's discourse in response to questioning about continuity of the self. At the initial interview participants were asked, 'In what ways have you always been the same?' and 'In what ways have you changed over the years?' On the follow-up visit, after they had described their average day, participants were asked, 'Do you feel that you are the same person as you were a year ago?' Although two-thirds (68 per cent) of those interviewed identified some change in attributes, only one-quarter (26 per cent) indicated that they might be unsure whether they saw themselves as essentially the same person and no one indicated that they had changed into a different kind of person. Consistent with the studies on dementia reported in the last chapter, even the most cognitively deteriorated persons included in the study used the pronoun 'I' with assurance.

The first Berlin longitudinal study of aging, already referred to in Chapter 6, also included a detailed study of self-description in the very old (Freund and Smith, 1999). The authors emphasised that their study was not simply about self-description but self-definition, by which they meant 'that part of self-related knowledge that contains attributes crucial for the definition of oneself. It involves the subjectively most important characteristics to which individuals feel committed and which subjectively distinguish their own person from that of others' (Freund and Smith, 1999, p. 55). They developed a category system for coding responses to the open question 'Who am I?' Participants were asked to generate ten answers to the question, and these were then taped and transcribed verbatim. Age differences were smaller than expected. Although the very old participants (85–103 years) expressed less positive evaluations than their younger-old counterparts (70–84 years) and referred more to health in their self-definitions, they still made more positive than negative statements and there were strong similarities in the category profiles of the two groups. An activity-oriented lifestyle was the central theme in both the younger-old and the older-old, with hobbies and interests, social participation and daily living routines being principal sources of self-definition. Individual differences were more prominent than age difference in the same authors' subsequent analysis of possible future selves among the same participants (Smith and Freund, 2002). The oldest old continued to display active, achievement-oriented future selves, and there was little evidence for any substantial shift towards greater disengagement.

More recent studies have begun examining in more depth the basis of this continuity of the self in late life. In the following subsections we describe three sets of studies. The first tests the theoretical model of accommodation to see whether changing standards of evaluation in later life produce benefits in terms of maintained well-being. The second examines changes in emotional functioning in the very old and its implications for the self. Age-related losses do in general lead to a decline in well-being but the latter appears less determined by the changes of later life than might be expected. This is further evidence for a process of positive adjustment to loss occurring in a significant proportion of people as they age. The third focuses on individual differences with age and in particular the role of perceived meaning in the lives of very old people. Trajectories of self-evaluation show marked variation with age, and include trajectories of recovery as well as decline in late life. Maintaining or recovering a sense to life seems to lie at the core of positive self-evaluation in the last years.

Changing standards of self-evaluation

One of the most substantial contributions to the study of late life adjustment, referred to in Chapters 4 and 6, has been Brandtstädter's two-stage model in which 'assimilative' processes of adjustment by correction of performance give way to 'accommodative' processes of acceptance of change as age decrements become more severe (Brandtstädter, 2006). His team at the University of Trier in Germany have tested this model in an impressively conducted study which used a cross-sequential design (see Table 2.2 in Chapter 2, p. 18). They followed six groups of over one hundred persons each, aged four years apart from each other at the outset of the study, over a four-year period. Thus their final analysis provided comparable results to those of a twenty-four year longitudinal study of persons on persons aged from 58 to 81 years.

The investigators found reports of depressive symptoms to increase slightly with age (Rothermund and Brandtstädter, 2003a). The level of change was similar to that found in other longitudinal studies of aging (but dissimilar to cross-sectional findings between age groups where older generations, at least in the past, have tended to underreport depressive symptoms). As the authors point out, the small size of the increase in depression, even in the oldest age groups, in itself indicates the considerable resilience of older people in adapting to health losses, disability, loss of family and friends, as well as a decreasing future perspective.

In their subsequent analysis Rothermund and Brandtstädter (2003b) produced evidence on possible factors underlying this resilience. They assessed various aspects of the participants' attitudes to their performance in daily life: their sense of personal control over performance in the four domains of physical fitness, mental efficiency, physical appearance and everyday competence; the effort they put into maintaining or improving their abilities in each of these fields; the degree of loss they experienced compared to earlier in their adult lives; the importance they attributed to keeping up personal standards; and their general contentment with their level of performance. The cross-sequential analyses (see Figure 7.1) suggested a linear decline with age in perceived control, but by contrast a curvilinear relationship over time in compensatory activities, which increased up to the age of about 70 years but declined thereafter, suggesting an initial attempt to keep up standards followed by a subsequent letting go. These findings were consistent with those from the first Berlin Aging Study which also indicated a reduction in compensatory efforts among the older people in their sample (Freund and Baltes, 1998).

But in spite of the declines in perceived performance, actual satisfaction with performance remained surprisingly constant across the entire age range of the sample, which Rothermund and Brandtstädter refer to as another example of 'the astonishing stability of self-evaluations in old age' (Rothermund and Brandtstädter, 2003b, p. 903). Despite the declines and losses which people experience as they

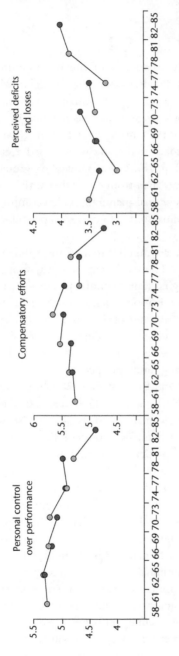

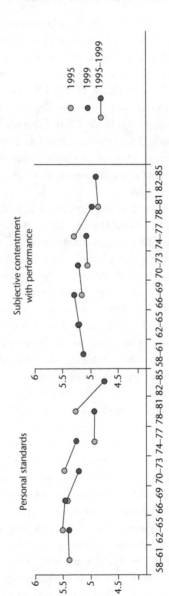

FIGURE 7.1 Cross-sequential patterns of changes with age in attitudes to personal performance in daily life.

Source: Rothermund and Brandstädter (2003b, p. 900): image reprinted with permission, American Psychological Association.

age, their impact on sense of self appears to be mitigated by an adjustment to the standards that they set for themselves. Efforts at compensation cease to be seen as worth the effort, and goals are modified to allow continued satisfaction with what is possible to achieve. The Trier study data suggest that for this sample of Germans growing old in the 1990s the shift to a predominantly accommodative mode of coping was occurring on average at the end of the seventh decade. Compensatory efforts declined after reaching a peak, personal standards dropped and contentment with what could still be achieved increased again.

As the researchers note, it is especially hard to demonstrate this critical psychological development in late life using data on groups because of huge inter-individual differences in the precise time of onset and nature of the changes that occur. That they were observable in this sample owes much to the amount of data collected and the care involved in assembling it. We will come back to the subject of inter-individual differences in adaptation to later life in the subsection after next.

Emotional functioning and the self

As we indicated in Chapter 6, an exaggerated distinction between the positive 'third' and negative 'fourth' stages of life risks stigmatising the later years as almost unworthy to be lived (Gilleard and Higgs, 2011; Higgs and Gilleard, 2015). Yet many very old people impress by their resilience and fortitude despite major physical and social losses. It therefore has become even more important to try to understand the variability of later life, in particular the factors influencing quality of life and well-being. How is it that some older people achieve high degrees of serenity? One important factor seems to be change in the nature of emotional functioning in later life. We will illustrate this by highlighting some recent Israeli research.

These studies have helped further expand the developmental theory of soci-oemotional selectivity (SES) theory that we presented first in Chapter 2. As we described it there, SES theory posits a developmental change with age away from prioritising information gains in favour of stabilising the quality of the person's emotional life. As a result older people tend to engage only in activities that are meaningful for them. Carstensen and colleagues have also argued that improved emotional regulation is reflected in greater affect complexity among older adults (Carstensen et al., 2000). By affect complexity is meant the greater ability to experience mixed emotions such as joy together with sadness (Ong and Bergeman, 2004; Schneider and Stone, 2015; see Box 7.1). Why this should be so is explained in terms of the heightened awareness of life's fragility that comes with age which results in the capacity to appreciate joy more fully but also, for example, the sadness that comes with the greater realisation of the increasing limits on the time left to live. Emotional life therefore becomes more complex in late life. Elderly people have a deeper realisation not only of what they have, but also that what they have cannot last for ever (Palgi et al., 2011).

BOX 7.1 MIXED EMOTIONS ACROSS THE ADULT LIFESPAN

The possibility of experiencing mixed emotions at the same time has long been debated in psychology, with some arguing that antagonistic emotions cannot be mixed together at a single point in time. The balance of current views is that the experience of, for example, bittersweet emotions is not only possible but more common than imagined. Recent evidence also suggests that the experience of mixed emotions increases with age and is a consequence of a more mature, sophisticated and realistic view of life. But does it increase into advanced age? Declining cognitive competence with age has led some to expect a decline in mixed emotion in late life whereas socio-emotional selectivity (SES) theory argues that increasing awareness of limitations to future prospects accompanied by emotions of 'poignancy' (i.e. happiness and sadness together) is intrinsic to psychological processes of aging.

Schneider and Stone carried out an investigation with two large nationally representative US samples, aged 15 years and over. Respondents were asked to provide a detailed time diary about the proceeding day and rate their happiness and sadness for three of the day's episodes. Results indicated small but significant steady increases in mixed emotions over the whole of the lifespan. The increases from 75 to 85 years, for example, were as great as those from 25 to 35 years. Several socio-demographic factors that might be expected to explain the differences, such as retirement and disability, did not alter the age-effects. This study therefore strongly suggests that the experience of mixed emotions is a major and unchanging characteristic of human aging.

(Schneider and Stone, 2015)

With these considerations in mind Bodner et al. (2013) carried out a study to examine the relationship between positive and negative affect in large samples both of young-old (65–79 years) and old-old Israelis (80–93 years). As we saw in Chapter 3 there has been an increasing interest among researchers in recent years in investigating age differences in emotional functioning, and this interest has now extended to comparisons between the young-old and the old-old. Besides expecting age differences in affect complexity Bodner and colleagues' study was also intended to investigate the hypothesis that affect complexity as an age-related developmental characteristic would be associated with higher self-esteem, and that this would apply especially to the older group.

Positive and negative affect, and self-esteem were measured by Hebrew versions of two well-established English language scales, the Positive and Negative Affect Schedule (PANAS) (Watson et al., 1988) and the Self-esteem Questionnaire (Rosenberg, 1965). As expected – and in line with previous studies – the young-old group had a higher level of self-esteem than the old-old group. The later stages of aging bring significant losses which tend to lower self-esteem. However, in support of their more challenging hypotheses they found that the relationship between positive and negative affect differed in the two groups. As in young and middle-aged adults, positive and negative affect were strongly negatively related in those in their sixties and seventies. But in those over the age of 80 years they positively correlated together. In addition, a more pronounced beneficial association between affect complexity and self-esteem was shown in the older group.

These results are particularly interesting. A closer examination of age trends showed the negative correlation beginning to disappear in the 77–82 years group and becoming markedly positive ($r = 0.45$) in the 89–93 years group. Moreover, affect complexity moderated the negative effects of age-related losses on self-esteem. This is a strong confirmation of Carstensen and colleague's views, not only that positive and negative affect occur increasingly together in later life, but that this phenomenon benefits very old people. It achieves this perhaps by mediating the extreme highs and lows of later life and contributing to stabilising an individual's emotional well-being in old age (Carstensen et al., 2011).

To provide further evidence on this topic Shmotkin and colleagues (Shmotkin et al., 2014) examined how well subjective wellness outcomes, assessed in terms of self-perceptions and self-evaluations, could be predicted by objective health status in participants aged 75 to 94 years drawn from a twelve-year national longitudinal study of the Jewish population in Israel. They found as they had hypothesised that objective health markers were progressively weak predictors as persons aged, and they discounted explanations in terms of decreased variability of health status at advanced age or lower measurement reliability. Why should such a change occur with advanced age? Some have suggested that the failing association between health and well-being reflects deteriorating cognitive functioning in late life (Labouvie-Vief, 2003). But, as Shmotkin (2005, 2011) has suggested, it could also indicate a well-functioning adaptive system at the end of life. It is to the advantage of those who are coming closer to death if their subjective well-being ceases to be dependent on their failing bodies, as this makes it easier for them to maintain an emotionally positive view of themselves and their lives.

There are similarities between Shmotkin's model on the pursuit of happiness in the face of adversity with the earlier developmental views of aging expressed by Gutmann and by Lieberman and Tobin which were referred to in Chapters 2 and 6. In the difficult circumstances of late life it may be more adaptive for older people to distance themselves from the 'objective reality' of their lives and instead to focus on their inner lives, their past memories and imaginative fantasies. Subjective well-being then ceases to be a mirror of the external world, and as a result 'psychological integration may still be sustained even when life is close to disintegration' (Shmotkin et al., 2014, p. 727). Shmotkin also points to an interesting paradox about late life. Survival to an advanced age indicates resilience whereas proximity to death implies vulnerability. The unprecedented position in which very old people find themselves may also help explain their unusual characteristics.

Individual trajectories of self and meaning

As we have stressed at various points in this book it is insufficient to build a psychology of aging based purely on the statistical study of differences between groups of people of specific ages. It has long been noted that variation increases with age in the rates of change shown by particular individuals on biological, psychological and social variables (Maddox, 1987). As Ian Stuart-Hamilton (in press) has argued, the gentle age curves shown in most statistical analyses on age differences in cognitive performance are especially misleading because they give an illusion of gradual small changes with age. By contrast, when the graphs for individuals are plotted the patterns are hugely erratic, with various forms of trajectory appearing, including rapid decline of performance, decline followed by recovery, and relative high performance. Moreover, according to group data analysis changes in performance on different skills may seem to follow similar age trajectories, but examined at the individual level may show large discrepancies with deterioration in skills occurring seemingly haphazardly within and across individuals. Therefore for the experience of aging to be properly understood it also needs to be studied at the level of the individual person. This applies even more strongly to late life as variation in personal experience continues to increase into the tenth decade.

To illustrate this point we present examples of case analyses from a twenty-year longitudinal study of aging conducted in one English city which has attempted to draw conclusions at the level of the individual case before attempting generalisations across them (Coleman et al., 1999, 2015). Self-description was a major focus of data collection at each of eight observation points during the study. At different interview points other forms of self-description were collected. These included written responses to sentence stems about the self (Dittmann-Kohli, 1990) and to questions exploring 'life strengths' adapted from Helen Kivnick's operationalisation of Erikson's eight life tasks (Kivnick, 1991) (see Chapter 2). Analysis of the group data showed, similarly to other comparable longitudinal studies of aging, a small decline in self-esteem which began towards the end of the eighth decade and continued to lower with age. Change was related especially to close bereavements and to the onset of personal frailty and loss of ability in self-care.

But of particular interest were the variations in individual trajectories of self-evaluation (Coleman et al., 2015). Among the trajectories observed were those who showed a pattern of decline in the earlier stages of aging followed by recovery, sometimes to an even higher level of expressed well-being than before. These deserve particular attention for what they reveal about the factors involved in creating high morale in late life. There follow abbreviated accounts of two of these persons' lives. Illustrative quotations from their interviews during their eighties and nineties are provided in Boxes 7.2 and 7.3.

The first case, 'Harold Rank', was a strongly family centred man who had been married twice, his first wife having died of meningitis in the Second World War. Together they had five children. When first interviewed at the age of 69 years he displayed very high self-esteem, centred on his family relationships as well as his outside interests. In particular he indicated a strong sense of self-efficacy – problems were there for him to solve. But in the following year his wife, who was ten years younger than him, was diagnosed with a form of early onset dementia. He struggled for a long time to accept this diagnosis, trying and failing to keep his wife functioning as before.

His morale decreased over subsequent years as his own physical health began to deteriorate. His wife had to be admitted to residential care where she died a few years later. When interviewed after a hip replacement at the age of 81 years he was greatly depressed. Despite the operation, he had been left with disability and pain. He had recriminations about failing to care for his wife at home, and feared that he too would lose his own independence. However, he still retained a sense of purpose in his life which suggested that he might recover his previous morale if his physical health were to improve.

BOX 7.2 RECOVERY OF POSITIVE SELF-EVALUATION IN LATE LIFE: CASE I

At 81 years, Harold Rank had low self-esteem, was depressed, still grieving for his wife and concerned he too might need institutional care, but still hoping his situation would improve (although fearing it would not).

'*I haven't coped you see, that's the point, I haven't coped, not without help, and I object to having help.*'

'*I worry if I've got to go into a home . . . I don't want to do that . . . don't break my heart! . . . this is my home and this is where I want to stay.*'

'*If I got rid of all these aches and pains I will be up again . . . I often wish I could go to bed and wake up and it's all gone and I shall get out of bed and jump and shout out "Hooray" and go back to what I was like.*'

'*I've had challenges all my life . . . I always enjoyed a challenge . . . but I can't say I'm going to challenge this . . . I know I'm not going to get rid of it.*'

At 85 years, he was less depressed, had recovered some of his previous sense of self based on his strong family ties, and was reminiscing and life reviewing.

'*What has been most meaningful about your life so far?*' . . . '*My family – I've been very fortunate to have two good wives – I've got to go on living because I've got children.*'

'*My wife was seven years like that. I visited her [his sister-in-law] this morning . . . I'm more concerned about her than about myself . . . She's such a lovely person. I visit her three times a week. It's no trouble. I'm going to do it as long as I can.*'

'*I can remember the first day I went to school . . . my mother was a lovely little woman . . . I remember how I met my first wife . . .* '

(continued)

(continued)

At 87 years, he was at peace with himself, accepting his more limited life, no longer concerned with external events, and had an even higher self-esteem.

'I wouldn't take any notice even if a bomb were to go off [in the street] outside.'

At 90 years, he felt more distant from the world, but still had a positive sense of self and was highly satisfied with his life.

'Through hard work, my children never wanted for anything.'

(Coleman et al., 2015)

Harold's situation had changed markedly for the better when he was interviewed at 85 years. He was able to do some cooking and shopping for himself, walked outside with a stick, and was coping at home with the support of his family and local welfare services. More remarkably, he was also contributing to the care of his wife's sister, who had developed a similar form of dementia and was living in a residential care home. He visited her regularly and did all he could to make sure she was comfortable. His self-esteem was recovering.

At 87 years his health problems had increased again. He had been operated on twice that year, for prostate cancer, and for pain in his back and legs. His depressive symptoms were raised, but his self-evaluation had risen even further closer to his rating at the beginning of the study, based as before on his family, including his care for his sister-in-law, but also his ability to continue managing at home. He also spoke more of the importance of prayer in his life, especially since his second wife had died, and how he had made contact again with his local parish church. He felt the benefits of prayer in which he said he believed strongly.

Interviewed again at 90 years – in the year before he died – his mobility had decreased further and he was falling more often. His son now helped him to visit his sister-in-law. He had had two further operations on his prostate but had refused another because he 'still wanted to look like a man'. However, he was now much more accepting of the care he received at home from paid carers, something he said he would have found very difficult in the past. Despite his increasing frailty he now showed no sign of depression and his self-esteem was further enhanced. He had continued his positive uses of reminiscence and prayer and expressed himself very satisfied with his life, present and past.

'Ethel Willis' showed a similarly striking recovery of sources of meaning to sustain a positive view of her life in her nineties. She had incurred major role losses in the earlier stages of aging, being widowed at 62 years and around the same period retired from major organisational roles she had held within political and other associations in her local community. She greatly missed her previous active social life. Her self-evaluations through her seventies and eighties were only moderately high, based mainly on her continued ability to maintain her own home and relationships with her two children. However, she encountered recurrent bouts of minor depression and looked with apprehension to the future.

At 85 years she became frailer as a result of a series of medical events. She had been admitted with a throat infection to hospital but there developed a chest infection and then a stomach haemorrhage for which she needed surgery. Discharged to a convalescent hospital she had experienced a heart attack there and needed to be returned to the general hospital. Her main thoughts were about death and dying with dignity without the need for prolonged care.

A year later her self-esteem had actually strengthened. This appeared to be a result both of her ability to continue maintaining her independence at home and of the care her family was now providing. But at the age of 88 she experienced a further crisis of morale following a stroke. Both her sight and mobility were damaged and she was obliged to restrict herself to living in the downstairs part of her house. When interviewed a year later her depression score was raised and her self-esteem lowered. Nevertheless, her determination to remain at home remained and she knew that she could still rely on her family.

Ethel's self-evaluation strengthened again in her nineties. At 92 years she was suffering further medical problems with inoperable gall stones, cystitis, back pain and constipation, and her depression score was raised. But her self-esteem was higher than ever before in the study, illustrated by the confidence she expressed in herself, her family and local services. Interviewed at 95 years, in the year before her death, she had encountered no further major medical problems, showed no signs of depression and her self-esteem remained high. She was still able to read and particularly enjoyed biographies. For the first time she spoke positively about the experience of aging. She felt close to her children, was very satisfied with her past life, and was serene about her approaching death.

BOX 7.3 RECOVERY OF POSITIVE SELF-EVALUATION IN LATE LIFE: CASE II

At 81 years, Ethel Willis had diminished self-esteem, missed her previous busy life, concerned to preserve good ties with her children, but worried about the future.

'Maybe I can' . . . 'be remembered as a good mother.'

'The goal that I would like to accomplish in my life' . . . 'love and affection in the years left to me.'

At 86 years, she was recovering from serious illness, more worried about her future care, but pleased she had retained her independence so far.

'I thought isn't it awful what I'm putting my kids through you know . . . I'm not frightened to die . . . but I hope I do it with dignity . . . And I don't want to sit around waiting for it. I'm fully active and going to a rest home would frighten me. I'd be the worst patient they ever had!'

(continued)

(continued)

> **At 88 years,** following a stroke, her life was more restricted, she was depressed and had low self-esteem, but still determined to remain at home and was reassured by the support of her family.
>
> *'What kinds of things do you enjoy doing?' . . . 'Very little. With failing eyesight my sewing and knitting have almost come to a standstill.'*
>
> *'What is it in your life that gives you hope?' . . . 'Not to lose my independence; to stand for myself.'*
>
> *'What is it about your life that makes you fell most alive?' . . . 'My son and daughter. They are my only means of getting out of the house.'*
>
> **At 92 years,** she had encountered further health problems and was depressed, but with higher self-esteem based on belief in herself, her family, and local welfare services.
>
> *'I am as bright and alert as ever' . . . 'a good advert for my age.'*
>
> *'I am of importance to others' . . . 'the caring people around me.'*
>
> *'I feel useless' . . . 'but I hope to feel useful again when I'm feeling better.'*
>
> **At 95 years,** she was grateful for her good health, appreciative of the services she received from family and welfare services, and for the first time agreed with positive statements about her experience of aging.
>
> *'Old age is a happy time for me . . . it is nice to grow old.'*
>
> *(Coleman et al., 2015)*

Such a positive outcome to Ethel's journey through aging would not have been expected ten or even twenty years earlier. She came to find pride in her success in remaining at home, despite the difficulties she encountered, while retaining the love and help of her family. The same could be said about Harold's recovery from the deep-seated malaise that he expressed in his early eighties. The predictions made about his future at that time had been very negative, based on the assumption that he would not be able to adapt to further loss. Yet in fact he was able to restore equilibrium to his life, both by recovering the central theme of family which had run through his life but also by accommodating to his increasingly dependent condition, to an extent that surprised even himself, and by finding new spiritual resources in his inner life. For both Harold and Ethel the investigators predicted further decline, for Harold at the age of 81 and for Ethel as late as 88, which proved incorrect. Their underlying resilience won through and by the end of their lives both showed a strengthening of their sense of self.

Meeting psychological needs in assisted-living and care settings

The high morale which both Harold Rank and Ethel Willis displayed could be attributed in part at least to their success in both maintaining their independence at home while continuing to feel part of a united family. They thus were able to continue to fulfil two of the major needs, for autonomy and relatedness, identified as essential to goal-related activity in Deci and Ryan's 'self-determination theory' (SDT) of human motivation and personality (Deci and Ryan, 2000). This theory emphasises the greater importance of intrinsic over extrinsic motivation in human behaviour and proposes that there are three universal inner motivators of behaviour, the needs for autonomy, competence and relatedness. Autonomy is defined principally by the awareness of one's ability to choose how to behave, competence by the perception of the effectiveness of one's actions within a given setting, and relatedness by the experience of positive relationships with others along with a sense of belonging. The theory has been an important influence on many areas of applied psychology, although it has been relatively little applied to the experience of aging (O'Connor and Vallerand, 1994; Coleman, 2000; Neubauer et al., 2016).

Current theory on adaptation in late life, as we have seen in the previous chapter, emphasises the importance, even the necessity, of changing goals in late life. Does this also apply to the experience of autonomy, competence and relatedness? SDT theory appears to assume that these primary needs are lifelong and that their loss in later life leads to a decline in well-being. Neubauer et al. (2016) have recently queried this assumption. In a four-year German longitudinal study of persons aged 87 to 97 years at outset they found that the links of autonomy with indicators of subjective well-being were non-existent or much weaker than expected. In explanation they suggest that 'the dependency of well-being on the fulfilment of basic needs may decline under "chronic" deprivation of these needs' (Neubauer et al., 2016, p. 8). Loss of autonomy in particular may be accepted as a necessary consequence of living to extreme old age. Perceived competence on the other hand does seem to have more important consequences than autonomy for well-being. Although they did not investigate relatedness in their study they suggest that sufficient is now known from studies conducted in the framework of socio-emotional selectivity theory (see Chapters 2 and 3) to conclude that the importance of interpersonal relationships increases in late life.

An important additional point to consider is that conflict between needs, as well as variation between them, may increase in later life. SDT theory recognises that individual persons will acquire stronger needs in particular areas as a result of the interaction between their personality and the social environment in which they have grown to adulthood. For example, persons with a great need for independence may acquire more anxiety about others taking control of their lives as they grow older. As a consequence they may be more inclined to hide evidence of their failing ability and even avoid others. Eventually they may come to lead lives of extreme isolation and incompetence (as in cases of late-life squalor) (Pertusa et al., 2010). In contrast those with relatively stronger needs for relatedness, as they become more in need of help, may feel obliged to allow others overmuch into their lives. As a result of lack of use their everyday skills in basic activities will decline more to the extent that they lose any remaining sense of autonomy and competence. Neubauer et al.

(2016) appear to suggest from their greater emphasis on the need for relatedness at the end of life that the latter scenario is the more likely outcome.

Nevertheless, as they become older many people do become concerned about losing their ability to live independently. Our earlier cited cases of 'Harold Rank' and 'Ethel Willis' expressed anxieties during their early to middle eighties about having to leave their own homes in order to live in a residential care home. They both succeeded in avoiding this outcome. But increasing numbers of older people do face the prospect of losing their homes and relocating to an assisted-living or residential-care setting especially if they lack the family or other means of social support that would enable them to continue living at home. Although such a relocation does have negative consequences for many older people, it is still possible, given the right circumstances in the care setting, for them to continue to feel independent, to undertake some tasks for themselves, and to make contributions to the life of the community home in which they live as well as to the society outside. Another example of a case analysis from the previous study (Coleman et al., 2015) illustrates this point (see Box 7.4).

BOX 7.4 FLOURISHING IN RESIDENTIAL CARE

At 89 years, Irene Monroe had recently moved into a new residential care home whose ethos reflected her own Christian religious allegiance. Health problems (angina and arthritis) had led her to move into sheltered housing in her early eighties after her husband died and at 87 into local authority residential care. She enjoyed life more in her new home, as she could give witness to her faith and also take up new activities.

'Oh yes, very happy. I have some wonderful friends, oh yes very happy.'

'When I feel unhappy' . . . 'I get to the root of the cause and then ask God to take my thoughts and renew them; which he does.'

'I really feel good' . . . 'when I have had fulfilment in painting.'

At 92 years, she was still active within the home, helped prepare the chapel room for Holy Communion, and took seriously her self-appointed task of reading the Bible systematically and sharing her faith with other residents. She was also drawing more on past experiences as a source of satisfaction.

'What is it about your life that makes you feel most alive?' . . . 'When I experience the joy of being a Christian.'

'What have been the major contributions you have made to life?' . . . 'It is difficult. I would say my faith . . . I have been able to share my faith with others . . . it has made me very, very happy.'

'What have been some of the main features of your life?' . . . 'Falling in love with my husband and having twin girls unexpected.'

At 95 years, one year before she died, her mobility was much reduced following a stroke and fall in the previous year, and she experienced breathlessness, and pain and unsteadiness in her legs. She felt depressed on occasions because of being alone in her room much of the time, but retained a positive sense of self. She still took responsibility for preparing the chapel in the home for Holy Communion, and had recently helped establish a new prayer group within the home. She enjoyed making new acquaintances.

'I thank God I have courage because God is in my heart.'

'Last night I gave myself over to prayer, the wonderful prayers of all these people. I've never heard prayers like them.'

'I love to look back on life as I have been very, very fortunate.'

'There's a person came yesterday that gave me great joy. He gave a wonderful prayer and his relatives said, "Oh I am pleased he's at your table."'

'I feel I could say that – I can say "Lord now let Thy servant (depart in peace)."'

(Coleman et al., 2015)

SDT theory provides a suitable framework for investigating how modifying social environments may allow for the better fulfilment of people's psychological needs. We focus in the rest of this section on recent research on older people in assisted-living settings, considering first studies examining needs for autonomy and control, and second needs for relatedness and belonging.

Self-determination: autonomy and control

The research on institutional care conducted by Langer and Rodin in the 1970s and 1980s, described in the previous chapter, emphasised the benefits of residents retaining a sense of control. Deci and Ryan (2000, p. 233ff) describe four types of behaviour that vary along a continuum of self-determination. 'Intrinsically motivated' behaviour is carried out for the pleasure and satisfaction derived from the performance. 'Extrinsically motivated but self-determined' behaviour is performed to receive some benefit or avoid some ill, but not because the activity is intrinsically rewarding. 'Extrinsically motivated non-self-determined' behaviour on the other hand is externally determined. Finally 'amotivated' behaviour lacks any sense of awareness of contingency between behaviour and outcomes. O'Connor and Vallerand's research work on nursing homes in Montreal is one of the few examples of applications of SDT theory to the experience of aging. They used the above definitions to develop indicators of 'motivational style'. Although these four measures displayed no significant correlations with age or physical health, they all correlated strongly with indices of psychological adjustment, comprising self-esteem, depression, life satisfaction, existential meaning in life, intrinsic motivation and self-determined extrinsic motivation both relating positively, non-self-determined extrinsic motivation and amotivation both relating negatively (O'Connor and Vallerand, 1994).

Assessment of the nursing home environment was an important element in their project, and based on interviews with both the head nurse and administrator regarding the rules and treatment of residents. An elaborate description of the rules in each nursing home was then written, focusing on how much choice residents had regarding their daily activities, the extent to which the nursing home staff took responsibility for residents' personal care, and the degree to which the staff encouraged or discouraged personal initiative. Three psychologists who were highly familiar with SDT theory independently read the written descriptions, and rated the degree of self-determination provided by each home on each of these dimensions. Since the intra-class correlations were high, mean self-determination scores for each home could be computed.

As expected, residents in high self-determination nursing homes tended to score higher on self-determined motivation. Much more interesting however was the finding of interaction effects with motivational styles. There was a tendency for low self-determined motivation individuals to report better psychological adjustment in low self-determination nursing homes than in high self-determination nursing homes, and for high self-determined motivation individuals to report better psychological adjustment in high self-determination nursing homes than in low self-determination nursing homes. This is a strong demonstration of the importance of person–environment congruence theory mentioned in the previous chapter (Lawton, 1980). However, although one cannot expect all elderly nursing home residents to benefit from high levels of autonomy, O'Connor and Vallerand suggested the interesting hypothesis that long-term adjustment is better served by an environment which provides opportunities for autonomy that are always slightly greater than one's initial level of self-determined motivation.

Studies such as these have indicated ways in which the features of assisted-living settings could be developed better to enhance the adaptation and well-being of residents. More recent studies have taken this topic further. A particular problem is the passive position new residents are often placed in from the time that they realise they need to move into supportive living circumstances. There is a tendency to emphasise how their security and care needs will be met rather than the new opportunities they will be provided with to live more fully as if at home but also with the advantages of living in community (Peace and Holland, 2001; Cook et al., 2015).

Older people themselves tend not to use psychological terms such as 'autonomy' or 'control', but rather, as Harold Rank and Ethel Willis did, of their need to feel 'independent'. It is clear that meanings of terms such as 'independence' vary a good deal and researchers have become more interested in examining what precisely older people mean by them. In a recent study conducted in Wales (UK) Hillcoat-Nallétamby (2014) analysed qualitative interviews with frail older people collected as part of a large national survey. They constituted three groups: those still living privately in their own homes and receiving support to enable them to continue living there; those who had moved to residential care homes (communal environments which provided assistance with daily living tasks, but not to the level of nursing home care); and those who had moved to assisted-living settings ('extra care' purpose-built housing schemes with their own private apartment but with access to communal facilities and the presence of 24-hour-a-day support staff).

The participants made many references to the term 'independence' and the analysis focused on distinguishing the different understandings contained in their interviews. Thus it could mean doing things for one's self and avoiding reliance on others. But it could also mean the ability to remain independent by accepting help or having help available if needed. A somewhat different meaning was implied by an emphasis on wanting to avoid feeling dependent on others or feeling obligated to them, as also by a fear of 'institutional' care and associated ideas of loss of identity and imposition of control over the pattern of daily life. For others independence was about freedom in choosing what and when to do things. Common to all three settings was the link between a sense of independence and access to the necessary resources to maintain it. These could be constituted by the help provided by family or friends, or from social services, or by simply possessing the financial means to pay for help when needed. Another important perspective on independence was future oriented, having a strategy or plan in place that would enable the person to continue to be independent even if they became more disabled, ill or had an accident.

Both those who had remained living in their own homes and those who had moved to extra-care housing emphasised their independence in terms of making their own decisions and doing what they pleased. Those in extra-care housing emphasised the similarities with living in their previous home in that they had a private, personal living space. Within residential care homes by contrast independence was shown in terms of doing things alone and being self-reliant, and loss of independence expressed by an inability to do things as before. For many who had chosen to enter a care home it was the lesser of two evils, in that staying at home would have meant becoming reliant on others and/or being a burden to family members.

In discussing these findings Hillcoat-Nallétamby refers to the previous work of Collopy (1988) in distinguishing different forms of autonomy in care settings. These include 'authentic autonomy', when only doing things alone is to be true to one's character; 'decisional autonomy', where the emphasis is on being able to do what one pleases even if it requires the help of others; and 'delegated autonomy', when a person is content to accept help in decision making from chosen family members or others. She concludes that loss or compromised independence can occur in any setting, and that much depends on the type of autonomy the person desires.

Other researchers have continued to follow the example of Langer and Rodin in conducting natural experiments to investigate the consequences of different experiences of autonomy and control in assisted-living settings. Thus Knight et al. (2010) took the opportunity to investigate a situation in which residents of a UK care home were scheduled to move into a new building. Those who had previously been living on the one floor were given the opportunity to contribute to decision making about the design of the new setting into which they were relocating. The authors refer to this group as the 'empowered'. The 'unempowered' control group, who had been living on another floor, received the quality of care and support through the relocation that was the care home's standard practice. As there had been a difference in previous satisfaction with living conditions between the two floors the researchers decided to make the less satisfied into the experimental group to provide a stronger test of the hypothesis that empowerment in decision making would provide greater benefit than receiving care as usual.

The empowered group were given the opportunity to make decisions about how to decorate their home's shared social spaces (dining room, lounge and corridors), taking part in initial meetings with the designers but then meeting on their own to select the designs they preferred. Although the numbers of residents involved in the research were relatively small they were sufficient to produce a statistically significant effect for all four hypotheses developed for the experiment. The empowered residents identified more with one another and with their new setting. They interacted more together, reported greater life satisfaction and improved health, and used the lounge more to interact with one another. These effects were still evident over four months later.

This striking piece of research has introduced a new element into the study of self-determination, namely the role of collective decision making. This had the benefit of helping the residents identify more with their peers by undertaking a task which needed their joint collaboration. As a result it encouraged continuing productive interaction between them also after the intervention was completed. This contrasted with the situation of those cared for as isolated individuals who were less motivated to relate to one another.

Relationships and belonging in care settings

Relationships constitute perhaps an even more important aspect of assisted-living and care settings. The experience of loneliness can be prevalent even among those living together with others. In Chapter 5 we referred to the considerable evidence on the benefits of positive relationships for well-being (Antonucci et al., 2009). In later life the risk of social isolation tends to increase as a result of decline in social networks as well as personal mobility. One good reason for entering an assisted-living setting is the possibility it provides for social contact within its communal spaces. Indeed, it is often loss of spouse and increased social isolation that precipitates the move (Ball et al., 2009). Detailed surveys of quality of life in such settings have indicated that social cohesion, assessed by measures of how helpful and supportive staff members were towards residents and how involved and supportive residents were with each other are much more important to residents than the facilities available and the organisational characteristics of the establishment (Mitchell and Kemp, 2000).

Relationships with other residents are clearly an important source of social contact – family members may not be able to visit often and staff are frequently too busy to socialise – but are often hampered by a variety of factors, including the design of the communal spaces and the encouragement residents receive to interact with one another. A common view is that residents rarely form strong links with one another (Frank, 2002), which is often explained in socio-emotional selectivity terms as the result of lack of connection with key aspects of the person's previous identity. Residents often have quite different backgrounds and few attempts are made by staff to find possible matches for new residents. A greater homogeneity, including shared ethnicity and religious beliefs, provides more opportunities for creating bonds (Hazan, 1980 (see previous chapter); Ball et al., 2005; Eckert et al., 2001). Box 7.4 (pp. 174–5) presents extracts from interviews with 'Irene Monroe', another of the longitudinal case study analyses referred to earlier in the chapter (Coleman et al., 2015). It illustrates how Irene benefitted from moving to a home with similar religious values to her own). Further complicating factors include the typically low proportion of men in such facilities and the tendency of higher-functioning residents to avoid those in poorer health, especially those with dementia.

A major recent study into the issue of co-resident relationships in assisted-living settings has examined intensively over three years eight such US communities varying in size, location and resident profiles. It made use of mixed research methods: participant observation, informal as well as formal interviews, and quantitative surveys. Initial analysis (Kemp et al., 2012) using 'grounded theory' method developed an explanatory framework employing the concept of 'social careers' which the resident developed within the assisted-living setting. The course these careers took varied greatly between individual residents, showing patterns both of decrease and increase in interaction. For example, one woman initially engaged in a lot of social activities which she enjoyed, but because of increasing hearing problems gradually withdrew and became content spending her time sitting and reading and just interacting with those she called 'friends' at the meals table. Another by contrast began her life in the new setting in a very withdrawn and isolated way, staying virtually all of the time in her room, but a staff member persuaded two of the more outgoing female residents to make an effort to include her, and as a result she became very sociable.

The quality of friendships also varied greatly. Many of the residents viewed everyone in the home they entered as 'strangers' and for some this remained so. They denied that they had any relationships in the home. Others used only the term 'acquaintances'. As one resident said, 'I have acquaintances here, but don't get too involved'. Some did develop what they called friendships but still perceived them as 'artificial' or 'by circumstances'. One woman distinguished the friendships she had in the home from those she considered 'real': 'I consider a lot of them friends but don't have the "I have something I want to tell you relationship"'. Others did develop real friendships but these were still limited by history and circumstances, as one spoke of a deceased co-resident: 'I don't think it was the intensity that one would have with a 40-year-old friend . . . there wasn't any reason for it to be'. Yet others did develop friendships which were similar to past friendships or seen as different but still as meaningful. Understanding better the factors underlying these differences in perceived quality of new friendships developed in later life is an important task for future research.

The study also highlighted the importance of the design of spaces and staff policy on residents' use of them. More attention needs to be given to the value of creating dedicated space for relationships with comfortable seating and wheel-chair accessibility. Mealtimes nevertheless remained very important for forming and developing relationships. Taking meals together builds a sense of community, reflects and continues the meaning of earlier family life, and constitutes the most intimate activity that older residents can share with one another. The decisions made by staff in allocating residents to different tables could make the difference between social integration and isolation. Promoting involvement in the varied leisure activities the home offered was also a hugely influential part of staff duties.

Other research has focused more on staff interactions with residents. Often care assistants have to make sensitive distinctions between what different residents require from them. This is well illustrated in O'Connor and Rigby's (1996) earlier study on so-called 'baby talk'. This is a common feature of staff behaviour in care settings, often commented on critically by observers but rarely examined for its impact on residents themselves. A particular strength of this study research, conducted in Canadian nursing homes, was that not only did it assess staff behaviour but also the personality characteristics and needs of residents. In so doing it provided another test of the importance of person–environment congruence. The elderly resident's need for succour was found to be associated with perceptions of warmth in 'baby talk', whereas the younger age of the resident and a higher level of functional health were associated with negative perceptions of being spoken down to. Significant interactions were evident in the statistical analyses conducted, suggesting the harmful effect of receiving 'baby talk' on the self-esteem of those who perceived it negatively. The opposite result – self-esteem gains – was found for those with positive perceptions of 'baby talk'.

A more recent study has also used a variety of methods, including participant observation, interviews and focus groups to examine types of relationships, including relationships with staff, within English care homes (Brown Wilson et al., 2009). Their main contribution was to delineate three types of relationships observed between care assistants and residents. The first type they described as 'pragmatic'. This was focused on the practical aspect of care, which usually dominated conversations between staff and residents, and included family members as well. Although they spoke about their main aim as 'getting the job done', they did try to respect persons' wishes and preferences, but could not be described as establishing real personal ties. By contrast the second type, 'personal and responsive' relationships, focused more on the sharing of personal information. Staff who worked in this way sought out details of residents' habits and preferences, spending more time talking to residents and family about their past lives. The third type, to which they gave the name 'reciprocal relationships', went further in recognising the needs of family members and staff as well as residents and in stressing the importance of shared understandings between all three. For example, one resident spoke about how she helped care assistants by waiting patiently while they completed a care task with another resident. Staff in return acknowledged the help of residents in supporting them in their work.

It was clear from this study that the quality of personal relationships with staff, centred in the provision of personal care, was the key to quality of life in care homes. The authors also made a number of other observations, including the importance of story telling which helped staff create personalised care routines for each resident. Listening to an older person's story gave a sign of respect but even more showed understanding when the implications drawn from it were applied in everyday practice. As we stressed in Chapter 3, talking about the past is a powerful tool in confirming identity and there are many opportunities for staff to encourage residents to reminisce during the care routines of the day. Involving family in three-way interactions provides further possibilities. Other studies have also highlighted the potential of more effective involvement of families in long-term care (Gaugler et al., 2003), including at the end of life (Williams et al., 2012). An important skill both nursing and care assistants need to acquire is to be sensitive to the extent to which family want to be involved in caregiving.

The third fundamental human need stressed by Deci and Ryan is competence. Certainly a sense that one can still perform at least some self-care and home-care activities adequately is important. However, what may be even more important than practical competence in everyday skills is a sense that the person is still contributing, whether to their own family or the broader community (Coleman et al., 2015). This also applies within care settings where it is sometimes other residents who alert staff to the pressing needs of those they need to attend to. If it is to be a genuine community then this is how life should be conducted in a home. Contribution comes in many different forms, in listening, in showing empathy and in including others in activities. The importance of a sense of contribution is perhaps one of the more underrated aspects of individual identity in later life and one that deserves more attention both in research and practice. The case study presented in Box 7.4 also illustrates the value of contributing to, as well as belonging within, a residential care setting.

Living well with dementia

In Chapter 6 we described the contribution of psychology to studying dementia not just in terms of assessing cognitive failure but also by promoting understanding of lived experience. A better appreciation of how the person with dementia sees the world and what might be their underlying psychological needs is necessary to good care. Particularly important is awareness of emotional reactions, their origin and nature, as well as the most appropriate types of response to emotional disturbance.

As already stressed in Chapter 3, the study of emotions has been neglected in the history of psychological science in favour of the study of cognitive processes in isolation (Oatley and Jenkins, 1996). Yet emotions are an important and essential part of what makes us human. They are so because humans, as well as animals, are not automata. They often find themselves in situations where they lack appropriate patterns of behaviour, when they are not fully adapted to an environment that has changed or when no habit or instinct fits a situation. Emotions are important at such junctures because they prompt us towards certain types of actions when perhaps we should do something but lack already established modes of action. In short emotions help us to act in a world that can be only imperfectly known. Where something has not gone as expected, a change in readiness to act may be followed by a longer lasting mental preoccupation in which we can concentrate on reprogramming the way we think about our lives, for example the turning in on self and greater reflection produced by sadness, the capacity for vigorous action produced by anger, the restless searching resulting from anxiety.

This line of thinking has particularly important implications for dementia. Precisely because the world to a confused person is likely to appear less certain, one would expect people suffering from a dementing condition to be more emotional. Unexpected things will happen more often. There will be sadness over losing things, anger at being frustrated in achieving aims, and fear and anxiety because of increasing uncertainty over the future. It is also probable that negative emotions will be expressed in more extreme ways and resulting moods will become more prolonged and difficult to change, and carers need advice in handling them (Stokes, 2000; Cheston and Bender, 2003; Bird and Moniz-Cook, 2008). Important principles in responding to sadness and despondency include the provision of opportunity for activity, in particular successful activity, and contact with familiar and friendly others. Angry or violent behaviour needs to be treated as a catastrophic reaction, to be responded to calmly and if possible by removing the persons from the circumstances that are upsetting them. Very often anger is a reaction to a situation and the actions of others which have been misunderstood. Anxiety and nervousness are major problems and do not subside easily, which is why staff often have recourse to sedative medication when they see no alternative course of action. While some anxiety and nervousness may result from changes within the brain, a lot may arise from real feelings of loss and tension.

An important principle, therefore, which should guide dementia care is respect for emotions. Their very presence is a sign of continuing vitality. Both their expression and the type of responses they elicit from care staff have been used to develop systems of monitoring quality of dementia care within institutions, such as 'dementia care mapping' (Kitwood, 1997; Brooker, 2005). The field of dementia care research is now growing strongly (Woods and Clare, 2008; Cheston and Ivanecka, 2016). In this last section we consider examples of recent studies evaluating two aspects of dementia care: first, helping people make the difficult adjustment to awareness that their mental faculties are deteriorating and that they may have dementia; and, second, optimising care for the individual person within a community setting.

Adaptation to mental infirmity

Dementia used to be a hidden condition of late life, cloaked in stigma and shame. With the greater opening up of attitudes and a more constructive approach to support and therapy, acknowledgement of a diagnosis of dementia directly to the person affected is now recommended practice. But this necessarily requires that some subsequent support be offered in coming to terms with a more uncertain future. In recent years there have been various initiatives in different countries to develop forms of supportive intervention, with individuals, couples and groups. Group therapy has been thought to have particular benefits because of the understanding and support that sharing with persons in similar conditions can bring to someone who may often be suffering in isolation after receiving a diagnosis of dementia.

So far only few attempts have been made to evaluate the different forms of group therapy that have been tried, but these will undoubtedly increase in the future as the importance of optimising support to those in the early stages of dementia becomes more recognised. The most substantial evaluation so far has been a US study by Logsdon et al. (2010) comparing 96 patient and carer dyads who were randomly divided between those entering early-stage memory loss support groups and those kept on a waiting list. The intervention involved presentations on dementia as well as an occupational therapist speaking about daily living skills, followed by therapeutic discussion in groups over nine sessions. Significant differences were found in participant quality of life, depression and family communication. A pilot study of a 'Living Well with Dementia' group in the UK, which drew on the therapists' combined experience with psycho-educational courses and group psychotherapy with persons in early stage dementia, has also produced promising results (Marshall et al., 2015).

The Assimilation Model of psychotherapeutic change (Stiles, 2001) is the theoretical background to studies currently being conducted with persons with dementia in the UK (Cheston et al., 2016). It provides a model for understanding the underlying changes that occur in response to acknowledging a threatening situation and a framework for assessing change as it occurs. Influenced by Mikhail Bakhtin's thinking concept of the dialogical self and its psychological application by Hermans and Kempen (1992), this model represents the self not as a unified entity but as a 'community of voices'. Two of the different voices that are important in the assimilation model are the 'Dominant Voice' and the 'Problematic Voice'. Whereas the former represents continuity and preservation of the desired situation, the other presents the emotional consequences of change, the fear, anger and sadness that accompany acknowledgement of severe loss. In successful assimilation a 'dialogue' occurs between the two voices leading to an acceptance of the new information and their relatively harmonious integration into the self. However, some experiences are so traumatic and their implications so threatening to the person's sense of self that conflict arises between the voices and the material is 'warded off' (Stiles, 2001).

The role of psychotherapy is thus to overcome the block and ease the acceptance of the difficult material. This can be a long process involving repeated approaching and retreating from the threatening information. In the model this process of adaptation is represented in eight levels or stages from 'warding off' to 'unwanted thoughts', 'vague awareness', 'problem clarification', 'reaching insight', 'working through', 'problem solution' and 'mastery'. Thus in an earlier account of the application of this method in a psychotherapy group for people with dementia, one of the participants, 'Robert', moved from a position of warding off awareness that he had dementia of the Alzheimer's type to being able to joke about the changes he was experiencing (Watkins et al., 2006) (see Box 7.5). During these groups his expression of emotion had increased; but as Robert acknowledged, his initial internal fear of what was going to happen to him had been replaced by the reassuring knowledge that he was not alone.

BOX 7.5 COMING TO TERMS WITH A DIAGNOSIS OF DEMENTIA

Robert, a lawyer by previous occupation, was one of eight participants in a psychotherapy group for those with a diagnosis of dementia. In the first session he would not acknowledge his Alzheimer's diagnosis. Although by the fourth session he acknowledged that he had memory problems, he continued to deny a diagnosis of dementia and expressed signs of apprehension towards others in the group accepting it.

'There's a premise here that I just don't agree with . . . You sound as though you've accepted the fact that you've got Alzheimer's. Now I don't think anyone in this room has got Alzheimer's.'

In the following session Robert did acknowledge he had Alzheimer's but only to stress that it was a problem with his short-term memory.

'The problem with Alzheimer's as it affects me is that I have no problems with retrieving the information in the long term . . . it's quite common for me to park a car . . . and then I can't remember where I've put [it] . . . that's short-term memory.'

He became angry and he mentioned feeling frustrated. His anger appeared to be directed at members of the group whom he thought were associating Alzheimer's with a loss of intelligence.

'Even the most intelligent people . . . can still have Alzheimer's. It's got nothing to do with intelligence. It's short-term memory only.'

By the seventh session he had become more open in his acknowledgement of Alzheimer's. He asked permission to address the group.

'Can I tell you something that's happened to me in this last week. I've had a CT scan, which was quite an interesting thing in itself, but I got the results back yesterday and it said that my brain had shrunk very, very slightly in the cavity, which is fairly symptomatic of the onset of Alzheimer's. So I asked, "Well if it's the onset, what happens when you're there" [group laughs], and he said "very little more."'

The affect within the group was light-hearted. Dennis remarked, 'I mean look at us, we're all sitting here laughing, and we're all quite happy one way or the other, and yes we all have got Alzheimer's and no it's not all that bad'. In contrast to his comments in previous sessions also Robert praised other members of the group, including Julie, whom he believed had 'got to grips with the problem more than anyone else'.

Although Robert's depression had decreased, his anxiety level had risen as a consequence of acknowledging more of the problems associated with dementia. Both were to rise again as the psychotherapy group ended after ten sessions – probably too soon for Robert, who may have needed more help to come to terms with his diagnosis.

(Watkins et al., 2006)

In a recent analysis of change in participants' comments on dementia in an eight-session therapeutic group referred to earlier (Marshall et al., 2015), a range of level of expression from 'warding off' to 'problem solution' was observed (Cheston et al., 2016). The proportion of emergence markers (indicating the initial stages of assimilation) compared to later markers changed significantly between the first four sessions and the final sessions. For example, as the group discussions developed, 'Graham' came to express distressing emotion about what his future care would be like. But by their end he was able to express a measure of resolution: 'when I was told I got dementia it was as if you know the end of the world had come, where as far as I'm concerned I'm not on so many tablets, I'm probably jollier, not necessarily happy, but jollier than I've been for years'.

Persons age in very different ways and it is important to apply this same principle to those aging with the additional problems that come with dementia. Clare et al. (2005) for example distinguish between self-maintaining and self-adjusting styles of coping with dementia which they found to have remained largely constant over the course of a year: 'some explicitly confronted the extent of the changes they had noticed, and others made it clear that they preferred not to think too much about their present situation or about the future' (Clare et al., 2005, p. 513). Nevertheless, they also observed change in the course of the study they conducted. Persons in the early stages of dementia may begin with denial but over time come to use more accepting coping strategies. Therapeutic interventions may play an important role in facilitating this transition.

Individualising dementia care

The greater interest in understanding the experience of dementia has been accompanied by an increase in efforts not only to find effective medications but also to develop psychosocial interventions to enhance the quality of life of those with the condition and their carers. Many of these ideas have been adopted from practice with non-demented elders and include a variety of activities: creative art, life-story work, music therapy, animal-assisted therapy, and reminiscence groups. Unfortunately, despite many promising accounts of these forms of therapy, the evaluative studies conducted so far have not yet reached a sufficient standard of methodological sophistication to allow definitive statements on their value. By contrast the longer established forms of cognitive stimulation therapy, which use structured programmes of activities within small groups in care homes and day centres, have been more thoroughly researched and shown not only to improve scores on cognitive tests but to benefit quality of life as well. In controlled trials they have been shown to add to the benefits arising from currently available medication in persons with mild to moderate dementia (Woods et al., 2012). Also well demonstrated is the efficacy of emotional coping and support programmes for family caregivers with dementia which go beyond provision of information to provide insight and practical help in dealing with the emotionally stressful experiences associated with caregiving (Belle et al., 2006). High-quality evaluative research is a necessary component of identifying therapies which can be recommended with confidence.

An excellent example of research to test the effectiveness of individualising activities for persons with dementia in nursing homes has been published recently by Van Haitsma et al. (2015). The research is important both for its subject matter and the rigour with which the evaluation was conducted. Standardised programmes of activities in care settings, which can be applied without consideration of individual differences in interests and needs, involve less effort and are less costly of time to design. But individualised activities are clearly preferable for the person concerned. They help both show respect for and confirm individual identity. This is even more important for the person with dementia whose sense of self is threatened by declining memory abilities. Increasingly care assistants are being encouraged to take the time to understand each resident's particular needs and to 'customise' the care they provide. But how far should such individualising of dementia care go? To demonstrate the cost-effectiveness of taking the time to discover cognitively impaired residents' preferences in the activities they should be encouraged to undertake it is necessary to conduct carefully controlled comparative research.

Van Haitsma is a past colleague and member of the same Pennsylvanian research institute as the late Powell Lawton whose pioneering work on environmental design and congruence with individual needs was referred to in the previous chapter. In designing the study on individualised care Van Haitsma drew both on Lawton's model of 'person–environment fit' and two other theories, Deci and Ryan's 'self-determination theory' (Deci and Ryan, 2000), referred to earlier in this chapter, and Frederickson's 'broaden-and-build theory' (Frederickson, 2001; Frederickson and Losada, 2005). The former stresses the importance of autonomy and connectedness which are strengthened by listening to and supporting a person's preferences, as well as of competence which is reinforced by conducting known and liked activities. The latter emphasises the different roles of positive and negative emotions. The former opens up possibilities for further engagement whereas the latter tends to constrict activities.

One hundred and eighty nursing home residents with dementia were recruited from one large non-profit Jewish nursing home and divided randomly into three groups, those who were to receive the individualised interventions, those who received nursing-assistant-led standard activity sessions, and those who simply received usual care. The nursing assistants involved in the individualised intervention used an instrument to assess residents' preferences for activities (Van Haitsma, 2000), based on Logsdon and Teri's 'pleasant events schedule' for persons with dementia (Logsdon and Teri, 1997). Suitable for use with older adults as well as their family and carers it assessed a variety of types of activities, including self-care and social contact as well as personal interests. Choices were given for each type of activity. Thus physical exercise included the possibility to walk outside or work with clay; for music it could mean singing or listening to a favourite performer; for sensory stimulation it could involve a hand massage with a lotion or smelling fresh flowers.

A complex form of unobtrusive behaviour observation was instituted to record residents' observed emotion and behaviour during the three-week period in which the interventions were conducted. Participants selected for individualised activities, as well as those in the two control groups, were observed on a total of over 500 occasions for each of the three groups. The assessors coded the affect shown by the participants as well as any verbal and non-verbal behaviours during the 10-minute interventions, the 5 minutes before they began and the 5 minutes after they finished. Thirty minutes later the research assistant made a final 5-minute observation.

As predicted, the individualised preference-based intervention increased instances of positive responses: indicators of pleasure and alertness, positive touch and increased time spent on the task, as well as positive verbal comment. Those involved in more standard activities with care assistants also showed more positive responses than the control group who received usual care, but to a lesser extent than those receiving the individualised intervention. The pattern of results on negative responses however was different. Both interventions in fact produced a worsening of mood, not shown in the usual care control group. The participants in the standard activities group in particular showed more uncooperative and aggressive behaviour as well as more sadness, anger and negative verbal behaviour.

These results highlight the complexity of emotional responses in later life which were stressed earlier in the chapter (Bodner et al., 2013). Positive and negative affect become more dissociated than they were earlier in life. Negative affect appears to reflect more the older person's internal state (Wahl et al., 2012). Therefore external engagement is more likely to produce positive affect than reduce negative affect. Nevertheless, as Frederickson (2001) has argued, expression of positive emotions in itself can lead to a succession of other beneficial physiological and psychological effects, broaden and strengthen behavioural possibilities and in the long run increase resilience to adversity. The opportunity, even for a short time, to experience periods of elation is justification for the staff effort involved in inducing them. However, as the researchers themselves stress, it is important to monitor negative as well as positive effects of any intervention on the residents involved and on the total milieu of the nursing home. Policy decisions need to be made on the basis of an overall assessment. But a cautious 'no risk, no intervention' approach is clearly of no benefit to the well-being of persons with dementia. As Kitwood (1997) and later others have stressed, additional input from the social environment is needed to compensate for the incapacities mental infirmity brings with it.

The study of Van Haitsma and colleagues provides an appropriate example, on which to end this chapter, of how high-quality research can contribute to improving practice in care for older people. There are a number of other recent studies on promoting very old people's quality of life which are also well worth exploring. It is now accepted that persons with mild-to-moderate dementia are capable of reporting reliably on their well-being (Brod et al., 1999; Selai et al., 2001; Logsdon et al., 2002). Even aspects of existential well-being such as purpose in life, previously ignored in persons with dementia, have been shown to be assessable and to change positively with encouragement of goal-directed activity (Mak, 2011). Researchers have even begun considering what can be done for more severely mentally impaired persons. For example, Linda Clare (2010) has reviewed the evidence on the benefits of enhancing the expression of some aspects of awareness in people with moderate to severe dementia. The aim of both research and practice must remain focused on seeing what can be done to improve quality of life even in its last stages.

8

CONCLUDING THOUGHTS AND SUGGESTIONS FOR FURTHER READING

The study of aging is now a well-developed multidisciplinary subject with a developing theoretical basis (Bengtson and Settersten, 2016). Psychologists who choose to work in this field need to cultivate strong working links with other disciplines, especially within the biological and social sciences. The psychology of aging cannot be understood without attention to bodily aging and the social and cultural context in which it occurs. At the same time it is important that geropsychologists continue to pay attention to other specialisms within psychology. They have to keep pace with relevant developments in neuroscience, and in social as well as cognitive psychology. We particularly wish to emphasise the value of links with child psychology. As Maas pointed out more than thirty years ago, there is a curious 'childlessness' about gerontology (Maas, 1985), puzzling both because of the connections people readily make between life at both ends of the life course, and the vital importance of intergenerational, and especially grandparent–child, relationships. Of course old age is not a repeat of childhood and older people should not be treated as children, but this does not rule out there being fruitful parallels in understanding psychological development at these different stages of life.

In Chapters 4 and 6 we have pointed to attachment theory as a prime example of a theory originating in the study of childhood which has major implications for the whole of the lifespan, and not least for the experience of aging. Perhaps there are other developmental theories which could be mined in this way. But the concept of attachment in itself offers rich possibilities, and can encourage further dialogue across the lifespan. Why for example do some older people appear to accept separation and loss comparatively easily while others suffer greatly? Issues of relationship and loss are crucial to the study of aging, so attachment has to be a central concept in understanding these differences.

Readers may have observed a tension between the normative developmental theories discussed in Part I of this book and the greater emphasis on differential aging in Part II, also between those who propose general models of aging and those who argue that the experience of aging is more malleable than we currently imagine. Baltes has been one of the first psychologists to advocate the latter position:

> As was true for other age periods such as infancy and childhood, it takes a long evolutionary process and much technological investment before we will achieve the kind of differentiated culture of old age that is required to uncover the latent potential of old age and empower older persons to choose among a variety of opportunity structures.
>
> *(Baltes, 1991, p. 851)*

We respect both points of view. We greatly admire the efforts of Paul Baltes and colleagues to direct more attention to the difficulties caused by living to an advanced age, to develop a more positive attitude to correcting and compensating for the deficiencies of age. Cultural developments have lagged behind the realities of an aging population. We have to direct more of our human ingenuity to solving the problems which have multiplied as a consequence of an aging population, to develop what Baltes has referred to as the 'prosthetics' of aging. It should not be beyond the means of future technologies to greatly enhance the quality of life of very old people.

At the same time the developmental models do show respect for the positive qualities a long life may bring forth, a view which is reflected in many of the world's cultures but increasingly forgotten in modern society. Therefore we have given considerable attention to research on subjects such as wisdom, meaning and spirituality. The experience of aging raises the great existential questions of life: Why do we live? Why do we die? A gerontology which neglects these issues misses something essential from discussions of quality of life and successful aging. We therefore have kept such developmental models firmly in sight despite their current relative neglect. We have also maintained the link between the experience of aging and the concept of the midlife transition as its gateway, as developed in the writings of developmental theorists such as Carl Jung.

We have also advocated the use of multiple methodologies. Of course the developmental psychology of aging must develop as strong an expertise in quantitative research design and statistical analysis as other areas of psychology, but it must also make creative use of the range of qualitative methodologies available from ethnography to case study analysis. In our selection of particular studies to highlight in Chapters 3, 5 and 7, we have tried to give some flavour of this variation in methodological approach, and hopefully of its symbiotic character.

In writing this book, we have also tried to convey some sense of the history of gerontology. It is a relatively short history, mainly a product of the last sixty years of research, but already a history worth critical examination as well as celebration. We all stand on the achievements of those who have gone before, and it is important to be aware of previous ideas and avenues of research if only to avoid making similar mistakes. An awareness of the past helps to make us more sensitive to current fashions and trends. For example, the present interest in promoting 'productive aging' appears largely motivated by concerns about maintaining economic growth rather than by any intrinsic interest in creating the right balance of work, education and leisure throughout the lifespan. Thirty to forty years ago the pressure was in the opposite direction, towards earlier retirement and segregated services for older people. Psychologists often have little appreciation of the social policy considerations which underlie funding of their research. Psychology is a social science as well as a life science, and it must retain an important element of reflexive criticism as to the direction and purposes of its enquiries.

In composing a textbook on the developmental psychology of aging we have tried in Part III to give attention to the developmental aspects of advanced old age. Since the first edition of this textbook there has been major progress in this field, but more consideration needs to be given to appropriate research methods. New methodologies are required, a more composite approach perhaps, employing both qualitative and quantitative elements. We cannot expect very old people to happily fill in long questionnaires or undergo laboratory tests. We need to use observation more and reflect well on our observations. Individual differences continue to increase into very old age and we must seek to understand better the basis of different trajectories through later life. This requires longitudinal study, detailed case reports as well as large-scale surveys.

For those who wish to become more acquainted with developmental psychology of aging, we would recommend that they follow up particular topics that have caught their attention while reading this book, making use of the references we have provided as starting points for exploration. For reviews of particular areas of research we would recommend the *Handbook of the Psychology of Aging* which has been published at regular intervals in recent years (e.g. Birren and Schaie, 2006; Schaie and Willis, 2015) as well as more multidisciplinary and interdisciplinary texts on aging (e.g. Johnson et al., 2005), including the most recent editions of the *Handbook of Theories of Aging* (Bengtson et al., 2009; Bengtson and Settersten, 2016). The latter have the advantage of presenting the psychology of aging within its multidisciplinary context.

As regards journals, we recommend acquaintance with the two major US journals, *Psychology and Aging*, produced by the American Psychological Association, and the *Journals of Gerontology: Psychological and Social Sciences*, produced by the Gerontological Society of America. They report major scientific, predominantly quantitative, studies in the psychology of aging. But it is important not to neglect the more qualitative and multidisciplinary journals in which exploratory studies and ideas relevant to the psychology of aging are often expressed for the first time and also critiqued. These include *Ageing and Society* (a UK-based journal), the *Journal of Aging Studies*, and the *International Journal of Aging and Human Development*. Of course one should not forget the more general developmental journals. Hopefully lifespan developmental psychology will regain its earlier vigour and journals like *Human Development* and *Developmental Review* will have an important role in fostering connections across the lifespan. Last but not least we recommend

The Gerontologist, also produced by the Gerontological Society of America, as a journal which links together research and practice in service to older people. Some of the most lucid accounts of ideas and research developments in the field of aging studies are given here. Such a journal is an admirable advertisement for a science of aging which is sensitive to the dignity of human experience throughout the latter part of life.

SELECTED WEBSITES

Psychology of aging

American Psychological Association: www.apa.org
 Division 20 on aging: www.apa.org/about/division/div20.aspx
Australian Psychological Society: www.psychology.org.au
British Psychological Society: www.bps.org.uk
 Faculty for the Psychology of Older People: www.psige.org
Canadian Psychological Association: www.cpa.ca
New Zealand Psychological Society: www.psychology.org.nz
Psychological Society of Ireland: www.psihq.ie
Psychological Society of South Africa: www.psyssa.com

Gerontology

Australian Association of Gerontology: www.aag.asn.au
British Society of Gerontology: www.britishgerontology.org
Canadian Association of Gerontology: www.cagacg.ca
Gerontology Society of America: www.geron.org
International Association of Gerontology and Geriatrics: www.iagg-er.net
Irish Gerontology Society: www.irishgerontology.com
South African Gerontological Association: www.geronpta.org.za

GLOSSARY

accommodation modification of goals to suit changing circumstances

adaptation changes in behaviours or attitudes in response to challenges, constraints or losses

adjustment process by which an individual attempts to minimise losses and optimise functioning or well-being

affect/affective functioning any subjectively experienced feeling state or emotion such as anxiety, sadness or anger

aging negative stereotyping, attitudes or behaviours towards older adults due to chronological age

anxiety an emotion characterised by an unpleasant feeling of dread over anticipated events, and often accompanied by somatic complaints or nervous behaviour

assessment use of specified procedures to measure the abilities, behaviours or personal qualities of people

assimilation adaptation of goal-related behaviour in response to feedback on performance

attachment need requirement for a strong social bond with another person

attachment patterns typical responses which individuals show to a situation of loss or threat of loss of an important relationship

attitude a stable evaluative response towards a person, place, objective or idea

autonomy capacity to choose one course of action over another

case-study analysis of data collected on one individual, organisation or particular incident

cognition processes of thinking, reasoning, learning and remembering

cognitive behaviour therapy therapy based on the assumption that how events are perceived influences subsequent thoughts and feelings

cohort particular age group in the population defined by the year(s) in which members were born

conformity change of attitudes, opinions or behaviours in response to social pressures

control ability of an individual to determine outcomes of events or situations

coping managing stress-related situations, usually by attempts to change them or to minimise emotional reactions to them

correlation statistical term representing the strength and direction of the relationship between two measures

cross-cultural comparison of behaviour or attitudes of people from different cultural backgrounds

cross-sectional comparison of data between different age groups

cross-sequential comparison of data between age groups which takes into account differences in their pattern of change over time

curvilinear a path of change in an individual or group characteristic in which the middle range of scores is higher or lower than the starting or ending points

deficit a shortfall or limitation in either functioning or capacity

development change in behaviour as a result of experience and learning

developmental psychology branch of psychology examining how people change over time, as well as the predictors and consequences of those changes

developmental task development required by changes in social position or situation with age

diagnosis (psychological) label given to psychological abnormality by classifying and categorising the observed behaviour pattern into a recognised diagnostic system.

differentiation (age) increasing variability between individuals as they age

disengagement process of diminishing engagement in social roles with advancing age

distress state of affective and physiological arousal in which individuals perceive the demands of a given situation as being greater than their available resources

emotion regulation processes of changing or controlling emotional reactions likely to be elicited by outside circumstances

empathy ability to understand and share the feelings of another person

finitude awareness appreciation of limits to one's own lifespan and capacity for continued action in pursuit of goals

fourth age stage of later life beginning with the onset of physical or mental frailty

frailty state of physical or mental disability which places the person at major risk of adverse outcomes such as accident, illness or death

generativity behaviour which benefits the following generation(s)

gerotranscendence capacity to see beyond the interests of one's limited lifespan and to identify with human life as a whole

goals principal objectives towards which a person chooses to direct their behaviour

hassles continual or ongoing set of inconvenient stresses

health general condition of soundness and vigour of body and mind (not simply the absence of illness or injury)

identity a coherent sense of self which persons construct for themselves

immunisation process of avoiding acknowledging information which has painful consequences for self-understanding

integration of the self process of constructing identity

integrity acceptable self-understanding of the life one has lived

inter-generational research that compares the behaviour or attitudes of people from different generations or age groups

interiority tendency with advanced age to be more concerned with one's inner life and less with the world outside

learning a long-lasting change in behaviour or attitude that occurs as a consequence of experience

life review process of reconsidering the life one has lived in the light of growing awareness of finitude

lifespan developmental theory consideration of patterns in development from birth until death

locus of control perception whether what happens to oneself is self-determined ('intrinsic') or influenced by external factors/others ('extrinsic')

longitudinal comparison across time of data collected on an individual or group

maturation continuing influence of heredity and learning throughout development

motivation internal ('intrinsic') and external ('extrinsic') factors that influence whether an individual engages in a particular behaviour

normative that which is typical of a given population or group

nature–nurture debate concerning the relative importance of heredity (nature) and learning or experience (nurture) in determining development and behaviour

plasticity capacity of an individual to respond differently than previous patterns of behaviour would suggest is likely

population entire set of individuals to which generalisations are expected to be made

possible selves components of self-understanding which can include an ideal self (the person he/she would like to become), or a feared self (a person he/she is afraid of becoming)

prejudice pre-judgement or premature opinion based on limited information or evidence

psychoanalysis practice of studying individual behaviour in the light of unconscious processes

psychobiography study of the whole or part of an individual's life which makes use of psychological theory

psychodynamic theory psychological theory which takes account of changing sources of motivation across the lifespan

psychosocial interaction between an individual and their social environment

qualitative investigation research seeking to describe or explore subjective beliefs and ideas; typically involving small numbers so as to focus on issues in depth rather than breadth

quantitative investigation research involving formal or objective measurement of information; often involves large or very large samples to test statistical associations between different measures

reflexivity capacity to reflect critically on one's own thinking and previous conclusions which one may have drawn

reliability statistical term measuring the consistency and stability of a given scale

reminiscence thinking or talking about one's past life

resilience ability to withstand high levels of stress and life changes

representative that which is typical of a group or cohort

resources inner characteristics or outer supports which enable the individual to display resilience

sample group of individuals selected as participants in a study

selective optimisation with compensation strategy for successful aging in which one makes the most of gains while minimising the impact of losses or constraints that can accompany aging

self-efficacy set of beliefs about one's ability to perform in a particular situation

self-esteem generalised evaluation about the self that can exert a significant effect on range of physical, behavioural, psychological and social aspects of functioning

selfhood aspects of self-understanding, such as 'social self' versus 'personal self' or 'perceiving self' versus 'perceived self', which may change over the lifespan independently of one another

social comparison comparing oneself with others within a social situation or context

socio-emotional selectivity process of narrowing emotional priorities occasioned by the changing circumstances of later life

stereotype over-simplified, biased and inflexible view of a social group

structured dependency societal constraints on functioning resulting from limited opportunities provided, such as opportunities for social engagement or adequate financial support

successful aging growing older with optimal health, well-being and functioning

third age stage of life which begins after the pressures of work and other social responsibilities diminish

trajectory path followed over time by a characteristic of an individual or group

validity statistical measure of the degree to which a given scale measures what it purports to measure

well-being categories distinction between 'hedonic' and 'eudaimonic' types of well-being, the former sensation and satisfaction based, the latter meaning and purpose based

REFERENCES

Aanes, M., Hetland, J., Pallesen, S. and Mittelmark, M. 2011. Does loneliness mediate the stress–sleep quality relation? The Hordaland Health Study. *International Psychogeriatrics*. 23: 994–1002.

Abrams, D., Crisp, R., Marques, S., Fagg, E., Bedford, L. and Provias, D. 2008. Threat inoculation: experienced and imagined intergenerational contact prevents stereotype treat effects on older people's maths performance. *Psychology and Aging*. 23: 934–939.

Achenbaum, W.A. and Bengtson, V.L. 1994. Re-engaging the disengagement theory of aging: on the history and assessment of theory development in gerontology. *Gerontologist*. 34: 756–763.

Adler, A. 1927. *The practice and theory of individual psychology*. New York: Harcourt Brace World.

Adler, J., Turner, A., Brookshier, K., Monahan, C., Walder-Biesanz, I., Harmeling, L., Albaugh, M., McAdams, D.P. and Oltmanns, T. 2015. Variation in narrative identity is associated with trajectories of mental health over several years. *Journal of Personality and Social Psychology*. 108: 476–496.

Ainsworth, M.D.S. 1989. Attachments beyond infancy. *American Psychologist*. 44: 709–716.

Ainsworth, M.D.S., Bell, S.M. and Stayton, D.J. 1971. Individual differences in strange situation behaviour of one-year-olds. In H.R. Schaffer (ed), *The origins of human social relations*. London: Academic Press, 17–58.

Ainsworth, M., Blehar, M.C., Waters, E. and Wall, E. 1978. *Patterns of attachment: a psychological study of the Strange Situation*. Hillsdale, NJ: Erlbaum.

Aldwin, C.M., Sutton, K.J., Chiara, G. and Spiro, A. 1996. Age differences in stress, coping and appraisal: findings from the Normative Aging Study. *Journal of Gerontology: Psychological Sciences*. 51B: P179–488.

Alexander, B., Rubinstein, R., Goodman, M. and Luborsky, M. 1991. Generativity in cultural context: the self, death and immortality as experienced by older American women. *Ageing and Society*. 11: 417–442.

Allan, L., Johnson, J. and Emerson, S. 2014. The role of individual difference variables in ageism. *Personality and Individual Differences*. 59: 32–37.

Allen, A. and Leary, M. 2013. Self-compassionate responses to aging. *Gerontologist*. 54(2): 190–200.

Almeida, D.M. and Horn, M.C. 2004. Is daily life more stressful during middle adulthood? In O.G. Brim, C.D. Ryff and R.C. Kessler (eds), *How healthy are we? A national study of well-being at midlife.* Chicago, IL: University of Chicago Press, 425–451.

Anderson, D. and Wiscott, R. 2003. Comparing social work and nonsocial work students' attitudes about aging: implications to promote work with elders. *Journal of Gerontological Social Work.* 42: 21–36.

Andresen, E., Carter, W., Malmgren, J. and Patrick, D. 1994. Screening for depression in well older adults: evaluation of a short form of the CES-D. *American Journal of Preventive Medicine.* 10: 77–84.

Andrews, M. 1997. Life review in the context of acute social transition: the case of East Germany. *British Journal of Social Psychology.* 36: 273–290.

Andrews, P.W. and Thomson, J.A., Jr. 2009. The bright side of being blue: depression as an adaptation for analyzing complex problems. *Psychological Review.* 116: 620–654.

Antonucci, T.C. 2001. Social relations: an examination of social networks, social support and sense of control. In J.E. Birren and K.W. Schaie (eds), *Handbook of the psychology of aging,* 5th ed. New York: Academic Press, 427–453.

Antonucci, T.C., Birditt, K.S. and Akiyama, H. 2009. Convoys of social relations: an interdisciplinary approach. In V.L. Bengtson, M. Silverstein, N.M. Putney and D. Gans (eds), *Handbook of theories of aging.* 2nd ed. New York: Springer, 247–260.

Ardelt, M. 1997. Wisdom and life satisfaction in old age. *Journal of Gerontology: Psychological Sciences.* 52B: P15–27.

Ardelt, M. 2003. Empirical assessment of a three-dimensional wisdom scale. *Research on aging.* 25: 275–324.

Ardelt, M. and Edwards, C.A. 2016. Wisdom at the end of life: an analysis of mediating and moderating relations between wisdom and subjective well-being. *Journals of Gerontology, Series B: Psychological Sciences and Social Sciences.* 71: 502–513.

Atchley, R.C. 1991. The influence of aging or frailty on perceptions and expressions of the self: theoretical and methodological issues. In J.E. Birren, J.E. Lubben, J.C. Rowe and D.E. Deutchman (eds), *The concept and measurement of quality of life in the frail elderly.* New York: Academic Press, 207–225.

Atchley, R.C. 1997. Everyday mysticism: spiritual development in later adulthood. *Journal of Adult Development.* 4: 123–134.

Atchley, R.C. 1999. *Continuity and adaptation in aging: creating positive experiences.* Baltimore, MD: Johns Hopkins University Press.

Ayalon, L. 2014. Profiles of loneliness in the caregiving unit. *The Gerontologist.* 56: 201–214.

Bäckman, L. and MacDonald, S.W.S. 2006. Death and cognition: synthesis and outlook. *European Psychologist.* 11: 224–235.

Baer, B., Bhushan, A., Taleb, H., Vasquez, J. and Thomas, R. 2016. The right to health of older people. *Gerontologist.* 56(S2): S206–S217.

Baethge, A., Muller, A. and Rigotti, T. 2016. Nursing performance under high workload: a diary study on the moderating role of selection, optimization and compensation strategies. *Journal of Advanced Nursing.* 72(3): 545–557.

Bailly, N., Martinent, G., Ferrand, C., Kamel, G., Joulain, M. and Maintier, C. 2016. Tenacious goal persuit and flexible goal adjustment in older people over 5 years: a latent profile transition analysis. *Age and Ageing.* 45: 287–292.

Ball, M.M., Perkins, M.M., Hollingsworth, C., Whittington, F.J. and King, S.V. 2009. Pathways to assisted living: the influence of race and class. *Journal of Applied Gerontology.* 28: 81–108.

Ball, M.M., Perkins, M.M., Whittington, F.J., Hollingsworth, C., King, S.V. and Combs, B.L. 2005. *Communities of care: assisted living for African American elders.* Baltimore, MD: Johns Hopkins University Press.

Baltes, M.M. and Baltes, P.B. 1986. *The psychology of control and aging*. Hillsdale, NJ: Lawrence Erlbaum.

Baltes, M.M. and Carstensen, L.L. 1996. The process of successful ageing. *Ageing and Society*. 16: 397–422.

Baltes, M.M. and Carstensen, L.L. 1999. Social-psychological theories and their applications to aging: from individual to collective. In V.L. Bengtson, J.-E. Ruth and K.W. Schaie (eds), *Handbook of theories of aging*. New York: Springer, 209–226.

Baltes, M.M., Neumann, E.-V. and Zank, S. 1994. Maintenance and rehabilitation of independence in old age: an intervention program for staff. *Psychology and Aging*. 9: 179–188.

Baltes, M.M., Wahl, H.-W. and Reichert, M. 1991. Institutions and successful aging for the elderly? *Annual Review of Gerontology and Geriatrics*. 11: 311–337.

Baltes, P.B. 1987. Theoretical propositions of life-span developmental psychology: on the dynamics between growth and decline. *Developmental Psychology*. 23: 611–626.

Baltes, P.B. 1991. The many faces of human ageing: toward a psychological culture of old age. *Psychological Medicine*. 21: 837–854.

Baltes, P.B. 1997. On the incomplete architecture of human ontogeny: selection, optimization and compensation as foundation of developmental theory. *American Psychologist*. 52: 366–380.

Baltes, P.B. 2003. On the incomplete architecture of human ontogeny: selection, optimization, and compensation as foundation of developmental theory. In U.M. Staudinger and U. Lindenberger (eds), *Understanding human development: dialogues with lifespan psychology*. Boston, MA: Kluwer, 17–43.

Baltes, P.B. and Baltes, M.M. 1990. Psychological perspectives on successful aging: the model of selective optimization with compensation. In P.B. Baltes and M.M. Baltes (eds), *Successful aging: perspectives from the behavioural sciences*. Cambridge, UK: Cambridge University Press, 1–34.

Baltes, P.B., Reese, H.W. and Lipsitt, L.P. 1980. Life-span developmental psychology. *Annual Review of Psychology*. 31: 65–110.

Baltes, P.B. and Smith, J. 2003. New frontiers in the future of aging: from successful aging of the young old to the dilemmas of the fourth age. *Gerontology*. 49: 123–135.

Baltes, P.B. and Staudinger, U.M. 1993. The search for a psychology of wisdom. *Current Directions in Psychological Science*. 2: 75–80.

Baltes, P.B. and Staudinger, U.M. 2000. Wisdom: a meta-heuristic (pragmatic) to orchestrate mind and virtue towards excellence. *American Psychologist*. 55: 122–136.

Baltes, P.B., Staudinger, U.M., Maercker, A. and Smith, J. 1995. People nominated as wise: a comparative study of wisdom-related knowledge. *Psychology and Aging*. 10: 155–166.

Bandura, A. 2001. Social cognitive theory: an agentic perspective. *Annual Review of Psychology*. 52: 1–26.

Barker, M., O'Hanlon, A., McGee, H., Hickey, A. and Conroy, R. 2007. Cross-sectional validation of the Aging Perceptions Questionnaire: a multidimensional instrument for assessing self-perceptions of aging. *BMC Geriatrics*. 7: 9.

Bayley, J. 1998. *Iris: a memoir of Iris Murdoch*. London: Duckworth.

Beadle, J.N., Sheehan, A.H., Dahlben, B. and Gutchess, A.H. 2015. Aging, empathy, and prosociality. *Journals of Gerontology, Series B: Psychological Sciences and Social Sciences*. 70: 213–222.

Becker, G., Xander, C.J., Blum, H.E., Lutterbach, J., Momm, F., Gysels, M. and Higginson, I.J. 2007. Do religious or spiritual beliefs influence bereavement? A systematic review. *Palliative Medicine*. 21: 207–217.

Bédard, M., Molloy, D., Squire, L., Dubois, S., Lever, J. and O'Donnell, M. 2001. The Zarit Burden Interview: a new short version and screening version. *Gerontologist.* 41: 652–657.

Bell, D.C. and Richard, A.J. 2000. Caregiving: the forgotten element in attachment. *Psychological Inquiry.* 11: 69–83.

Belle, S.H., Burgio, L., Burns, R., Coon, D., Czaga, S.J., Gallagher-Thomson, D., Gitlin, L.N., Klinger, J., Koepke, K.M., Lee, C.C., Martindale-Adams, J., Nichols, L., Schulz, R., Stahl, S., Stevens, A., Winter, L. and Zhang, S. 2006. Enhancing the quality of life of dementia caregivers from different ethnic or racial groups. A randomized, controlled trial. *Annals of Internal Medicine.* 145: 727–738.

Bengston, V.L. 2001. Beyond the nuclear family: the increasing importance of multigenerational bonds. *Journal of Marriage and the Family.* 63: 1–16.

Bengtson, V.L., Copen, C.E., Putney, N.M. and Silverstein, M. 2009. A longitudinal study of the intergenerational transmission of religion. *International Sociology.* 24: 325–345.

Bengtson, V.L. and Settersten, R.A., Jr. (eds) 2016. *Handbook of theories of aging.* 3rd ed. New York: Springer.

Bengtson, V.L, Silverstein, M., Putney, N.P. and Harris, S.C. 2015. Does religiousness increase with age? Age changes and generational differences over 35 years. *Journal of the Scientific Study of Religion.* 52: 363–379.

Berger, P., Davie, G. and Fokas, E. 2008. *Religious America, secular Europe: a theme and variations.* Farnham, UK: Ashgate.

Biggs, S. 1999. *The mature imagination: dynamics of identity in midlife and beyond.* Bucks, UK: Oxford University Press.

Biggs, S. 2005. Psychodynamic approaches to the life-course and ageing. In M. Johnson, V.L. Bengtson, P.G. Coleman and T. Kirkwood (eds), *Cambridge handbook of age and ageing.* New York: Cambridge University Press, 149–155.

Bird, M. and Moniz-Cook, E. 2008. Challenging behaviour in dementia: a psychosocial approach to intervention. In R. Woods and L. Clare (eds), *Handbook of the clinical psychology of ageing.* Chichester, UK: Wiley, 571–594.

Birditt, J., Antonucci, T. and Tighe, L. 2012. Enacted support during stressful life events in middle and older adulthood: an examination of the interpersonal context. *Psychology and Aging.* 27(3): 728–774.

Birditt, K.S. 2014. Age differences in emotional reactions to daily negative social encounters. *Journals of Gerontology, Series B: Psychological Sciences and Social Sciences.* 69: 557–566.

Birren, J.E. and Deutchman, D.E. 1991. *Guiding autobiography groups for older adults: exploring the fabric of life.* Baltimore, MD: Johns Hopkins University Press.

Birren, J.E., Kenyon, G.M., Ruth, J.-E., Schroots, J.J.F. and Svensson, T. (eds) 1996. *Aging and biography: explorations in adult development.* New York: Springer.

Birren, J.E. and Schaie, K.W. (eds) 2006. *Handbook of the psychology of aging.* 6th ed. New York: Academic Press.

Birren, J.E. and Schroots, J.J.F. 1996. History, concepts, and theory in the psychology of aging. In J.E. Birren, K.W. Schaie, R.P. Abeles, M. Gatz and T.A. Salthouse (eds), *Handbook of the psychology of aging.* 4th ed. San Diego, CA: Academic Press, 3–23.

Birren, J.E. and Svensson, C. 2013. Reminiscence, life review, and autobiography: emergence of a new era. *International Journal of Reminiscence and Life Review.* 1: 1–16.

Black, H. and Rubinstein, R. 2009. The effect of suffering on generativity: accounts of elderly African American men. *Journal of Gerontology: Social Sciences.* 64B: 296–303.

Bluck, S. and Habermas, T. 2000. The life story schema. *Motivation and Emotion.* 24: 121–147.

Bluck, S. and Levine, L. 1998. Reminiscence as autobiographical memory: a catalyst for reminiscence theory development. *Ageing and Society.* 18: 185–208.

Bodner, E. and Bergman, Y. 2016. Loneliness and depressive symptoms among older adults: the moderating role of subjective life expectancy. *Psychiatry Research.* 237: 78–82.

Bodner, E., Palgi, Y. and Kaveh, D. 2013. Does the relationship between affect complexity and self-esteem differ in young-old and old-old participants? *Journals of Gerontology, Series B: Psychological Sciences and Social Sciences.* 68: 665–673.

Bol, T. and Kalmijn, M. 2016. Grandparents' resources and grandchildren's schooling: does grandparental involvement moderate the grandparent effect? *Social Science Research.* 55: 155–170.

Bond, J. and Rodriguez Cabrero, G. 2007. Health and dependency in later life. In J. Bond, S. Peace, F. Dittmann-Kohli and G. Westerhof (eds), *Ageing in society: European perspectives on gerontology.* London: Sage, 113–141.

Booth, L. and Kada, S. 2015. Student radiographers' attitudes towards the older patient: an intervention study. *Radiography.* 21: 160–164.

Bornat, J. (ed) 1994. *Reminiscence reviewed: perspectives, evaluations, achievements.* Buckingham, UK: Open University Press.

Boswell, S. 2012a. Predicting trainee ageism using knowledge, anxiety, compassion, and contact with older adults. *Educational Gerontology.* 38: 733–741.

Boswell, S. 2012b. "Old people are cranky": helping professional trainees' knowledge, attitudes, aging anxiety, and interest in working with older adults. *Educational Gerontology.* 38: 465–472.

Bowlby, J. 1969. *Attachment and loss. Volume 1. Attachment.* London: The Hogarth Press.

Bowlby, J. 1973. *Attachment and loss. Volume 2. Anxiety and anger.* London: The Hogarth Press.

Bowlby, J. 1980. *Attachment and loss. Volume 3. Sadness and depression.* London: The Hogarth Press.

Bowlby, J. 1986. *Attachment, life-span and old age.* Deventer, The Netherlands: Van Loghum Slaterus.

Bowlby, J. 1988. *A secure base: parent–child attachment and healthy human development.* London: Routledge.

Braam, A.W., Bramsen, I., van Tilburg, T.G., van der Ploeg, H.M. and Deeg, D.J.H. 2006. Cosmic transcendence and framework of meaning in life: patterns among older adults in the Netherlands. *Journal of Gerontology: Social Sciences.* 61B: S121–128.

Brandt, M., Deindl, C. and Hnakd, K. 2012. Tracing the origins of successful ageing: the role of childhood conditions and social inequality in explaining later life health. *Social Science & Medicine.* 74: 1418–1425.

Brandtstädter, J. 2006. Adaptive resources in later life: tenacious goal pursuit and flexible goal adjustment. In M. Csikszentmihalyi and I.S. Csikszentmihalyi (eds), *A life worth living: contributions to positive psychology.* New York: Oxford University Press, 143–164.

Brandtstädter, J. 2009. Goal pursuit and goal adjustment: self-regulation and intentional self-development in changing developmental contexts. *Advances in Life Course Research.* 14: 52–62.

Brandtstädter, J. and Greve, W. 1994. The aging self: stabilizing and protective processes. *Developmental Review.* 14: 52–80.

Brandtstädter, J. and Renner, G. 1990. Tenacious goal pursuit and flexible goal adjustment: explication and age-related analysis of assimilative and accommodative strategies of coping. *Psychology and Aging.* 5: 58–67.

Brandtstädter, J. and Rothermund, K. 1994. Self-percepts of control in middle and later adulthood: buffering losses by rescaling goals. *Psychology and Aging.* 9: 265–273.

Brandtstädter, J., Rothermund, K. and Schmitz, U. 1997. Coping resources in later life. *European Review of Applied Psychology.* 47: 107–114.

Brandtstädter, J., Rothermund, K. and Schmitz, U. 1998. Maintaining self-integrity and efficacy through adulthood and later life: the adaptive functions of assimilative persistence and accommodative flexibility. In J. Heckhausen and C. Dweck (eds), *Motivation and self-regulation across the life span*. New York: Cambridge University Press, 365–388.

Brim, O.G., Ryff, C.D. and Kessler, R.C. 2004. The MIDUS national survey: an overview. In O.G. Brim, C.D. Ryff and R.C. Kessler (eds), *How healthy are we? A national study of well-being at midlife*. Chicago, IL: University of Chicago Press, 1–36.

Brink, T.L. 1979. *Geriatric psychotherapy*. New York: Human Sciences Press.

Brod, M., Stewart, A.L., Sands, L. and Walton, P. 1999. Conceptualization and measurement of quality of life in dementia: the dementia quality of life instrument (DQoL). *Gerontologist*. 39: 25–35.

Bromley, D.B. 1986. *The case-study method in psychology and related disciplines*. Chichester, UK: Wiley.

Brooker, D. 2005. Dementia care mapping: a review of the research literature. *Gerontologist*. 45(special issue 1): 11–8.

Brothers, A., Chui, H. and Diehl, M. 2014. Measuring time future perspective across adulthood: development and evaluation of a Brief Multidimensional Questionnaire. *Gerontologist*. 54(6): 1075–1088.

Brown, C. and Lewis, M.J. 2003. Psychosocial development in the elderly: an investigation into Erikson's ninth stage. *Journal of Aging Studies*. 17: 415–426.

Brown, L., Bryan, C., Brown, V., Bei, B. and Judd, F. 2015. Self-compassion, attitudes to ageing and indicators of health and well-being among midlife women. *Aging & Mental Health*. 20(10): 1035–1043.

Browning, D.S. 1975. *Generative man: psychoanalytic perspectives*. New York: Delta.

Brown Wilson, C., Davies, S. and Nolan, M. 2009. Developing personal relationships in care homes: realising the contributions of staff, residents and family members. *Ageing and Society*. 29: 1041–1063.

Bryant, C., Bei, B., Giulson, K., Komiti, A., Jackson, H. and Judd, F. 2012. The relationship between attitudes to aging and physical and mental health in older adults. *International Psychogeriatrics*. 24: 1674–1683.

Buber, M. 1923/1937. *I and thou*. Edinburgh, UK: Clark.

Buchan, H., Sunderland, M., Carragher, N., Louie, E., Batterham, P. and Slade, T. 2015. Investigating factors that bias the reporting of depression symptomatology among older Australian adults. *American Journal of Geriatric Psychiatry*. 23(10): 1046–1055.

Buffel, T. and Phillipson, C. 2016. Can global cities be "age friendly cities"? Urban development and ageing populations. *Cities*. 55: 94–100.

Burnell, K.J., Coleman, P.G. and Hunt, N. 2011. Achieving narrative coherence following traumatic war experience: the role of social support. In G. Kenyon, E. Bohlmeijer and W.I. Randall (eds), *Storying later life: issues, investigations, and interventions in narrative gerontology*. New York: Oxford University Press, 195–212.

Burrow, J.A. 1986. *The ages of man: a study in medieval writing and thought*. Oxford, UK: Clarendon Press.

Butler, R.N. 1963. The life review: an interpretation of reminiscence in the aged. *Psychiatry*. 26: 65–76.

Butler, R.N. 1987. Ageism. In G. Maddox (ed), *The encyclopedia of aging*. New York: Springer, 22–23.

Bytheway, B. 1995. *Ageism*. Buckingham, UK: Open University Press.

Bytheway, B. 2011. *Unmasking age: the significance of age for social research*. Bristol, UK: Policy Press.

Cacioppo J., Hawkley, L. and Thisted, R. 2010. Perceived social isolation makes me sad: 5-year cross-lagged analyses of loneliness and depressive symptomatology in the Chicago health, aging and social relations study. *Psychology and Aging*. 25(2): 453–463.

Cacioppo, J., Hughes, M., Waite, L., Hawkley, C. and Thisted, A. 2006. Loneliness as a specific risk factor for depressive symptoms: cross-sectional and longitudinal analyses. *Psychology and Aging*. 21(1): 140–151.

Cappeliez, P. 2002. Cognitive-reminiscence therapy for depressed older adults in day hospital and long-term care. In J.D. Webster and B.K. Haight (eds), *Critical advances in reminiscence work: from theory to application*. New York: Springer, 300–313.

Cappeliez, P. and O'Rourke, N. 2006. Empirical validation of a comprehensive model of reminiscence and health in later life. *Journal of Gerontology: Psychological Sciences*. 61B: P237–244.

Carmel, S., Shrira, A. and Shmotkin, D. 2013. The will to live and death-related decline in life satisfaction. *Psychology and Aging*. 28: 1115–1123.

Carmichael, C., Reis, H. and Duberstein, P. 2015. In your 20s its quantity, in your 30s it's quality: the prognostic value of social activity across 30 years of adulthood. *Psychology and Aging*. 30(1): 95–105.

Carr, D., House, J., Wortman, C., Nesse, R. and Kessler, R. 2001. Psychological adjustment to sudden and anticipated spousal death among the older widowed. *Journal of Gerontology: Social Sciences*. 56B: S237–S248.

Carr, D. and Sharp, S. 2014. Do afterlife beliefs affect psychological adjustment in late-life spousal loss. *Journals of Gerontology, Series B: Psychological Sciences and Social Sciences*. 69: 103–112.

Carstensen, L.L. 1991. Selectivity theory: social activity in life-span context. *Annual Review of Gerontology and Geriatrics*. 11: 195–217.

Carstensen, L.L. 2006. The influence of a sense of time on human development. *Science*. 312: 1913–1195.

Carstensen, L.L., Fung, H. and Charles, S. 2003. Socioemotional selectivity theory and the regulation of emotion in the second half of life. *Motivation and Emotion*. 27: 103–123.

Carstensen, L.L., Isaacowitz, D.M. and Charles, S.T. 1999. Taking time seriously: a theory of socioemotional selectivity. *American Psychologist*. 54: 165–181.

Carstensen, L.L., Pasupathi, M., Mayr, U. and Nesselroade, J.R. 2000. Emotional experience in everyday life across the adult life span. *Journal of Personality and Social Psychology*. 79: 644–655.

Carstensen, L.L., Turan, B., Scheibe, S., Ram, N., Ersner-Hersfeld, H., Samanez-Larkin, G.R., Brooks, K.P. and Nesselroade, J.R. 2011. Emotional experience improves with age: evidence based on over 10 years of experience sampling. *Psychology and Aging*. 26: 21–33.

Carver, C.S. and Scheier, M.F. 1998. *On the self-regulation of behavior*. New York: Cambridge University Press.

Cesari, M., Vellas, B. and Gambassi G. 2013. The stress of aging. *Experimental Gerontology*. 48: 451–456.

Chan, T. and Bolivier, V. 2013. The grandparents effect in social mobility: evidence from British birth cohort studies. *American Sociological Review*. 78: 662–678.

Chandler, M.J. and Holliday, S. 1990. Wisdom in a post-apocalyptic age. In R.J. Sternberg (ed), *Wisdom: its nature, origins and development*. New York: Cambridge University Press, 121–140.

Charles, S.T. 2010. Strength and vulnerability integration: a model of emotional well-being across adulthood. *Psychological Bulletin*. 136: 1068–1091.

Charles, S.T. and Carstensen, L.L. 2008. Unpleasant situations elicit different emotional responses in younger and older adults. *Psychology and Aging*. 23: 495–504.

Charles, S.T. and Carstensen, L.L. 2010. Social and emotional aging. *Annual Review of Psychology*. 61: 383–409.

Charles, S.T., Reynolds, C.A. and Gatz, M. 2001. Age-related differences and change in positive and negative affect over 23 years. *Journal of Personality and Social Psychology*. 80: 136–151.

Chen, A., Kiersma, M., Yehle, K. and Plake, K. 2015. Impact of the Geriatric Medication Game® on nursing students' empathy and attitudes toward older adults. *Nurse Education Today*. 35: 38–43.

Chen, A., Plake, K., Yehle, K. and Kiersma, M. 2011. Impact of the Geriatric Medication Game on pharmacy students' attitudes toward older adults. *American Journal of Pharmacy Education*. 75(8): Article 158.

Cheng, C., Lau, H.P. and Chan, M.P. 2014. Coping flexibility and psychological adjustment to stressful life changes: a meta-analytic review. *Psychological Bulletin*. 140(6): 1582–1607.

Cheng, S.-T. 2009. Generativity in later life: perceived respect from younger generations as a determinant of goal disengagement and psychological well-being. *Journal of Gerontology: Psychological Sciences*. 64B(1): 45–54.

Cheston, R. and Bender, M. 2003. *Understanding dementia: the man with the worried eyes*. London: Jessica Kingsley.

Cheston, R. and Ivanecka, A. 2016. Individual and group psychotherapy with people diagnosed with dementia: a systematic review of the literature. *International Journal of Geriatric Psychiatry*. doi: 10.1002/gps4529.

Cheston, R., Gatting, L., Marshall, A., Spreadbury, J. and Coleman, P. 2016. Markers of assimilation of problematic experiences in dementia within the LivDem project. *Dementia*. doi: 10.1177/1471301215602473.

Chinen, A.B. 1989. *In the ever after: fairy tales and the second half of life*. Wilmette, IL: Chiron.

Clare, L. 2010. Awareness in people with severe dementia: review and integration. *Aging and Mental Health*. 14: 20–32.

Clare, L., Roth, I. and Pratt, R. 2005. Perceptions of change over time in early-stage Alzheimer's disease: implications for understanding awareness and coping style. *Dementia*. 4: 487–520.

Coats, A.H. and Blanchard-Fields, F. 2008. Emotion regulation in interpersonal problems: the role of cognitive-emotional complexity, emotion regulation goals, and expressivity. *Psychology and Aging*. 23: 39–51.

Cobb, L., Godino, J., Selvin, E., Kucharska-Newton, A., Coresh, J. and Koton, S. 2016. Spousal influence on physical activity in middle-aged and older adults: the Atherosclerosis Risk in Communities Study. *American Journal of Epidemiology*. 183: 444–451.

Cohen, G. 2005. *The mature mind: the positive power of the aging brain*. New York: Basic Books.

Cohen, S., Kamarck, T. and Mermelstein, R. 1983. A global measure of perceived stress. *Journal of Health and Social Behaviour*. 24: 385–396.

Cohen, S. and Pressman, S.D. 2006. Positive affect and health. *Current Directions in Psychological Science*. 15: 122–125.

Cole, M. and Dendukuri, N. 2003. Risk factors for depression among elderly community subjects: a systematic review and meta analyses. *American Journal of Psychiatry*. 160: 1147–1156.

Cole, T.R. 1984. Aging, meaning and well-being: musings of a cultural historian. *International Journal of Aging and Human Development*. 19: 329–336.

Cole, T.R. 1992. *The journey of life: a cultural history of aging in America*. New York: Cambridge University Press.

Cole, T.R. and Edwards, C. 2005. The 19th century. In P. Thane (ed), *A history of old age*. London: Thames & Hudson, 211–261.

Coleman, P.G. 1974. Measuring reminiscence characteristics from conversation as adaptive features of old age. *International Journal of Aging and Human Development*. 5: 281–294.

Coleman, P.G. 1986. *Ageing and reminiscence processes: social and clinical implications*. Chichester, UK: Wiley.

Coleman, P.G. 1993. Adjustment in later life. In J. Bond, P. Coleman and S. Peace (eds), *Ageing in society. An introduction to social gerontology*. 2nd ed. London: Sage, 97–132.

Coleman, P.G. 1999. Creating a life story: the task of reconciliation. *Gerontologist*. 39: 133–139.

Coleman, P.G. 2000. Aging and the satisfaction of psychological needs. *Psychological Inquiry*. 11: 291–293.

Coleman, P.G. 2002. Doing case study research in psychology. In A. Jamieson and C.R. Victor (eds), *Researching ageing and later life*. Buckingham, UK: Open University Press, 135–154.

Coleman, P.G. 2010. Religion and age. In D. Dannefer and C. Phillipson (eds), *The Sage handbook of social gerontology*. London: Sage, 164–176.

Coleman, P.G. 2011. The changing social context of belief in later life. In P.G. Coleman and colleagues, *Belief and ageing: spiritual pathways in later life*. Bristol, UK: Policy Press, 11–33.

Coleman, P.G., Aubin, A., Robinson, M., Ivani-Chalian, C. and Briggs, R. 1993. Predictors of depressive symptoms and low self-esteem in a follow-up study of elderly people over ten years. *International Journal of Geriatric Psychiatry*. 8: 343–349.

Coleman, P.G., Ivani-Chalian, C. and Robinson, M. 1999. Self and identity in advanced old age: validation of theory through longitudinal case analysis. *Journal of Personality*. 69: 819–848.

Coleman, P.G., Ivani-Chalian, C. and Robinson, M. 2004. Religious attitudes among British older people: stability and change in a 20-year longitudinal study. *Ageing and Society*. 24: 167–188.

Coleman, P.G., Ivani-Chalian, C. and Robinson, M. 2015. *Self and meaning in the lives of older people: case studies over twenty years*. Cambridge, UK: Cambridge University Press.

Coleman, P.G. and Jerrome, D. 1999. Applying theories of aging to gerontological practice through teaching and research. In V.L. Bengtson and K.W. Schaie (eds), *Handbook of theories of aging*. New York: Springer, 379–395.

Coleman, P.G., Koleva, D. and Bornat, J. (eds) 2013. *Ageing, ritual and social change: comparing the secular and religious in Eastern and Western Europe*. Farnham, UK: Ashgate.

Coleman, P.G., McKiernan, F., Mills, M.A. and Speck, P. 2007. In sure and uncertain faith: belief and coping with loss of spouse in later life. *Ageing and Society*. 27: 869–890.

Coleman, P.G. and Mills, M.A. 2001. Philosophical and spiritual perspectives. In C. Cantley (ed), *Handbook of dementia care*. Buckingham, UK: Open University Press, 62–76.

Coleman, P.G. and Podolskij, A. 2007. Identity loss and recovery in the life stories of Soviet World War II veterans. *Gerontologist*. 47: 52–60.

Collopy, B.J. 1988. Autonomy in long term care: some crucial distinctions. *Gerontologist*. 28(Suppl): 10–17.

Connelly, J. 2015. Promoting self-transcendence and well-being in community dwelling older adults: a pilot study of a psychoeducational intervention. *Geriatric Nursing*. 36: 431–437.

Connor, K.M., Davidson, J.R.T., Churchill, L.E., Sherwood, A., Foa, E. and Weisler, R. 2000. Psychometric properties of the Social Phobia Inventory (SPIN). *British Journal of Psychiatry*. 176: 379–386.

Consedine, N.S., Magai, C. and Bonanno, G.A. 2002. Moderators of the emotion inhibition–health relationship: a review and research agenda. *Review of General Psychology*. 6: 204–228.

Cook, G., Thompson, J. and Reed, J. 2015. Re-conceptualising the status of residents in a care home: older people wanting to 'live with care'. *Ageing and Society*. 35: 1587–1613.

Cooper, S.A. and Coleman, P.G. 2001. Caring for the older person: an exploration of perceptions using personal construct theory. *Age and Ageing*. 30: 399–402.

Cosco, T., Prina, A., Perales, J., Stephan, B. and Bravne, C. 2014. Operational definitions of successful aging: a systematic review. *International Psychogeriatrics*. 26: 373–381.

Coupland, J. 2004. Age in social and sociolinguistic theory. In J.F. Nussbaum and J. Coupland (eds), *Handbook of communication and aging research*. 2nd ed. Mahwah, NJ: Lawrence Erlbaum, 69–90.

Courbalay, A., Deroche, T., Prigent, E., Chalabaev, A. and Amorim, M. 2015. Big five personality traits contribute to prosocial responses to others' pain. *Personality and Individual Differences*. 78: 94–99.

Craig, L. and Jenkins, B. 2016. The composition of parents' and grandparents' child-care time: gender and generational patterns in activity, multi-tasking, and co-presence. *Ageing and Society*. 36: 785–810.

Craik, F. and Byrd, M. 1982. Aging and cognitive deficits: the role of attentional resources. In F. Craik and S. Trehub (eds), *Aging and cognitive processes*. New York: Plenum, 191–211.

Crimmins, E.M. and Beltrán-Sánchez, H. 2011. Mortality and morbidity trends: is there compression of morbidity? *Journal of Gerontology: Social Sciences*. 66B: 75–86.

Crittenden, P.M. 1995. Attachment and risk for psychopathology: the early years. *Journal of Developmental and Behavioral Pediatrics: Supplemental Issue on Developmental Delay and Psychopathology in Young Children*. 16: S12–S16.

Crittenden, P.M. 1997. The effect of early relationship experiences on relationships in adulthood. In S. Duck (ed), *Handbook of personal relationships*. 2nd ed. Chichester, UK: Wiley, 99–119.

Crittenden, P.M. 1998. Dangerous behavior and dangerous contexts: a thirty-five year perspective on research on the developmental effects of child physical abuse. In P. Trickett (ed), *Violence to children*. Washington, DC: American Psychological Association, 11–38.

Crittenden, P.M. 2015. Raising parents: attachment, representation, and treatment. 2nd ed. London: Routledge.

Crittenden, P.M. and Claussen, A.H. (eds) 2000. *The organization of attachment relationships: maturation, culture, and context*. New York: Cambridge University Press.

Crittenden, P.M., Dallos, R., Landini, A. and Kozlowska, K. 2014. *Attachment and family therapy*. London: Open University Press.

Crittenden, P.M. and Landini, A., 2011. *Assessing adult attachment: a dynamic-maturational approach to discourse analysis*. New York: W.W. Norton.

Crocker, J. and Canevello, A. 2008. Creating and undermining social support in communal relationships: the role of compassionate and self-image goals. *Journal of Personality and Social Psychology*. 95: 555–575.

Crockett, A. and Voas, D. 2006. Generations of decline: religious change in 20th century Britain. *Journal for the Scientific Study of Religion*. 45: 567–584.

Cruwys, T., Dingle, G., Haslam, C., Haslam, A., Jetten, J. and Morton, T. 2013. Social group memberships protect against future depression, alleviate depression symptoms and prevent depression relapse. *Social Science & Medicine*. 98: 179–186.

Csikszentmihalyi, M. 1990. *Flow: the psychology of optimal experience*. New York: Harper & Row.

Cumming, E. and Henry, W. 1961. *Growing old: the process of disengagement.* New York: Basic Books.

Dalby, P. 2006. Is there a process of spiritual change or development associated with ageing? A critical review of research. *Aging & Mental Health.* 10: 4–12.

Dannefer, D. and Perlmutter, M. 1990. Development as a multidimensional process: individual and social constituents. *Human Development.* 33: 108–137.

Davie, G. and Vincent, J. 1998. Religion and old age. Progress report. *Ageing and Society.* 18: 101–110.

Deek H., Hamilton S., Brown N., Inglis S.C., Digiacomo M., Newton P.J., Noureddine S., MacDonald P.S. and Davidson P.M. 2016. Family-centred approaches to healthcare interventions in chronic diseases in adults: a quantitative systematic review. *Journal of Advanced Nursing.* 72: 968–979.

DeGrezia, M. and Scrandis, D. 2015. Successful coping in urban, community-dwelling older adults with HIV. *Journal of the Association of Nurses in AIDS Care.* 26: 151–163.

De Leon, C.F.M. and Rajan, K.B. 2014. Psychosocial influences in onset and progression of late life disability. *Journals of Gerontology, Series B: Psychological Sciences and Social Sciences.* 69: 287–302.

De Medeiros, K., Rubinstein, R. and Ermoshkina, P. 2015. The role of relevancy and social suffering in 'generativity' among older post-Soviet women immigrants. *Gerontologist.* 55: 526–536.

DePasquale, N., Davis, K., Zarit, S., Moen, P., Hammer, L. and Almeida, D. 2016. Combining formal and informal caregiving roles: the psychosocial implications of double- and triple-duty care. *Journal of Gerontology, Series B: Psychological Sciences and Social Sciences.* 71(2): 201–211.

De Raedt, R., Koster, E.H.W. and Ryckewaert, R. 2013. Aging and attentional bias for death related and general threat-related information: less avoidance in older as compared with middle-aged adults. *Journals of Gerontology, Series B: Psychological Sciences and Social Sciences.* 68: 41–48.

De Vries, N.M., Staal, J.B., van Ravensberg, C.D., Hobbelen, J.S.M., Olde Rickert, M.G.M. and Nijhuis-van der Sanden, M.W.G. 2011. *Ageing Research Reviews.* 10: 104–114.

Deci, E.L. and Ryan, R.M. 2000. The 'what' and 'why' of goal pursuits: human needs and the self-determination of behaviour. *Psychological Inquiry.* 11: 227–268.

Di Castelnuovo, A., Quacquaruccio, G., Donati, M., de Gaetano, G. and Iacoviello, L. 2009. Spousal concordance for major coronary risk factors: a systematic review and meta-analysis. *American Journal of Epidemiology.* 169: 1–8.

Diener, E., Suh, E.M., Lucas, R.E. and Smith, H.E. 1999. Subjective well-being: three decades of progress. *Psychological Bulletin.* 125: 276–302.

Di Gessa, G., Glaser, K. and Tinker, A. 2016. The impact of caring for grandchildren on the health of grandparents in Europe: a life course approach. *Social Science & Medicine.* 152: 166–175.

Dikken, J., Hoogerduijn, J. and Schuurmans, M. 2015. Construct development, description and initial validation of the Knowledge about Older Patients Quiz (KOP-Q) for nurses. *Nurse Education.* 35: e54–e59.

Dillon, M. and Wink, P. 2007. *In the course of a lifetime: tracing religious belief, practice, and change.* Berkeley, CA: University of California Press.

Dittmann-Kohli, F. 1990. The construction of meaning in old age: possibilities and constraints. *Ageing and Society.* 10: 279–294.

Donnellan, M.B. and Lucas, R.E. 2008. Age differences in the Big Five across the life-span: evidence from two national samples. *Psychology and Aging.* 23: 558–566.

Drew, L. and Silverstein, M. 2007. Grandparents' psychological well-being after loss of contact with their grandchildren. *Journal of Family Psychology*. 21: 372–379.

Drew, L.A. and Smith, P.K. 1999. The impact of parental separation/divorce on grandparent–grandchild relationships. *International Journal of Aging and Human Development*. 48: 191–216.

Dunkle, R., Feld, S., Lehning, A., Kim, H., Shen, H.-W. and Kim, M.H. 2014. Does becoming an ADL spousal caregiver increase the caregiver's depressive symptoms? *Research on Aging*. 36: 655–682.

Eckert, J.K., Zimmerman, S. and Morgan, L.A. 2001. Connectedness in residential care: a qualitative perspective. In S. Zimmerman, P.D. Sloane and J.K. Eckert (eds), *Assisted living: needs, practices, and policies in residential care for the elderly*. Baltimore, MD: Johns Hopkins University Press, 292–313.

Edel, L. 1985. *Henry James: a life*. New York: Harper & Row.

Edmondson, R. 2009. Wisdom: a humanist approach to valuing older people. In R. Edmondson and H.-J. von Kondratowitz (eds), *Valuing older people: a humanist approach to ageing*. Bristol, UK: Policy Press, 201–216.

Edmondson, R. 2015. *Ageing, insight and wisdom. Meaning and practice across the lifecourse*. Bristol, UK: Policy Press.

Einolf, C.J. 2010. Does extensivity form part of the altruistic personality? An empirical test of Oliner and Oliner's theory. *Social Science Research*. 39: 142–151.

Einolf, C.J. 2014. Stability and change in generative concern: evidence from a longitudinal survey. *Journal of Research in personality*. 51: 54–61.

Eisenhandler, S. 2003. *Keeping the faith in late life*. New York: Springer.

Eli, K., Howell, K., Fisher, P. and Nowicka, P. 2016. A question of balance: explaining differences between parental and grandparental perspectives on preschoolers' feeding and physical activity. *Social Science & Medicine*. 154: 28–35.

Erikson, E.H. 1950/1963. *Childhood and society*. New York: Norton (rev. ed. 1963, Harmondsworth: Penguin).

Erikson, E.H. 1970. *Gandhi's truth: on the origins of militant nonviolence*. New York: Norton.

Erikson, E.H. 1997. *The life cycle completed: a review*. Extended ed. New York: Norton.

Erikson, E.H. and Erikson, J.M. 1998. *The life cycle completed*. Norton: New York.

Erikson, E.H., Erikson, J.M. and Kivnick, H.Q. 1986. *Vital involvement in old age: the experience of old age in our time*. New York: Norton.

European Union. 2012. *Social protection committee's pension adequacy report on pension adequacy 2010–2050: country profiles*. Brussels, Belgium: European Union.

Fauth, E.B., Gerstorf, D., Ram, N. and Malmberg, B. 2012. Changes in depressive symptoms in the context of disablement processes: role of demographic characteristics, cognitive function, health and social support. *Journals of Gerontology, Series B: Psychological Sciences and Social Sciences*. 67: 167–177.

Femia, E.E., Zarit, S.H. and Johansson, B. 2001. The disablement process in very later life: a study of the oldest-old in Sweden. *Journal of Gerontology: Psychological Sciences*. 56B: P12–23.

Ferraro, K. and Wilkinson, L. 2015. Alternative measures of self-rated health for predicting mortality among older people: is past or future orientation more important? *Gerontologist*. 55(5): 836–844.

Ferreira-Alves, J., Magalhães, P., Viola, L. and Simoes, R. 2014. Loneliness in middle and old age: demographics, perceived health, and social satisfaction as predictors. *Archives of Gerontology and Geriatrics*. 59: 613–623.

Fingerman, K.L., Miller, L.M., Birditt, K.S. and Zarit, S. 2009. Giving to the good and the needy: parental support of grown children. *Journal of Marriage and Family*. 71: 1220–1233.

Fischer, D.H. 1978. *Growing old in America*. New York: Oxford University Press.

Flett, G., Goldstein, A., Pechenkova, I., Nepona, T. and Wekerlec, C. 2016. Antecedents, correlates, and consequences of feeling like you don't matter: associations with maltreatment, loneliness, social anxiety, and the five-factor model. *Personality and Individual Differences*. 92: 52–56.

Folkman, S., Lazarus, R.S., Pimley, S. and Novacek, J. 1987. Age differences in stress and coping processes. *Psychology and Aging*. 2: 171–184.

Forbat, L. and Henderson, J. 2003. 'Stuck in the middle with you': the ethics and process of qualitative research with two people in an intimate relationship. *Qualitative Health Research*. 3: 1453–1462.

Foster, L. and Walker, A. 2015. Special issue: successful aging. *Gerontologist*. 55(1): 83–90.

Fraboni, M., Saltstone, R. and Hughes, S. 1990. The Franboni Scale of Ageism (FSA): an attempt at a more precise measure of ageism. *Canadian Journal on Aging*. 9: 56–66.

Frank, J.B. 2002. *The paradox of aging in place in assisted living*. Westport, CT: Bergin & Garvey.

Frankl, V.E. 1964. *Man's search for meaning*. London: Hodder & Stoughton.

Fredrickson, B. 2001. The role of positive emotions in positive psychology: the broaden-and-build theory of positive emotions. *American Psychologist*. 56: 218–226.

Fredrickson, B.L. and Losada, M.F. 2005. Positive affect and complex dynamics of human flourishing. *American Psychologist*. 60: 678–686.

Freeman, A., Santini, Z., Tyrovolas, S., Rummel-Kluge, C., Haro, J. and Koyanagi, A. 2016. Negative perceptions of ageing predict the onset and persistence of depression and anxiety: findings from a prospective analysis of the Irish Longitudinal Study on Ageing (TILDA). *Journal of Affective Disorders*. 199: 132–138.

Freeman, A., Santini, Z., Tyrovolas, A., Rummel-Kluge, C., Haro, J. and Koyanagi, A. 2016. Negative perceptions of ageing predict the onset and persistence of depression and anxiety: findings from a perspective analysis of the Irish Longitudinal Study on Ageing (TILDA). *Journal of Affective Disorders*. 199: 132–138.

Freeman, M. 1997. Death, narrative integrity and the radical challenge of self-understanding: a reading of Tolstoy's 'Death of Ivan Ilych'. *Ageing and Society*. 17: 373–398.

Freeman, M. 2010. *Hindsight: the promise and peril of looking backward*. New York: Oxford University Press.

Freund, A.M. and Baltes, P.B. 1998. Selection, optimization and compensation as strategies of life management: correlations with subjective indicators of successful aging. *Psychology & Aging*. 13: 531–543.

Freund, A.M. and Baltes, P.B. 1999. Selection, optimization, and compensation as strategies of life management: correction to Freund and Baltes (1998). *Psychology and Aging*. 14: 700–702.

Freund, A.M. and Baltes, P.B. 2000. The orchestration of selection, optimization, and compensation: an action-theoretical conceptualization of a theory of developmental regulation. In W.J. Perrig and A. Grob (eds), *Control of human behavior, mental processes and consciousness*. Mahwah, NJ: Erlbaum, 35–58.

Freund, A.M. and Baltes, P.B. 2002. The adaptiveness of selection, optimization, and compensation as strategies of life management: evidence from a preference study on proverbs. *Journal of Gerontology: Psychological Sciences*. 57B: 426–434.

Freund, A.M. and Blanchard-Fields, F. 2014. Age-related differences in altruism across adulthood: making personal financial gain versus contributing to the public good. *Developmental Psychology*. 50: 1125–1136.

Freund, A.M. and Smith, J. 1999. Content and function of the self-definition in old and very old age. *Journal of Gerontology: Psychological Sciences*. 54B: P55–67.

Fruhauf, C., Jarrott, S. and Allen, K. 2006. Grandchildren's perceptions of caring for grand-parents. *Journal of Family Issues*. 27: 887–911.

Fry, P.S. 2000. Religious involvement, spirituality and personal meaning for life: existential predictors of psychological wellbeing in community-residing and institutional care elders. *Aging & Mental Health*. 4: 375–387.

Fry, P.S. 2001. The unique contribution of key existential factors to the prediction of psychological well-being of older adults following spousal loss. *Gerontologist*. 41: 69–81.

Galatzer-Levy, I. and Bonanno, G. 2012. Beyond normality in the study of bereavement: heterogeneity in depression outcomes following loss in older adults. *Social Science and Medicine*. 74: 1987–1994.

Galenkamp, H., Deeg, D.J.H., Huisman, M., Hervonen, A., Braam, A.W. and Jylhä, M. 2013. Is self-rated health still sensitive for changes in disease and functioning among nonagenarians? *Journals of Gerontology, Series B: Psychological Sciences and Social Sciences*. 68: 848–858.

Gana, K., Saada, Y. and Amieva, H. 2015. Does positive affect change in old age? Results from a 22-year longitudinal study. *Psychology and Aging*. 30: 172–179.

Gatz, M. and Karel, M.J. 1993. Individual change in perceived control over 20 years. *International Journal of Behavioral Development*. 16: 305–322.

Gaugler, J.E., Anderson, K.A. and Leach, C.R. 2003. Predictors of family involvement in residential long-term care. *Journal of Gerontological Social Work*. 42: 3–26.

Gavett, B.E. and Stern, R.A. 2012. Dementia has a categorical, not dimensional, latent structure. *Psychology and Aging*. 27: 791–797.

George, L.K. 1998. Self and identity in later life: protecting and enhancing the self. *Journal of Aging and Identity*. 3: 133–152.

George, L.K., Larson, D.B., Koenig, H.G. and McCullough, M.E. 2000. Spirituality and health: what we know, what we need to know. *Journal of Social and Clinical Psychology*. 19: 102–116.

Gerstorf, D., Heckhausen, J., Ram, N. and Wagner, G. 2014. Perceived personal control buffers terminal decline in well-being. *Psychology and Aging*. 29: 612–625.

Gerstorf, D., Hoppmann, C.A., Löckenhoff, C.E., Infurna, F.J., Schupp, J. and Wagner, G.G. 2016. Terminal decline in well-being: the role of social orientation. *Psychology and Aging*. 31: 149–165.

Gerstorf, D., Hülür, G., Drewelies, J., Eibich, P., Duezel, S., Demuth, I., Ghisletta, P., Steinhagen-Thiessen, E., Wagner, G.G. and Lindenberger, U. 2015. Secular changes in late-life cognition and well-being: towards a long bright future with a short brisk ending? *Psychology and Aging*. 30: 301–310.

Gerstorf, D., Ram, N., Estabrook, R., Schupp, J., Wagner, G.G. and Lindenberger, U. 2008. Life satisfaction shows terminal decline in old age: longitudinal evidence from the German Socio-Economic Panel Study (SOEP). *Developmental Psychology*. 44: 1148–1159.

Gerstorf, D., Ram, N., Mayraz, G., Hidajat, M., Lindenberger, U., Wagner, G.G. and Schupp, J. 2010. Late-life decline in well-being across adulthood in Germany, the UK, and the US: something is seriously wrong at the end of life. *Psychology and Aging*. 25: 477–485.

Geurts, T., Poortman, A.-R., van Tilburg, T. and Dykstra, P. 2009. Contact between grandchildren and their grandparents in early adulthood. *Journal of Family Issues*. 30: 1698–1713.

Geurts, T. and van Tilburg, T. 2015. Grandparent–grandchild relationships. In James D. Wright (editor-in-chief), *International encyclopedia of the social and behavioural sciences*. 2nd ed. Vol. 10. Oxford, UK: Elsevier, 336–340.

Gignac, M.A.M., Cott, C. and Badley, E.M. 2000. Adaptation to chronic illness and disability and its relationship to perceptions of independence and dependence. *Journal of Gerontology: Psychological Sciences.* 55B: P362–372.

Gilleard, C.J. 1984. *Living with dementia.* London: Croom Helm.

Gilleard, C.J. and Higgs, P. 2011. Ageing abjection and embodiment in the fourth age. *Journal of Aging Studies.* 25: 135–142.

Goffman, E. 1961. *Asylums: essays on the social situation of mental patients and other inmates.* New York: Double Day Anchor Books.

Golden, J., Conroy, R.M., Bruce, I., Denihan, A., Greene, E., Kirby, M. and Lawlor, B.A. 2009. Loneliness, social support networks, mood and well-being in community-dwelling elderly. *International Journal of Geriatric Psychiatry.* 24: 694–700.

Grossbaum, M.F. and Bates, G.W. 2002. Correlates of psychological wellbeing at midlife: the role of generativity, agency and communion and narrative themes. *International Journal of Behavioural Development.* 26: 120–127.

Grühn, D., Sharifian N. and Chu, Q. 2015. The limits of a limited future time perspective in explaining age differences in emotional functioning. *Psychology and Aging.* 31: 583–593.

Gutmann, D. 1987. *Reclaimed powers: towards a new psychology of men and women in later life.* Basic Books, New York. (2nd ed. 1994.)

Gutmann, D. 1997. *The human elder in nature, culture and society.* Boulder, CO: Westview Press.

Haase, C.M., Shiota, M.N. and Levenson, R.W. 2012. Anger and sadness in response to an emotionally neutral film: evidence for age-specific associations with well-being. *Psychology and Aging.* 27: 305–317.

Habermas, T. and Bluck, S. 2000. Getting a life: the emergence of the life story in adolescence. *Psychological Bulletin.* 126: 748–769.

Haight, B.K. 1988. The therapeutic role of a structured life review process in homebound elderly subjects. *Journal of Gerontology.* 43: 40–44.

Haight, B.K. 1992. Long-term effects of a structured life review process. *Journal of Gerontology.* 47: 312–315.

Hamblin, K.A. 2013. *Active ageing in the European Union: policy convergence and divergence.* London: Palgrave Macmillan.

Hank, K. and Buber, I. 2009. Grandparents caring for their grandchildren: findings from the 2004 survey of health, ageing and retirement in Europe. *Journal of Family Issues.* 30: 53–73.

Harris, D. 2005. Age norms. In E. Palmore, L. Branch and D. Harris (eds), *Encyclopedia of ageism.* Binghamton, NY: Haworth Press, 14–15.

Harris, L.A. and Dollinger, S. 2001. Participation in a course on aging: knowledge, attitudes, and anxiety about aging in oneself and others. *Educational Gerontology.* 27: 657–667.

Hart, H. and McAdams, D.P. 2001. Generativity and social involvement among African American and white adults. *Journal of Research in Personality.* 35: 208–230.

Hautamäki, A. and Coleman, P.G. 2001. Explanations for low prevalence of PTSD among older Finnish war veterans: social solidarity and continued significance given to wartime sufferings. *Aging and Mental Health.* 5: 165–174.

Havighurst, R.J. 1948/1972. *Developmental tasks and education.* New York: David McKay. (3rd ed. 1972.)

Havighurst, R.J. and Albrecht, R. 1953. *Older people.* New York: Longmans.

Hayflick, L. 2000. The future of ageing. *Nature.* 408: 267–269.

Haynie, D.A., Berg, S., Johansson, B., Gatz, M. and Zarit, S.H. 2001. Symptoms of depression in the oldest old: a longitudinal study. *Journal of Gerontology: Psychological Sciences.* 56B: P111–118.

Hayward, R.D. and Krause, N. 2013. Trajectories of late-life change in God-mediated control. *Journals of Gerontology, Series B: Psychological Sciences and Social Sciences*. 68: 49–58.

Hazan, H. 1980. *The limbo people: a study of the constitution of the time universe among the aged*. London: Routledge.

Hearn, S., Saulnier, G., Strayer, J., Glenham, M., Koopman, R. and Marcia, J.E. 2012. Between integrity and despair: toward construct validation of Erikson's eighth stage. *Journal of Adult Development*. 19: 1–20.

Heckhausen, J. 1999. *Developmental regulation in adulthood: age normative and sociostructural constraints as adaptive challenges*. New York: Cambridge University Press.

Heckhausen, J. 2005. Psychological approaches to human development. In M. Johnson, V.L. Bengtson, P.G. Coleman and T. Kirkwood (eds), *Cambridge handbook of age and ageing*. New York: Cambridge University Press, 181–189.

Heckhausen, J., Dixon, R.A. and Baltes, P.B. 1989. Gains and losses in development throughout adulthood as perceived by different adult age groups. *Developmental Psychology*. 25: 109–121.

Heckhausen, J. and Schulz, R. 1995. A life-span theory of control. *Psychological Review*. 102: 284–304.

Heckhausen, J., Wrosch, C. and Fleeson, W. 2001. Developmental regulation before and after a developmental deadline: the sample case of 'biological clock' for child-bearing. *Psychology and Aging*. 16: 400–413.

Heelas, P. and Woodhead, L. 2005. *The spiritual revolution: why religion is giving way to spirituality*. Oxford, UK: Blackwell.

Heikkinnen, R.-L. 2000. Ageing in an autobiographical context. *Ageing and Society*. 20: 467–483.

Hendrix, S. and Haight, B.K. 2002. A continued review of reminiscence. In J.D. Webster and B.K. Haight (eds), *Critical advances in reminiscence work: from theory to application*. New York: Springer, 3–29.

Henry, B., Ozier A. and Johnson, A. 2011. Empathetic responses and attitudes about older adults: how experience with the aging game measures up. *Educational Gerontology*. 37(10): 924–941.

Henry, J.P. 1988. The archetypes of power and intimacy. In J.E. Birren and V.L. Bengtson (eds), *Emergent theories of aging*. New York: Springer, 269–298.

Hermans, H. and Kempen, H. 1992. The dialogical self: beyond individualism and rationalism. *American Psychologist*. 47: 23–33.

Heyslip, B., Jr., Blumenthal, H. and Garner, A. 2015. Social support and grandparent caregiver health: one-year longitudinal findings for grandparents raising their grandchildren. *Journal of Gerontology: Social Sciences*. 70: 804–812.

Higgs, P. and Gilleard, C. 2015. *Rethinking old age: theorising the fourth age*. London: Palgrave.

Hill, T.D., Angel, J.L., Ellison, C.G. and Angel, R.J. 2005. Religious attendance and mortality: an 8-year follow-up of older Mexican Americans. *Journal of Gerontology: Social Sciences*. 60B: S102–109.

Hillcoat-Nallétamby, S. 2014. The meaning of 'independence' for older people in different residential settings. *Journals of Gerontology, Series B: Psychological Sciences and Social Sciences*. 69: 102–109.

Hinds, P.S., Britton, D.R., Coleman, L., Engh, E., Humbel, T.K. et al. 2015. Creating a career legacy map to help assure meaningful work in nursing. *Nursing Outlook*. 63: 211–218.

Hilt, M. and Lipschultz, J. 1999. Revising the Kogan scale: a test of local television news producers' attitudes toward older adults. *Educational Gerontology*. 25: 143–153.

Hoare, C.H. 2002. *Erikson on development in adulthood*. New York: Oxford University Press.

Hofer, J., Holger, B., Au, A., Poláčková Šolcová, I., Tavel, P. and Wong, T.T. 2014. For the benefit of others: generativity and meaning in life in the elderly in four cultures. *Psychology and Ageing.* 29: 764–775.

Holliday, S.G. and Chandler, M.J. 1986. *Wisdom: explorations in adult competence.* Basel, Switzerland: Karger.

Howe, N. and Strauss, W. 2000. *Millenials rising: the next great generation.* New York: Basic Books.

Huang, Y., Liang, J. and Shyu Y. 2014. Ageism perceived by the elderly in Taiwan following hip fracture. *Archives of Gerontology and Geriatrics.* 58(1): 30–36.

Hughes, C., Herron, S. and Younge, J. 2014. *CBT for mild to moderate depression and anxiety.* McGraw-Hill Education: Open University Press.

Hunt, L., Marshall, M. and Rowlings, C. (eds) 1997. *Past trauma in late life: European perspectives on therapeutic work with older people.* London: Jessica Kingsley.

Hunt, N.C. 2010. *Memory, war and trauma.* Cambridge, UK: Cambridge University Press.

Hunter, E. and Rowles, G. 2005. Leaving a legacy: toward a typology. *Journal of Aging Studies.* 19: 327–347.

Hyde, M. and Jones, I.R. 2007. The long shadow of work? Does time since labour market exit affect the association between socio-economic position and health in a post-working population? *Journal of Epidemiology and Community Health.* 61: 533–539.

Idler, E.L., McLaughlin, J. and Kasl, S. 2009. Religion and the quality of life in the last year of life. *Journal of Gerontology: Social Sciences.* 64B: 528–537.

Iida, M., Stephens, M., Rock, J.K., Frank, M. and Salen, J. 2010. When the going gets tough, does the support get going? Determinants of spousal support provision to type 2 diabetic patients. *Personality and Social Psychology Bulletin.* 36: 780–791.

Infurna, F.J., Gerstorf, D., Ram, N., Schupp, J., Sprangers, M.A.G. and Wagner, G.G. 2014. Linking concurrent self-reports and retrospective proxy reports about the last year of life: a prevailing picture of life satisfaction decline. *Journals of Gerontology, Series B: Psychological Sciences and Social Sciences.* 69: 695–709.

Ingersoll-Dayton, B., Krause, N. and Morgan, D. 2002. Religious trajectories and transitions over the life course. *International Journal of Aging and Human Development.* 55: 51–70.

Irwin, M., Artin, K. and Oxman, M. 1999. Screening for depression in the older adult: criterion validity of the 10-item Center for Epidemiological Studies Depression Scale (CES-D). *Archives of Internal Medicine.* 159: 1701–1704.

James, W. 1890. *The principles of psychology.* Cambridge, MA: Harvard University Press.

Janse, M., Ranchor, A., Smink, A., Sprangers, M. and Fleer, J. 2016. People with cancer use goal adjustment strategies in the first 6 months after diagnosis and tell us how. *British Journal of Health Psychology.* 21(2): 268–284.

Jerrome, D. 1992. *Good company: an anthropological study of old people in groups.* Edinburgh, UK: Edinburgh University Press.

Jeste, D.V., Ardelt, M., Blazer, D., Kraemer, H.C., Vaillant, G. and Meeks, T.W. 2010. Expert consensus on characteristics of wisdom: a Delphi method study. *Gerontologist.* 50: 668–680.

Jiang, D., Fung, H., Sims, T., Tsai, J. and Zhang, F. 2016. Limited time perspective increases the value of calm. *Emotion.* 16(1): 52–62.

Jivraj, S., Nazroo, J., Vanhoutte, B. and Chandola, T. 2014. Aging and subjective well-being in later life. *Journals of Gerontology, Series B: Psychological Sciences and Social Sciences.* 69: 930–941.

John, D. and Lang, F. 2015. Subjective acceleration of time experience in everyday life across adulthood. *Developmental Psychology.* 12: 1824–1839.

Johnson, C.L. and Barer, B.M. 1992. Patterns of engagement and disengagement among the oldest old. *Journal of Aging Studies.* 6: 351–364.

Johnson, C.L. and Barer, B.M. 1997. *Life beyond 85 years: the aura of survivorship.* New York: Springer.

Johnson, D.R. and Whiting, W.L. 2013. Detecting subtle expressions: older adults demonstrate automatic and controlled positive reponse bias in emotional perception. *Psychology and Aging.* 28: 172–178.

Johnson, M.L., Bengtson, V.L., Coleman, P.G. and Kirkwood, T.B.L. (eds) 2005. *The Cambridge handbook of age and ageing.* New York: Cambridge University Press.

Johnson, M.L. 2009. Spirituality, finitude, and theories of the life span. In V.L. Bengtson, M. Silverstein, N.M. Putney and D. Gans (eds), *Handbook of theories of aging.* 2nd ed. New York: Springer, 659–674.

Jones, B. and McAdams, D.P. 2013. Becoming generative: socializing influences recalled in life stories in late midlife. *Journal of Adult Development.* 20: 158–172.

Jones, B.K. and McAdams, D.P. 2013. Becoming generative: socializing influences recalled in life stories in late midlife. *Journal of Adult Development.* 20: 158–172.

Jönson, H. and Magnusson, J.A. 2001. A new age of old age? Gerotranscendence and the re-enchantment of aging. *Journal of Aging Studies.* 15: 317–331.

Jordan, J. 2005. The quest for wisdom in adulthood: a psychological perspective. In R.J. Sternberg and J. Jordan (eds), *A handbook of wisdom: psychological perspectives.* New York: Cambridge University Press, 160–188.

Jung, C.G. 1938. *Psychology and religion. Volume 2.* New Haven, CT: Yale University Press.

Jung, C.G. 1972. The transcendent function. In H. Read, M. Fordham, G. Adler and W. McGuire (eds), *The structure and dynamics of the psyche. Volume 8. The collected works of C.G. Jung.* 2nd ed. London: Routledge and Kegan Paul, 139–158.

Kada, S. and Booth, L. 2016. Student radiographers' attitudes towards the older patient: six and twelve months post intervention. *Radiography.* 22: 147–151.

Kahn, R.L. and Antonucci, T.C. 1980. Convoys over the life course: attachment, roles, and social support. In P.B. Baltes and O.B. Brim (eds), *Life-span development and behavior,* Vol. 3. New York: Academic Press, 253–268.

Kato, T. 2012. Development of the coping flexibility scale: evidence for the coping flexibility hypothesis. *Journal of Counseling Psychology.* 59: 262–273.

Katz, S., Ford, A., Moskowitz, R., Jackson, B. and Jaffe, M. 1963. Studies of illness in the aged. The index of ADL: a standardized measure of biological and psychosocial function. *Journal of the American Medical Association.* 185: 914–919.

Kaufman, S.R. 1987. *The ageless self: sources of meaning in late life.* Madison, WI: University of Wisconsin Press.

Keller, B. 2002. Personal identity and social discontinuity: on memories of the 'war generation' in former West Germany. In J.D. Webster and B.K. Haight (eds), *Critical advances in reminiscence work: from theory to application.* New York: Springer, 165–179.

Kemp, C.L., Ball, M.M., Hollingsworth, C. and Perkins, M.M. 2012. Strangers and friends: residents' social careers in assisted living. *Journals of Gerontology, Series B: Psychological Sciences and Social Sciences.* 67: 491–502.

Kenyon, G., Bohlmeijer, E. and Randall, W.L. (eds) 2011. *Storying later life: issues, investigations, and interventions in narrative gerontology.* New York: Oxford University Press.

Kenyon, G.M. and Randall, W.L. 1997. *Restorying our lives: personal growth through autobiographical reflection.* Westport, CT: Praeger.

Kessler, E.-M. and Staudinger, U.M. 2007. Intergenerational potential: effects of social interaction between older adults and adolescents. *Psychology and Aging.* 22: 690–704.

Kessler, E.M. and Staudinger, U.M. 2009. Affective experience in adulthood and old age: the role of affective arousal and perceived affect regulation. *Psychology and Aging.* 24: 349–362.

Keyes, C.L. and Ryff, C.D. 1998. Generativity in adult lives: social structural contours and quality of life consequences. In D.P. McAdams and E. de St. Aubin (eds), *Generativity and adult development: how and why we care for the next generation.* Washington, DC: American Psychological Association, 227–257.

Kiely, K.M. and Butterworth, P. 2015. Validation of four measures of mental health against depression and generalized anxiety in a community based sample. *Psychiatry Research.* 225: 291–298.

Kilpi, F., Konttinen, H., Silventoinen, K. and Martikainen, P. 2015. Living arrangements as determinants of myocardial infarction incidence and survival: a prospective register study of over 300,000 Finnish men and women. *Social Science & Medicine.* 133: 93–100.

Kim, K., Bangerter, L., Liu, Y., Polenick, C., Zarit, S. and Fingerma, K. 2016. Middle-aged offspring's support to aging parents with emerging disability. *The Gerontologist.* doi: 10.1093/geront/gnv686.

Kim, Y., Lucette, A. and Loscalzo, M. 2013. Bereavement needs of adults, children and families after cancer. *Cancer Journal.* 19(5): 444–457.

King, M., Speck, P. and Thomas, A. 1999. The effect of spiritual beliefs on outcome from illness. *Social Science & Medicine.* 48: 1291–1299.

Kirby, S.E., Coleman, P.G. and Daley, D. 2004. Spirituality and well-being in frail and non-frail older adults. *Journal of Gerontology: Psychological Sciences.* 59B: P123–129.

Kirkpatrick, L.A. 2005. *Attachment, evolution and the psychology of religion.* New York: Guilford Press.

Kitwood, T. 1988. The contribution of psychology to the understanding of senile dementia. In B. Gearing, M. Johnson and T. Heller (eds), *Mental health problems in old age: a reader.* Chichester, UK: Wiley, 123–130.

Kitwood, T. 1997. *Dementia reconsidered: the person comes first.* Buckingham, UK: Open University Press.

Kitwood, T. and Bredin, K. 1992. Towards a theory of dementia care: personhood and well-being. *Ageing and Society.* 12: 269–287.

Kivnick, H.Q. 1991. *Living with care, caring for life: the inventory of life strengths.* Minneapolis, MN: University of Minnesota.

Klass, D., Silverman, P. and Nickman, S. (eds) 1996. *Continuing bonds: new understandings of grief.* New York: Routledge.

Kleemeier, R.W. 1962. Intellectual changes in the senium. *Proceedings of the Social Statistics section of the American Statistical Association.* 1: 290–295.

Knight, C., Haslam, S.A. and Haslam, C. 2010. In home or at home? How collective decision making in a new care facility enhances social interaction and wellbeing amongst older adults. *Ageing and Society.* 30: 1393–1418.

Knight, S.J. and Emanuel, L. 2007. Processes of adjustment to end-of-life losses: a reintegration model. *Journal of Palliative Medicine.* 10: 1190–1198.

Koenig, H., King, D. and Carson, V. 2012. *Handbook of religion and health.* 2nd ed. New York: Oxford University Press.

Kogan, N. 1961. Attitudes toward old people: the development of a scale and an examination of correlates. *Journal of Abnormal and Social Psychology.* 62(1): 44–54.

Kohlberg, L., Levine, C. and Hewer, A. 1983. *Moral stages: a current formulation and a response to critics.* Basel, Switzerland: Karger.

Kotre, J. 1984/1996. *Outliving the self: generativity and the interpretation of lives.* Baltimore, MA: Johns Hopkins University Press (1996, New York: Norton).

Korte, J., Bohlmeijer, E.T., Westerhof, G.J. and Pot, A.M. 2011. Reminiscence and adaptation to critical life events in older adults with mild to moderate depressive symptoms. *Aging and Mental Health.* 15: 638–646.

Korte, J., Westerhof, G.J. and Bohlmeijer, E.T. 2012. Mediating processes in an effective life-review intervention. *Psychology and Aging*. 27: 1172–1181.

Kotter-Grühn, D., Kleinspehn-Ammerlahn, A., Gerstorf, D. and Smith, J. 2009. Self-perceptions of aging predict mortality and change with approaching death: 16-year longitudinal results from the Berlin Aging Study. *Psychology and Aging*. 24(3): 654–667.

Koukouli, S., Pattakou-Parasyri, V. and Kalaitzaki, A. 2014. Self-reported aging anxiety in Greek students, health care professionals, and community residents: a comparative study. *The Gerontologist*. 54(2): 201–210.

Kramer, D.A. 2000. Wisdom as a classical source of human strength: conceptualization and empirical inquiry. *Journal of Social and Clinical Psychology*. 19: 83–101.

Kranz, D., Bollinger, A. and Nilges, P. 2010. Chronic pain acceptance and affective well-being: a coping perspective. *European Journal of Pain*. 14: 1021–1025.

Krause, N. 1995a. Assessing stress-buffering effects: a cautionary note. *Psychology and Aging*. 10: 518–526.

Krause, N. 1995b. Religiosity and self-esteem among older adults. *Journal of Gerontology: Psychological Sciences*. 50B: P236–246.

Krause, N. 2009. Meaning in life and mortality. *Journal of Gerontology: Social Sciences*. 64B: 517–527.

Krause, N., Ellison, C.G., Shaw, B.A., Marcum, J.P. and Boardman, J.D. 2001. Church-based social support and religious coping. *Journal for the Scientific Study of Religion*. 40: 637–656.

Kruse A. 1989. Coping with chronic disease, dying, and death: a contribution to competence in old age. *Comprehensive Gerontology*. 1: 1–11.

Kruse, A. and Schmitt, E. 2000. *Wir haben uns als Deutsche gefühlt: lebensrückblick und lebenssituation jüdischer emigranten und lagerhäftlinge*. Darmstadt, Germany: Steinkopf Verlag.

Kunzmann, U. 2007. Wisdom: adult developmental and emotional-motivational dynamics. In R. Fernández-Ballesteros (ed), *Geropsychology: European perspectives for an aging world*. Hogrefe & Huber: Göttingen, 224–238.

Kunzmann, U., Little, T. and Smith J. 2000. Is age-related stability of subjective well-being a paradox? Cross-sectional and longitudinal evidence from the Berlin Aging Study. *Psychology and Aging*. 3: 511–526.

Kunzmann, U. and Thomas, S. 2014. Multidirectional age differences in anger and sadness. *Psychology and Aging*. 29: 16–27.

Kurina, L., Knutson, K., Hawkley, L., Cacioppo, J., Lauderdale, S. and Ober, C. 2011. Loneliness is associated with sleep fragmentation in a communal society. *Sleep*. 34: 1519–1526.

Labouvie-Vief, G. 2003. Dynamic integration: affect, cognition, and the self in adulthood. *Current Directions in Psychological Science*. 12: 201–206.

Labouvie-Vief, G. 2005. The psychology of emotions and aging. In M. Johnson, V.L., Bengtson, P.G. Coleman and T. Kirkwood (eds), *Cambridge handbook of age and ageing*. New York: Cambridge University Press, 229–236.

Labouvie-Vief, G. 2009. Dynamic integration theory: emotion, cognition, and equilibrium in later life. In V.L. Bengtson, M. Silverstein, N.M. Putney and D. Gans (eds), *Handbook of theories of aging*. 2nd ed. New York: Springer, 277–293.

Lachman, M.E. 2004. Development in midlife. *Annual Review of Psychology*. 55: 305–331.

Lagacé, M., Tanguay, A., Lavallée, M.-L. and Robichaud, S. 2012. The silent impact of ageist communication in long-term care facilities: elders' perspectives on quality of life and coping strategies. *Journal of Aging Studies*. 26(3): 335–342.

Laidlaw, K. and Kishita, N. 2015. Age-appropriate augmented cognitive behavior therapy to enhance treatment outcome for late-life depression and anxiety disorders. *GeroPsych*. 28(2): 57–66.

Laidlaw, K., Power, M.J. and Schmidt, S. 2007. The attitudes to ageing questionnaire (AAQ): development and psychometric properties. *International Journal of Geriatric Psychiatry*. 22(4): 367–379.

Lamers, S.M.A., Bohlmeijer, E.T., Korte, J. and Westerhof, G.J. 2015. The efficacy of life-review as online-guided self-help for adults: a randomized trial. *Journals of Gerontology, Series B: Psychological Sciences and Social Sciences*. 70: 24–34.

Landes, S.D., Ardelt, M., Vaillant, G.E. and Waldinger, R. 2014. Childhood adversity, midlife generativity and later life well-being. *Journals of Gerontology, Series B: Psychological Sciences and Social Sciences*. 69: 942–952.

Lang, F.R. and Carstensen, L.L. 1994. Close emotional relationships in late life: further support for proactive aging in the social domain. *Psychology and Aging*. 9: 315–324.

Langer, E.J. 1983. *The psychology of control*. Beverly Hills, CA: Sage.

Langer, E.J. 1989. Minding matters: the consequences of mindlessness–mindfulness. *Advances in experimental social psychology*. 22: 137–173.

Langlois, F., Vu, T.T.M., Chassé, K., Dupuis, G., Kergoat, M.-J. and Bherer, L. 2012. Benefits of physical exercise training on cognition and quality of life in frail older adults. *Journals of Gerontology, Series B: Psychological Sciences and Social Sciences*. 68: 400–404.

Lasher, K.P. and Faulkender, P.J. 1993. Measurement of aging anxiety: development of the Anxiety about Aging Scale. *International Journal of Aging and Human Development*. 37: 247–259.

Laslett, P. 1989. *A fresh map of life: the emergence of the third age*. London: Weidenfeld & Nicolson.

Lawton, M.P. 1980. *Environment and aging*. Belmont, CA: Brooks-Cole.

Lazarus, R.S. 1966. *Psychological stress and the coping process*. New York: McGraw-Hill.

Lazarus, R.S. 1999. *Stress and emotion: a new synthesis*. New York: Springer.

Lazarus, R.S. and DeLongis, A. 1983. Psychological stress and coping in aging. *American Psychologist*. 38: 245–254.

Lazarus, R.S. and Folkman, S. 1984. *Stress, appraisal and coping*. New York: Springer.

Lazarus, R.S. and Lazarus, B.N. 2006. *Coping with aging*. New York: Oxford University Press.

Lee, G., DeMaris, A., Bavin, S. and Sullivan, R. 2001. Gender differences in the depressive effect of widowhood in later life. *Journals of Gerontology: Series B: Psychological Sciences and Social Sciences*. 56: S56–S61.

Levinson, D.J. 1996. *The seasons of a woman's life*. New York: Ballantine Books.

Levinson, D.J., Darrow, D.N., Klein, E.B., Levinson, M.H. and McKee, B. 1978. *The seasons of a man's life*. New York: Knopf.

Levy, B.R. 2009. Stereotype embodiment: a psychosocial approach to aging. *Current Directions in Psychological Science*. 18: 332–336.

Levy, B.R., Ferrucci, L., Zonderman, A.B., Slade, M.D., Troncoso, J. and Resnick, S.M. 2016. A culture–brain link: negative age stereotypes predict Alzheimer's disease bio-markers. *Psychology and Aging*. 31: 82–88.

Levy, B.R., Pilver, C., Chung, P.H. and Slade, M.D. 2014. Subliminal strengthening: improving older individuals' physical function over time with an implicit-age-stereotype intervention. *Psychological Science*. 25: 2127–2135.

Levy, B.R., Slade, M., Kunkel, S. and Kasl, S. 2002a. Longevity increased by positive self-perceptions of aging. *Journal of Personality and Social Psychology*. 83: 261–270.

Levy, B.R., Slade, M.D. and Kasl, S.V. 2002b. Longitudinal benefit of positive self-perceptions of aging on functioning health. *Journal of Gerontology: Psychological Sciences*. 57: 409–417.

Li, T. and Fung, H.H. 2013. Age differences in trust: an investigation across 38 countries. *Journals of Gerontology, Series B: Psychological Sciences and Social Sciences*. 68: 347–355.

Liddle, J., Parkinson, L. and Sibbritt, D. 2013. Purpose and pleasure in late life: conceptualising older women's participation in art and craft activities. *Journal of Aging Studies.* 27: 330–338.

Lieberman, M.A. and Tobin, S.S. 1983. *The experience of old age: stress, coping and survival.* New York: Basic Books.

Lim, L. and Kua, E. 2011. Living alone, loneliness and psychological well-being of older persons in Singapore. *Current Gerontology and Geriatrics Research.* 1–9.

Logsdon, R., Gibbons, L., McCurry, S. and Teri, L. 2002. Assessing quality of life in older adults with cognitive impairment. *Psychosomatic Medicine.* 64: 510–519.

Logsdon, R., Pike, K.C., McCurry, S.M., Hunter, P., Maher, J., Snyder, L. and Teri, L. 2010. Early-stage memory loss support groups: outcomes from a randomized controlled clinical trial. *Journal of Gerontology: Psychological Sciences.* 65B: 691–697.

Logsdon, R. and Teri, L. 1997. The pleasant events schedule-AD: psychometric properties and relationship to depression and cognition in Alzheimer's disease patients. *Gerontologist.* 37: 40–45.

Long, M.V. and Martin, P. 2000. Personality, relationship closeness, and loneliness of oldest old adults and their children. *Journal of Gerontology: Psychological Sciences.* 55B: P311–319.

Luong, G., Charles, A., Rook, K., Reynolds, C. and Gatz, M. 2015. Age differences and longitudinal change in the effects of data collection mode on self-reports of psychosocial functioning. *Psychology and Aging.* 30: 106–119.

Lynch, G. 2007. *The new spirituality: an introduction to progressive belief in the twenty-first century.* London: I.B. Tauris.

Lyons, J., Cauley, J. and Fredman, L. 2015. The effect of transitions in caregiving status and intensity on perceived stress among 992 female caregivers and noncaregivers. *Journals of Gerontology: Medical Sciences.* 1018–1023.

Lyyra, T., Lyyra, A., Lumme-Sandt, K., Tiikkainen, P. and Heikkinen, R. 2010. Social relations in older adults: secular trends and longitudinal changes over a 16-year follow-up. *Archives of Gerontology and Geriatrics.* 51: e133–138.

Maas, H.S. 1985. The development of adult development: recollections and reflections. In J.M.A. Munnichs, P. Mussen, E. Olbrich and P.G. Coleman (eds), *Life-span and change in a gerontological perspective.* Orlando, FL: Academic Press, 161–175.

Maddox, G.L. 1987. Aging differently. *Gerontologist.* 27: 557–564.

Magai, C. and Cohen, C.I. 1998. Attachment style and emotion regulation in dementia patients and their relation to caregiver burden. *Journal of Gerontology: Psychological Sciences.* 53B: P147–154.

Main, M., Kaplan, N. and Cassidy, J. 1985. Security in infancy, childhood, and adulthood: a move to the level of representation. In I. Bretherton and E. Waters (eds), *Growing points in attachment theory and research. Monographs of the Society for Research in Child Development.* 50: 66–106.

Mak, W. 2011. Self-reported goal pursuit and purpose in life among people with dementia. *Journal of Gerontology: Psychological Sciences.* 66B: 177–184.

Marcoen, A. 1993. The search for meaning: some reflections from a psycho-gerontological perspective. *Ultimate Reality and Meaning – Interdisciplinary Studies in the Philosophy of Understanding.* 16: 228–240.

Marcoen, A. 2005. Religion, spirituality and older people. In M. Johnson, V.L. Bengtson, P.G. Coleman and T. Kirkwood (eds), *Cambridge handbook of age and ageing.* New York: Cambridge University Press, 363–370.

Markus, H. and Nurius, P. 1986. Possible selves. *American Psychologist.* 41: 954–969.

Markus, H. and Wurf, E. 1987. The dynamic self-concept: a social psychological perspective. *Annual Review of Psychology.* 38: 299–337.

Marshall, J., Robinson, O. and Thompson, T. 2015. Happiness and age in European adults: the moderating role of gross domestic product per capita. *Psychology and Aging*. 30: 544–551.

Marshall, A., Spreadbury, J., Cheston, R., Coleman, P., Ballinger, C., Mullee, M., Pritchard, J., Russell, C. and Bartlett, E. 2015. A pilot randomised controlled trial to compare changes in quality of life for participants with early diagnosis dementia who attend a 'Living Well with Dementia' group compared to waiting-list control. *Aging and Mental Health*. 19: 526–535.

Marsiske, M., Lang, F.R., Baltes, M.M. and Baltes, P.B. 1995. Selective optimization with compensation: life-span perspectives on successful human development. In R.A. Dixon and L. Bäckman (eds), *Compensation for psychological defects and declines: managing losses and promoting gains*. Hillsdale, NJ: Erlbaum, 35–79.

Martin, P., Rott, C., Hagberg, B. and Morgan, K. (eds) 2000. *Centenarians: autonomy versus dependence in the oldest old*. New York: Springer.

Mather, M. 2012. The emotion paradox in the aging brain. *Annals of the New York Academy of Sciences*. 1251: 33–49.

Mather, M. and Carstensen, L.L. 2005. Aging and motivated cognition: the positivity effect in attention and memory. *Trends in Cognitive Science*. 9: 496–502.

Mausbach, B.T., Chattillion, E., Ho, J., Flynn, L., Tiznado, D., von Känel, R., Patterson, T. and Grant, I. 2014. Why does placement of persons with Alzheimer's disease into long-term care improve caregivers' well-being? Examination of psychological meditators. *Psychology and Aging*. 29: 776–786.

Mausbach, B.T., Chattillion, E., Moore, R., Roepke, S., Depp, C. and Roesch, S. 2011. Activity restriction and depression in medical patients and their caregivers: a meta-analysis. *Clinical Psychology Review*. 31: 900–908.

McAdams, D.P. 2006. The redemptive self: generativity and the stories Americans live by. *Research in human development*. 3: 81–100.

McAdams, D.P. and de St. Aubin, E. 1992. A theory of generativity and its assessment through self-report, behavioral acts, and narrative themes in autobiography. *Journal of Personality and Social Psychology*. 62: 1003–1015.

McAdams, D.P., de St. Aubin, E. and Logan, R. 1993. Generativity among young, midlife and older adults. *Psychology and Aging*. 8: 221–230.

McAdams, D.P. and Guo, J. 2015. Narrating the generative life. *Psychological Science*. 26: 475–483.

McAdams, D.P., Hart, H. and Maruna, S. 1998. The anatomy of generativity. In D.P. McAdams and E. de St. Aubin (eds), *Generativity and adult development: how and why we care for the next generation*. Washington, DC: American Psychological Association, 7–43.

McCarthy, V.L., Ling, J., Bowland, S., Hall, L.A. and Connelly, J. 2015. Promoting self-transcendence and well-being in community dwelling older adults: a pilot study of a psychoeducational intervention. *Geriatric Nursing*. 36: 431–437.

McCullough, M., Enders, C., Brion, S. and Jain, A. 2005. The varieties of religious development in adulthood. *Journal of Personality and Social Psychology*. 89: 78–89.

McFadden, S.H. 1996a. Religion and spirituality. In J.E. Birren (ed), *Encyclopedia of gerontology. Volume 2*. San Diego, CA: Academic Press, 387–397.

McFadden, S.H. 1996b. Religion, spirituality and aging. In J.E. Birren and K.W. Schaie (eds), *Handbook of the psychology of aging*. 4th ed. San Diego, CA: Academic Press, 162–177.

McFadden, S.H. and Levin, J.S. 1996. Religion, emotions and health. In C. Magai and S.H. McFadden (eds), *Handbook of emotion, adult development, and aging*. San Diego, CA: Academic Press, 349–365.

McGuire, S., Klein, D. and Chen, S.-L. 2008. Ageism revisited: a study measuring ageism in East Tennessee, USA. *Nursing and Health Sciences*. 10: 11–16.

McMahon, A.W. and Rhudick, P.J. 1967. Reminiscing: adaptational significance in the aged. In S. Levin and R.J. Kahana (eds), *Psychodynamic studies on aging: creativity, reminiscence and dying.* New York: International Universities Press, 64–78.

Mehta, K.K. 1997. The impact of religious beliefs and practices on aging: a cross-cultural comparison. *Journal of Aging Studies.* 11: 101–114.

Merriam, S.B. 1993. Race, sex and age-group differences in the occurrences and uses of reminiscence. *Activities, Adaptation and Aging.* 18: 1–18.

Miesen, B.M. 1992. Attachment theory and dementia. In G.M. Jones and B.M. Miesen (eds), *Care-giving in dementia: research and applications.* London: Tavistock, 38–56.

Miesen, B.M. 1998. *Dementia in close-up.* London: Routledge.

Miller, L.R. 2016. *Definition of family: the Wiley-Blackwell encyclopedia of family studies.* Chichester, UK: Wiley-Blackwell.

Minois, G. 1989. *History of old age from antiquity to the renaissance.* Chicago, IL: University of Chicago Press (reissued by Polity Press, Cambridge).

Mitchell, J.M. and Kemp, B.J. 2000. Quality of life in assisted living homes: a multidimensional analysis. *Journal of Gerontology: Psychological Sciences.* 55B: P117–127.

Moberg, D.O. 2001. Research on spirituality. In D.O. Moberg (ed), *Aging and spirituality: spiritual dimensions of aging theory, research, practice, and policy.* New York: The Haworth Press, 55–69.

Moberg, D.O. 2005. Research in spirituality, religion, and aging. *Journal of Gerontological Social Work.* 45: 11–40.

Modin, B., Erikson, R. and Vagero, D. 2013. Intergenerational continuity in school performance: do grandparents matter? *European Sociological Review.* 29: 858–870.

Molloy, G., Stamatakis, E., Randall, G. and Hamer, M. 2009. Marital status, gender and cardiovascular mortality: behavioral, psychological distress and metabolic explanations. *Social Science & Medicine.* 69: 223–228.

Monin, J., Schulz, R. and Feeney, B. 2015. Compassionate love in individuals with Alzheimer's disease and their spousal caregivers: associations with caregivers' psychological health. *Gerontologist.* 55(6): 981–989.

Moore, R., Martin, A., Kaup, A., Thompson, W., Peters, M., Jeste, D., Golshan, S. and Eyler, L. 2015. From suffering to caring: a model of differences among adults in levels of compassion. *International Journal of Geriatric Psychiatry.* 30: 185–191.

Moorman, S. and Stokes, J. 2016. Solidarity in the grandparent–adult grandchild relationship and trajectories of depressive symptoms. *Gerontologist.* 56: 408–420.

Morgan, J., Robinson, O. and Thompson, T. 2015. Happiness and age in European adults: the moderating role of gross domestic product per capita. *Psychology and Aging.* 30: 544–551.

Morrow-Howell, N. 2010. Volunteering in later life: research frontiers. *Journal of Gerontology: Social Sciences.* 65B: 461–469.

Müller, A., Heiden, B., Herbig, B., Poppe, F. and Angerer, P. 2016. Improving well-being at work: a randomized controlled intervention based on selection, optimization, and compensation. *Journal of Occupational Health Psychology.* 21: 169–181.

Müller, A., Weigl, M., Heiden, B., Herbig, B., Glaser, J. and Angerer, P. 2013. Selection, optimization, and compensation in nursing: exploration of job-specific strategies, scale development, and age-specific associations to work ability. *Journal of Advanced Nursing.* 69(7): 1630–1642.

Munnichs, J.M.A. 1964. Loneliness, isolation and social relations in old age: a pilot survey. *Vita Humana.* 7: 228–238.

Munnichs, J.M.A. 1966. *Old age and finitude: a contribution to psychogerontology.* Basel: Karger.

Munnichs, J.M.A. 1992. Ageing: a kind of autobiography. *European Journal of Gerontology.* 1: 244–250.

Muniz-Terrera, G., van den Hout, A., Piccinin, A.M., Matthews, F.E. and Hofer, S.M. 2013. Investigating terminal decline: results from a UK population-based study of aging. *Psychology and Aging.* 28: 377–385.

Murray, H.A. 1938. *Explorations in personality.* New York: Oxford University Press.

Murray, H.A. 1943. *The Thematic Apperception Test: manual.* Cambridge, MA: Harvard University Press.

Neff, K.D. 2003. The development and validation of a scale to measure self-compassion. *Self and Identity.* 2: 223–225.

Neijmeyer, R.A. and Werth, J.L. 2005. The psychology of death. In M. Johnson, V.L. Bengtson, P.G. Coleman and T. Kirkwood (eds), *Cambridge handbook of age and ageing.* New York: Cambridge University Press, 387–393.

Neubauer, A.B., Schilling, O.K. and Wahl, H.-W. 2016. What do we need at the end of life? Competence, but not autonomy, predicts intraindividual fluctuations in subjective well-being in very old age. *Journals of Gerontology, Series B: Psychological Sciences and Social Sciences.* doi: 10.1093/geron/gbv052.

Neugarten, B.L. 1968. Adult personality: toward a psychology of the life cycle. In B.L. Neugarten (ed), *Middle age and aging: a reader in social psychology.* Chicago, IL: University of Chicago Press, 137–147.

Neugarten, B.L. and Associates 1964. *Personality in middle and late life.* New York: Atherton Press.

Neugarten, B.L. and Neugarten, D.A. 1987. The changing meanings of age in the aging society. In A. Pifer and L. Bronte (eds), *Our aging society: paradox and promise.* New York: Norton, 33–51.

Neugarten, B.L. and Weinstein, K. 1964. The changing American grandparent. *Journal of Marriage and the Family.* 26: 41–47.

Newberry, G., Martin, C. and Robbins, L. 2015. How do people with learning disabilities experience and make sense of the ageing process? *British Journal of Learning Disabilities.* 43: 285–292.

Niederhoffer, K.G. and Pennebaker, J.W. 2002. Sharing one's story: on the benefits of writing or talking about emotional experience. In C.R. Snyder and S.J. Lopez (eds), *Handbook of positive psychology.* New York: Oxford University Press, 573–583.

Nielsen, L., Knutson, B. and Carstensen, L.L. 2008. Affect dynamics, affective forecasting, and aging. *Emotion.* 8: 318–330.

Nielsen, M.K., Neergaard, M., Jensen, A., Bro, F. and Guldin, M.-B. 2016. Do we need to change our understanding of anticipatory grief in caregivers? A systematic review of caregiver studies during end-of-life caregiving and bereavement. *Clinical Psychology Review.* 44: 75–93.

Nomura, T. 2013. The power of reminiscence groups to overcome the disaster of tsunami. *International Journal of Reminiscence and Life Review.* 1: 39–41.

Norlyk, A., Haahr, A. and Hall, E. 2016. Interviewing with or without the partner present? – an underexposed dilemma between ethics and methodology in nursing research. *Journal of Advanced Nursing.* 72: 936–945.

North, M. and Fiske, S. 2012a. Modern attitudes toward older adults in the aging world: a cross-cultural meta-analysis. *Psychological Bulletin.* 141(5): 993–1021.

North, M. and Fiske, S. 2012b. An inconvenienced youth? Ageism and its potential inter-generational roots. *Psychological Bulletin.* 138: 982–997.

Norton, M.C., Singh, A., Skoog, I., Corcoran, C., Tschanz, J.T., Zandi, P.P., Breitner, J.C.S., Welsh-Bohmer, K.A. and Steffens, D.C. 2008. Church attendance and new episodes of major depression in a community study of older adults: the Cache County Study. *Journal of Gerontology: Psychological Sciences.* 63B: P129–137.

Nybo, H., Gaist, D., Jeune, B., McGue, M., Vaupel, J.W. and Christensen, K. 2001. Functional status and self-rated health in 2,262 nonagenarians: the Danish 1905 Cohort Study. *Journal of the American Geriatrics Society*. 49: 601–609.

Nybo, H., Petersen, H.C., Gaist, D., Jeune, B., Andersen, K., McGue, M., Vaupel, V.W. and Christensen, K. 2003. Predictors of mortality in 2,249 nonagenarians: the Danish 1905 Cohort Study. *Journal of the American Geriatrics Society*. 51: 1365–1373.

Oatley, K. and Jenkins, J.M. 1996. *Understanding emotions*. Oxford, UK: Blackwell.

O'Brien, E., Konrath, S.H., Grühn, D. and Hagen, A.L. 2013. Empathic concern and perspective taking: linear and quadratic effects of age across the adult life span. *Journals of Gerontology, Series B: Psychological Sciences and Social Sciences*. 68: 168–175.

Ochse, R. and Plug, C. 1986. Cross-cultural investigation of the validity of Erikson's theory of personality development. *Journal of Personality and Social Psychology*. 50(6): 1240–1252.

O'Connor, B.P. and Rigby, H. 1996. Perceptions of baby talk, frequency of receiving baby talk, and self-esteem among community and nursing home residents. *Psychology and Aging*. 11: 147–154.

O'Connor, B.P. and Vallerand, R.J. 1994. Motivation, self-determination, and person–environment fit as predictors of psychological adjustment among nursing home residents. *Psychology and Aging*. 9: 189–194.

O'Connor, T.G. and Croft, C.M. 2001. A twin study of attachment in preschool children. *Child Development*. 72: 1501–1511.

Okun, M., Yeung, E. and Brown, S. 2013. Volunteering by older adults and risk of mortality: a meta-analysis. *Psychology and Aging*. 28: 564–577.

Ong, A. and Bergeman, C.S. 2004. The complexity of emotions in later life. *Journal of Gerontology: Psychological Sciences*. 59B: P117–122.

Ong, A., Rothstein, J. and Uchino, B. 2012. Loneliness accentuates age differences in cardiovascular responses to social evaluative threat. *Psychology and Aging*. 27: 190–198.

O'Rourke, N., Cappeliez, P. and Claxton, A. 2011. Functions of reminiscence and the psychological well-being of young–old and older adults over time. *Aging and Mental Health*. 15: 271–281.

O'Rourke, N., Carmel, S., Chaudhury, H., Polchenko, N. and Bachner, Y.G. 2013. A cross-national comparison of reminiscence functions between Canadian and Israeli older adults. *Journals of Gerontology, Series B: Psychological Sciences and Social Sciences*. 68: 184–192.

Ostchega, Y., Harris, T.B., Hirsch, R., Parsons, V.L. and Kington, R. 2000. The prevalence of functional limitations and disability in older persons in the US: data from the National Health and Nutrition Examination Survey III. *Journal of the American Geriatrics Society*. 48: 1132–1135.

Palgi, Y., Shrira, A., Ben-Ezra, M., Fridel, S. and Bodner, E. 2011. The relationships between daily optimism, daily pessimism, and affect differ in young and old age. *Personality and Individual Differences*. 50: 1294–1299.

Palmore, E. 2001. The ageism survey: first findings. *Gerontologist*. 41: 572–575.

Pargament, K.I. 2002a. The bitter and the sweet: an evaluation of the costs and benefits of religiousness. *Psychological Inquiry*. 13: 168–181.

Pargament, K.I. 2002b. Is religion nothing but . . . ? Explaining religion versus explaining religion away. *Psychological Inquiry*. 13: 239–244.

Pargament, K.I., Van Haitsma, K. and Ensing, D.S. 1995. When age meets adversity: religion and coping in the later years. In M.A. Kimble, S.H. McFadden, J.W. Ellor and J.J. Seeber (eds), *Aging, spirituality and religion: a handbook*. Minneapolis, MN: Fortress Press, 47–67.

Parker, R.G. 1995. Reminiscence: a continuity theory framework. *Gerontologist*. 35: 515–525.

Parmelee, P.W. and Lawton, M.P. 1990. The design of special environments for the aged. In J.E. Birren and K.W. Schaie (eds), *Handbook of the psychology of aging*. 3rd ed. San Diego, CA: Academic Press, 465–489.

Payman, V. and Ryburn, B. 2010. Religiousness and recovery from inpatient geriatric depression: findings from the PEJAMA Study. *Australian and New Zealand Journal of Psychiatry*. 44: 560–567.

Peace, S.M., Dittmann-Kohli, F., Westerhof, G.J. and Bond, J. 2007. The ageing world. In J. Bond, S. Peace, F. Dittmann-Kohli and G. Westerhof (eds), *Ageing in society. European perspectives on gerontology*. London: Sage, 1–14.

Peace, S.M. and Holland, C. (eds) 2001. *Inclusive housing in an ageing society: innovative approaches*. Bristol, UK: Policy Press.

Pearlin, L. and McKean Skaff, M. 1996. Stress and the life course: a paradigmatic alliance. *Gerontologist*. 36: 239–247.

Pearlin, L. Mullan, J., Semple, S. and Skaff, M. 1990. Caregiving and the stress process: an overview of concepts and their measures. *Gerontologist*. 30: 583–594.

Penezić, Z., Lacković-Grgin, K., Tucak, I., Nekić, M., Žorga, S., Škraban, O. and Vehovar, U. 2008. Predictors of generative action among adults in two transitional countries. *Social Indicators Research*. 87: 237–248.

Peng, R., Ling, L. and He, Q. 2010. Self-rated health status transition and long-term care need of the oldest Chinese. *Health Policy*. 97: 259–266.

Pennebaker, J.W. and Stone, L.D. 2003. Words of wisdom: language use over the life span. *Journal of Personality and Social Psychology*. 85: 291–301.

Pertusa, A., Frost, R.O., Fullana, M.A., Samuels, J., Steketee, G., Tolin, D., Saxena, S., Leckman, J.F. and Mataix-Cols, D. 2010. Refining the diagnostic boundaries of compulsive hoarding: a critical review. *Clinical Psychology Review*. 30: 371–386.

Peterson, B. and Stewart, A. 1990. Using personal and fictional documents to assess psychological development: a case study of Vera Brittain's generativity. *Psychology and Aging*. 5: 400–411.

Peterson, B. and Stewart, A. 1996. Antecedents and context of generativity motivation at midlife. *Psychology and Aging*. 11(1): 21–33.

Phillipson, C. and Walker, A. (eds) 1986. *Ageing and social policy. A critical assessment*. Aldershot, UK: Gower.

Piccinin, A.M., Muniz, G., Matthews, F.E. and Johansson, B. 2011. Terminal decline from within- and between-person perspectives, accounting for incident dementia. *Journal of Gerontology: Psychological Sciences*. 66B: 391–401.

Pilkington, P., Windsor, T. and Crisp, D. 2012. Volunteering and subjective well-being in midlife and older adults: the role of supportive social networks. *Journals of Gerontology, Series B: Psychological Sciences and Social Sciences*. 67: 249–260.

Ploubidis, G.B. and Grundy, E. 2009. Later-life mental health in Europe: a country-level comparison. *Journal of Gerontology: Social Sciences*. 64B: 666–676.

Pomeroy, V.M., Conroy, M.C. and Coleman, P.G. 1997. Setting handicap goals with elderly people: a pilot study of the Life Strengths Interview. *Clinical Rehabilitation*. 11: 156–161.

Poon, L.W., Jang, Y., Reynolds, S.G. and McCarthy, E. 2005. Profiles of the oldest-old. In M. Johnson, V.L. Bengtson, P.G. Coleman and T. Kirkwood (eds), *Handbook of age and ageing*. New York: Cambridge University Press, 346–353.

Prior, K. and Sargent-Cox, K. 2014. Students' expectations of ageing: an evaluation of the impact of imagined intergenerational contact and the mediating role of ageing anxiety. *Journal of Experimental Social Psychology*. 55: 99–104.

Prosser, J. and McArdle, P. 1996. The changing mental health of children and adolescents: evidence for a deterioration? *Psychological Medicine*. 26: 715–725.

Putnam, R. and Campbell, D. 2010. *American grace: how religion divides and unites us*. New York: Simon & Schuster.

Pyszczynski, T., Solomon, S. and Greenberg, J. 2015. Thirty years of terror management theory: from genesis to revelation. *Advances in Experimental Social Psychology*. 52: 1–70.

Rabbitt, P. 2015. *The aging mind: an owner's manual*. London: Routledge.

Radloff, L.S. 1977. The CES-D Scale: a self-report depression scale for research in the general population. *Applied Psychological Measurement*. 1(3): 385–401.

Ram-Prasad, C. 1995. A classical Indian philosophical perspective on ageing and the meaning of life. *Ageing and Society*. 15: 1–36.

Randall, W.L. and Kenyon, G.M. 2001. *Ordinary wisdom: biographical aging and the journey of life*. Westport, CT: Praeger.

Raposo, S., El-Gabalawy, R., Erickson, J., Mackenzie, C. and Sareen, J. 2014. Associations between anxiety disorders, suicide ideation, and age in nationally representative samples of Canadian and American adults. *Journal of Anxiety Disorders*. 28(8): 823–829.

Rechel, B., Grundy E., Robine, J.-M., Cylus J., Mackenback, J., Knai, C. and McKee, M. 2013. Ageing in the European Union. *Lancet*. 381(9874): 1312–1322.

Redzanowski, U. and Glück, J. 2013. Who knows who is wise? Self and peer ratings of wisdom. *Journals of Gerontology, Series B: Psychological Sciences and Social Sciences*. 68: 391–394.

Reed, J., Cook, G., Sullivan, A. and Burridge, C. 2003. Making a move: care-home residents' experiences of relocation. *Ageing and Society*. 23: 225–241.

Reichstadt, J., Sengupta, G., Depp, C., Palinkas, L. and Jeste, D. 2010. Older adults' perspectives on successful aging: qualitative interviews. *American Journal of Geriatric Psychiatry*. 18: 567–575.

Reker, G.T. and Chamberlain, K. 2000. *Exploring existential meaning: optimizing human development across the life span*. Thousand Oaks, CA: Sage.

Reker, G.T. and Wong, P.T.P. 1988. Aging as an individual process: toward a theory of personal meaning. In J.E. Birren and V.L. Bengtson (eds), *Emergent theories of aging*. Springer, New York, 214–246.

Reuter, T., Ziegelmann, J.P., Wiedemann, A.U., Lippke, S., Schüz, B. and Aiken, L.S. 2010. Planning bridges the intention–behaviour gap: age makes a difference and strategy use explains why. *Psychology & Health*. 25: 873–887.

Richardson, M.J and Pasupathi, M. 2005. Young and growing wiser: wisdom during adolescence and young adulthood. In R.J. Sternberg and J. Jordan (eds), *A handbook of wisdom: psychological perspectives*. New York: Cambridge University Press, 139–159.

Riediger, M. 2007. Interference and facilitation among personal goals: age differences and associations with well-being and behavior. In B.R. Little, K. Salmela-Aro, J.-E. Nurmi and S.D. Philipps (eds), *Personal project pursuit: goals, action, and human flourishing*. Mahwah, NJ: Erlbaum, 119–143.

Riediger, M., Freund, A.M. and Baltes, P.B. 2005. Managing life through personal goals: intergoal facilitation and intensity of goal pursuit in younger and older adulthood. *Journal of Gerontology: Psychological Sciences*. 60B: P84–91.

Riley, M.W. 1973. Aging and cohort succession: interpretations and misinterpretations. *Public Opinion Quarterly*. 37: 35–49.

Riley, M.W., Foner, A. and Riley, J.W., Jr. 1999. The aging and society paradigm. In V.L. Bengtson and K.W. Schaie (eds), *Handbook of theories of aging*. New York: Springer, 327–343.

Robins, W., Trzesniewski, K.H., Tracy, J.L., Gosling, S.D. and Potter, J. 2002. Global self-esteem across the life-span. *Psychology and Aging*. 17: 423–434.

Robinson, O. 2013. *Development through adulthood: an integrative sourcebook*. Basingstoke, UK: Palgrave Macmillan.

Rockwood, K., Song, X. and Mitnitski, A. 2011. Changes in relative fitness and frailty across the adult lifespan: evidence from the Canadian National Population Health Survey. *Canadian Medical Association Journal*. 183: E487–494.

Rodin, J. 1986. Aging and health: effects of the sense of control. *Science*. 233: 1271–6.

Rodin, J., Timko, C. and Harris, S. 1985. The construct of control: biological and psychosocial correlates. In C. Eisdorfer, M.P. Lawton and G.L. Maddox (eds), *Annual review of gerontology and geriatrics. Volume 5*. New York: Springer, 3–55.

Rosenberg, M. 1965. *Society and the adolescent self-image*. Princeton, NJ: Princeton University Press.

Rosso, A., Lee, B., Stefanick, M., Kroenke, C., Coker, L., Woods, N. and Michael, Y. 2015. Caregiving frequency and physical function: the Women's Health Initiative. *Journals of Gerontology: Medical Sciences*. 70: 210–215.

Rothermund, K. and Brandtstädter, J. 2003a. Depression in later life: cross-sequential patterns and possible determinants. *Psychology and Aging*. 18: 80–90.

Rothermund, K. and Brandtstädter, J. 2003b. Coping with deficits and losses in later life: from compensatory action to accommodation. *Psychology and Aging*. 18: 896–905.

Rott, C. and Thomae, H. 1991. Coping in longitudinal perspective: findings from the Bonn Longitudinal Study On Aging. *Journal of Cross-Cultural Gerontology*. 6: 23–40.

Rovner, M., Zisselman, P. and Shmuely-Dulitzki, Y. 1996. Depression and disability in older people with impaired vision: a follow-up study. *Journal of the American Geriatrics Society*. 44: 181–184.

Rowe, J.W. and Kahn, R.L. 1998. *Successful aging*. New York: Pantheon.

Rowe, J.W. and Khan, R.L. 2015. Successful aging 2.0: conceptual expansions for the 21st century. *Journal of Gerontology, Series B: Psychological Sciences and Social Sciences*. 70(4): 593–596.

Rupp, D.E., Vodanovich, S. and Credé, M. 2005. The multidimensional nature of ageism: construct validity and group differences. *Journal of Social Psychology*. 145: 335–362.

Ruth, J.-E., Birren, J.E. and Polkinghorne, D.E. 1996. The projects of life reflected in autobiographies of old age. *Ageing and Society*. 16: 677–699.

Ruth, J.-E. and Coleman, P.G. 1996. Personality and aging: coping and management of the self in later life. In J.E. Birren and K.W. Schaie (eds), *Handbook of the psychology of aging*. 4th ed. San Diego, CA: Academic Press, 308–322.

Ryff, C.D. 1989. Happiness is everything, or is it? Explorations on the meaning of psychological well-being. *Journal of Personality and Social Psychology*. 57: 1069–1081.

Ryff, C.D. 1991. Possible selves in adulthood and old age: a tale of shifting horizons. *Psychology and Aging*. 6: 286–295.

Ryff, C.D. 1995. Psychological well-being in adult life. *Current directions in psychological science*. 4: 99–104.

Ryff, C.D. and Migdal, S. 1984. Intimacy and generativity: self-perceived transitions. *Signs: Journal of Women in Culture and Society*. 9: 470–481.

Sabat, S.R. 2001. *The experience of Alzheimer's disease: life through a tangled veil*. Malden, MA: Blackwell.

Sabat, S.R. and Harre, R. 1992. The construction and deconstruction of self in Alzheimer's Disease. *Ageing and Society*. 12: 443–461.

Saito, T., Wakui, T. and Kai, I. 2015. Effects of spousal illness on self-rated health in older couples: roles of sex and proximity to adult children. *Geriatrics and Gerontology International.* doi: 10.1111/ggi.12646.

Santini, Z., Fiori, K., Feeney, J., Tyrovolas, S., Haro, J.M. and Koyanagi, A. 2016. Social relationships, loneliness, and mental health among older men and women in Ireland: a prospective community-based study. *Journal of Affective Disorders.* 204: 59–69.

Sargent-Cox, K., Rippon, M. and Burns, R. 2014. Measuring anxiety about aging across the adult lifespan. *International Psychogeriatrics.* 26: 135–145.

Schaie, K.W. 1996. *Intellectual development in adulthood: the Seattle Longitudinal Study.* New York: Cambridge University Press.

Schaie, K.W. and Willis, S.L. (eds) 2015. *Handbook of the psychology of aging.* 8th ed. New York: Academic Press.

Scheibe, S. and Carstensen, L.L. 2010. Emotional aging: recent findings and future trends. *Journal of Gerontology: Psychological Sciences.* 65B: 135–144.

Scheibe, S., English, T., Tsai, J.L. and Carstensen, L.L. 2013. Striving to feel good: ideal affect, actual affect, and their correspondence across adulthood. *Psychology and Aging.* 28: 160–171.

Scheibe, S., Kunzmann, U. and Baltes, P.B. 2007. Wisdom, life longings, and optimal development. In J.A. Blackburn and C.N. Dulmus (eds), *Handbook of gerontology: evidence based approaches to theory, practice, and policy.* New York: Wiley, 117–142.

Schilling, O.K. and Diehl, M. 2014. Reactivity to stressor pile-up in adulthood: effects on daily negative and positive affect. *Psychology and Aging.* 29: 72–83.

Schmitt, E., Hinner, J. and Kruse, A. 2015. Potentials of survivors, intergenerational dialogue, active ageing and social change. *Social and Behavioural Sciences.* 171: 7–16.

Schneider, S. and Stone, A.A. 2015. Mixed emotions across the adult life span in the United States. *Psychology and Aging.* 30: 369–382.

Schoklitsch, A. and Baumann, U. 2011. Measuring generativity in older adults: the development of new scales. *Journal of Gerontopsychology and Geriatric Psychiatry.* 24: 31–43.

Schryer, E. and Ross, M. 2012. Evaluating the valence of remembered events: the importance of age and self-relevance. *Psychology and Aging.* 27: 237–242.

Schulz, R. and Heckhausen, J. 1996. A life-span model of successful aging. *American Psychologist.* 51: 702–714.

Schulz, R. and Heckhausen, J. 1999. Aging, culture, and control: setting a new research agenda. *Journals of Gerontology Series B: Psychological Sciences and Social Sciences.* 54: P139–P145.

Sedikides, C. and Gebauer, J.E. 2013. Religion and the self. In V. Saroglou (ed), *Religion, personality, and social behavior.* New York: Psychology Press, 46–70.

Selai, C.E., Trimble, M.R., Rossor, M.N. and Harvey, R.J. 2001. Assessing quality of life in dementia: preliminary psychometric testing of the Quality of Life Assessment Schedule (QOLAS). *Neuropsychological Rehabilitation.* 11: 219–243.

Serrano, J.P., Latorre, J.M., Gatz, M. and Montanes, J. 2004. Life review therapy using autobiographical retrieval practice for older adults with depressive symptomatology. *Psychology and Aging.* 19: 272–277.

Sexton, E., King-Kallimanis, B., Morgan, K. and McGee, H. 2014. Development of the Brief Ageing Perceptions Questionnaire (B-APQ): a confirmatory factor analysis approach to item reduction. *BMS Geriatrics.* 14: 14.

Shah, S., Carey, I., Harris, T., DeWilde, S., Victor, C. and Cook, D. 2012. Do good health and material circumstances protect older people from the increased risk of death after bereavement? *American Journal of Epidemiology.* 176(8): 689–698.

Shang, L., Riedel, N., Loerbroks, A., Muller, A., Wege, N., Angerer, P. and Li, J. 2015. The association between effort–reward imbalance and depressive symptoms is modified by selection, optimization, and compensation strategy. *Journal of Occupational & Environmental Medicine*. 57(11): 1222–1227.

Shankar, A., McMunn, A., Banks, J. and Steptoe, A. 2011. Loneliness, social isolation, and behavioral and biological indicators in older adults. *Health Psychology*. 30: 377–385.

Sherman, E. 1981. *Counseling the aging: an integrative approach*. New York: Free Press.

Sherman, E. 1991. *Reminiscence and the self in old age*. New York: Springer.

Sherman, E. 2010. *Contemplative aging: a way of being in later life*. New York: Gordian Knot Books.

Shiota, M.N. and Levenson, R.W. 2009. Effects of aging on experimentally instructed detached reappraisal, positive reappraisal, and emotional behavior suppression. *Psychology and Aging*. 24: 890–900.

Shmotkin, D. 2005. Happiness in the face of adversity: reformulating the dynamic and modular bases of subjective well-being. *Review of General Psychology*. 9: 291–325.

Shmotkin, D. 2011. The pursuit of happiness: alternative conceptions of subjective well-being. In L.W. Poon and J. Cohen-Mansfield (eds), *Understanding well-being in the oldest old*. New York: Cambridge University Press, 27–45.

Shmotkin, D., Shrira, A., Eyal, N., Blumstein, T. and Shorek, A. 2014. The prediction of subjective wellness among the old-old: implications for the 'fourth-age' conception. *Journals of Gerontology, Series B: Psychological Sciences and Social Sciences*. 69: 719–729.

Siegler, I.C. 1975. The terminal decline hypothesis: fact or artefact? *Experimental Aging Research*. 1: 169–185.

Silverstein, M. and Long, J. 1998. Trajectories of grandparents' perceived solidarity with adult grandchildren: a growth curve analysis over 23 years. *Journal of Marriage and Family*. 60: 912–923.

Slater, C.L. 2003. Generativity versus stagnation: an elaboration of Erikson's adult stage of human development. *Journal of Adult Development*. 10(1): 53–65.

Small, J.A., Geldart, K., Gutman, G. and Scott, M.A.C. 1998. The discourse of self in dementia. *Ageing and Society*. 18: 291–316.

Smith, C.A. and Lazarus, R.S. 1993. Appraisal components, core relational themes, and the emotions. *Cognition and Emotion*. 7: 233–269.

Smith, J. and Baltes, P.B. 1997. Profiles of psychological functioning in the old and oldest old. *Psychology and Aging*. 12: 458–472.

Smith, J. and Baltes, P.B. 1999. Trends and profiles of psychological functioning in very old age. In P.B. Baltes and K.U. Mayer (eds), *The Berlin Aging Study: aging from 70 to 100*. Cambridge, UK: Cambridge University Press, 197–226.

Smith, J. and Freund, A.M. 2002. The dynamics of possible selves in old age. *Journal of Gerontology: Psychological Sciences*. 57B: P492–500.

Smith, P.K. (ed) 1991. *The psychology of grandparenthood: an international perspective*. London. Routledge.

Smith, P.K. 1994. Grandparenting. In M. Bornstein (ed), *Handbook of parenting. Volume 3. Social status and conditions of parenting*. Hillsdale, NJ: Lawrence Erlbaum, 89–112.

Smith, P.K. and Drew, L. 2004. Grandparenting and extended support networks. In M. Hoghughi and N. Long (eds), *Handbook of parenting: theory and research for practice*. London: Sage, 146–160.

Sneed, J.R., Whitbourne, S.K. and Culang, M.E. 2006. Trust, identity, and ego integrity: modeling Erikson's core stages over 34 years. *Journal of Adult Development*. 13: 148–157.

Sneed, J.R., Whitbourne, S.K., Schwartz, S.J. and Huang, S. 2012. The relationship between identity, intimacy, and midlife well-being: findings from the Rochester Adult Longitudinal Study. *Psychology and Aging*. 27: 318–323.

Snyder, C.R. and Lopez, S.J. 2002. *Handbook of positive psychology*. New York: Oxford University Press.

Spreadbury, J.H. 2013. Belief in the context of bereavement: the potential therapeutic properties associated with religious belief and ritual. In P.G. Coleman, D. Koleva and J. Bornat (eds), *Ageing, ritual and social change: comparing the secular and religious in Eastern and Western Europe*. Farnham, UK: Ashgate, 155–176.

Spreadbury, J.H. and Coleman, P.G. 2011. Religious responses in coping with spousal bereavement. In P.G. Coleman and colleagues, *Belief and aging: spiritual pathways in later life*. Bristol, UK: Policy Press, 79–96.

Sprecher, S. and Fehr, B. 2005. Compassionate love for close others and humanity. *Journal of Social and Personal Relationships*. 22: 629–651.

St. Jacques, P.L., Bessette-Symons, B. and Cabeza, R. 2009. Functional neuroimaging studies of aging and emotion: fronto-amygdalar differences during emotional perception and episodic memory. *Journal of the International Neuropsychological Society*. 15: 819–825.

Stahl, S.T. and Schulz, R. 2014. Changes in routine health behaviors following late-life bereavement: a systematic review. *Journal of Behavioural Medicine*. 37: 736–755.

Staudinger, U.M. 2005. Personality and aging. In M. Johnson, V.L. Bengtson, P.G. Coleman and T. Kirkwood (eds), *Cambridge handbook of age and ageing*. New York: Cambridge University Press, 237–244.

Staudinger, U.M. and Baltes, P.B. 1996. Interactive minds: a facilitative setting for wisdom-related performance? *Journal of Personality and Social Psychology*. 71: 746–762.

Staudinger, U.M. and Glück, J. 2011. Psychological wisdom research: commonalities and differences in a growing field. *Annual Review of Psychology*. 62: 215–241.

Stawski, R.L., Sliwinski, M.J., Almeida, D.M and Smyth, J.M. 2008. Reported exposure and emotional reactivity to daily stressors: the roles of adult age and global perceived stress. *Psychology and Aging*. 23: 52–61.

Steels, S. 2015. Key characteristics of age-friendly cities and communities: a review. *Cities*. 47: 45–52.

Stephan, Y. 2009. Openness to experience and active older adults' life satisfaction: a trait and facet-level analysis. *Personality and Individual Differences*. 47: 637–641.

Steptoe, A., Deaton, A. and Stone, A.A. 2015. Subjective wellbeing, health and ageing. *Lancet*. 385: 640–648.

Sternberg, R.J. (ed) 1990. *Wisdom: its nature, origins and development*. Cambridge, UK: Cambridge University Press.

Sternberg, R.J. and Grigorenko, E.L. 2005. Intelligence and wisdom. In M. Johnson, V.L. Bengtson, P.G. Coleman and T. Kirkwood (eds), *Cambridge handbook of age and ageing*. New York: Cambridge University Press, 209–215.

Stewart, A.J., Ostrove, J.M. and Helson, R. 2001. Middle aging in women: patterns of personality change from the 30s to the 50s. *Journal of Adult Development*. 8: 23–37.

Stewart, A.J. and Vandewater, E.A. 1998. The course of generativity. In D.P. McAdams and de St. Aubin (eds), *Generativity and adult development: how and why we care for the next generation*. Washington, DC: American Psychological Association, 75–100.

Stickley, A. and Koyanagi, A. 2016. Loneliness, common mental disorders and suicidal behavior: findings from a general population survey. *Journal of Affective Disorders*. 197: 81–87.

Stiles, W.B. 2001. Assimilation of problematic experiences. *Psychotherapy*. 38: 462–465.

Stokes, G. 2000. *Challenging behaviour in dementia: a person centred approach*. Bicester, UK: Winslow Press.

Stone, A.A., Schwartz, J.E., Broderick, J.E. and Deaton, A. 2010. A snapshot of the age distribution of psychological well-being in the United States. *Proceedings of the National Academy of Sciences in the United States of America*. 107: 9985–9990.

Strawbridge, W.J., Shema, S.J., Balfour, J.L., Higby, H.R. and Kaplan, G.A. 1998. Antecedents of frailty over three decades in an older cohort. *Journal of Gerontology: Social Sciences*. 53B: S9–16.

Streubel, B. and Kunzmann, U. 2011. Age differences in emotional reactions: arousal and age-relevance count. *Psychology and Aging*. 26: 966–978.

Strobe, M. and Schut, H. 1999. The dual process model of coping with bereavement: rationale and description. *Death Studies*. 23: 197–224.

Stuart-Hamilton, I. 2012. *The psychology of ageing: an introduction*. London: Jessica Kingsley.

Stuart-Hamilton, I. (in press). *Problems in studying the psychology of ageing*. London: Routledge

Sutton, L. 2004. Cultures of care in severe depression and dementia. In J. Hepple and L. Sutton (eds), *Cognitive analytic therapy in later life: a new perspective on old age*. London: Brunner-Routledge, 201–220.

Tang, W. and Chan, J. 2016. Effects of psychosocial interventions on self-efficacy of dementia caregivers: a literature review. *International Journal of Geriatric Psychiatry*. 31(5): 475–493.

Taylor, R.J., Chatters, L.M. and Jackson, J.S. 2007a. Religious participation among older black Caribbeans in the United States. *Journal of Gerontology: Social Sciences*. 62B: S251–256.

Taylor, R.J., Chatters, L.M. and Jackson, J.S. 2007b. Religious and spiritual involvement among older African Americans, Caribbean blacks, and Non-Hispanic whites: findings from the national survey of American life. *Journal of Gerontology: Social Sciences*. 62B: S328–350.

Taylor, R.J., Chatters, L.M. and Levin, J.S. 2004. *Religion in the lives of African Americans: social, psychological, and health perspectives*. Thousand Oaks, CA: Sage.

Tedeschi, R.G. and Calhoun, L.G. 1995. *Trauma and transformation: growing in the aftermath of suffering*. Thousand Oaks, CA: Sage.

Teerawichitchainan, B., Pothisiri, W. and Long, G. 2015. How do living arrangements and intergenerational support matter for psychological health of elderly parents? Evidence from Myanmar, Vietnam, and Thailand. *Social Science and Medicine*. 136(137): 106–116.

Thane, P. (ed) 2005. *A history of old age*. London: Thames & Hudson.

Thomae, H. (ed) 1976. *Patterns of aging*. New York: Karger.

Thomae, H. 1987. Conceptualizations of responses to stress. *European Journal of Personality*. 1: 171–192.

Thomas, S. and Kunzmann, U. 2014. Age differences in wisdom-related knowledge: does the age relevance of the task matter? *Journals of Gerontology, Series B: Psychological Sciences and Social Sciences*. 69: 897–905.

Thompson, P., Itzin, C. and Abdenstern, M. 1990. *'I don't feel old': the experience of later life*. Oxford, UK: Oxford University Press.

Thornton, S. and Brotchie, J. 1987. Reminiscence: a critical review of the empirical literature. *British Journal of Clinical Psychology*. 26: 93–111.

Tilak, S. 1989. *Religion and aging in the Indian tradition*. Albany, NY: State University of New York Press.

Tobin, S.S. 1991. *Personhood in advanced old age: implications for practice*. New York: Springer.

Tobin, S.S. 1999. *Preservation of the self in the oldest years: with implications for practice*. New York: Springer.

Tobin, S. and Raymundo, M. 2010. Causal uncertainty and psychological well-being: the moderating role of accommodation (secondary control). *Personality and Social Psychology Bulletin*. 36: 371–383.

Tolmunen, T., Lehto, S., Julkunen, J., Hintikka, J. and Kauhanen, J. 2014. Trait anxiety and somatic concerns associate with increased mortality risk: a 23-year follow-up in aging men. *Annals of Epidemiology*. 24: 463–468.

Torges, C.M., Stewart, A.J. and Nolen-Hoeksema, S. 2008. Regret resolution, aging, and adapting to loss. *Psychology and Aging*. 23: 169–180.

Tornstam, L. 1996a. Caring for the elderly: introducing the theory of gerotranscendence as a supplementary frame of reference for the care of elderly. *Scandinavian Journal of Caring Sciences*. 10: 144–150.

Tornstam, L. 1996b. Gerotranscendence: a theory about maturing in old age. *Journal of aging and identity*. 1: 37–50.

Tornstam, L. 1997. Gerotranscendence in a broad cross-sectional perspective. *Journal of aging and identity*. 2: 17–36.

Tornstam, L. 1999. Gerotranscendence and the functions of reminiscence. *Journal of Aging and Identity*. 4: 155–166.

Tornstam, L. 2005. *Gerotranscendence: the contemplative dimension of aging*. New York: Springer.

Townsend, P. 1962. *The last refuge: a survey of residential institutions and homes for the aged in England and Wales*. London: Routledge and Kegan Paul.

Townsend, P. 1981. The structured dependency of the elderly: the creation of social policy in the twentieth century. *Ageing and Society*. 1: 5–28.

Traphagan, J. 2004. *The practice of concern: ritual, well-being and aging in rural Japan*. Durham, NC: Carolina Academic Press.

Troll, L.E. and Skaff, M.M. 1997. Perceived continuity of self in very old age. *Psychology and Aging*. 12: 162–169.

Tsai, F.-J. 2016. The maintaining and improving effect of grandchild care provision on elders' mental health: evidence from longitudinal study in Taiwan. *Archives of Gerontology and Geriatrics*. 64: 59–65.

Tsai, J.L., Knutson, B. and Fung, H.H. 2006. Cultural variation in affect valuation. *Journal of Personality and Social Psychology*. 90: 288–307.

Tsai, J.L., Levenson, R.W. and Carstensen, L.L. 2000. Autonomic, subjective and expressive responses to emotional films in older and younger Chinese Americans and European Americans. *Psychology and Aging*. 15: 684–693.

Tufana, F., Yuruyenb, M., Kizilarslanogluc, M.C., Akpinara, T., Emiksiyea, S., Yesild, Y., Ozturke, Z., Bozbulutc, U., Bolayird, V., Tasarf, P., Yavuzerb, H., Sahinf, S., Ulgerc, Z., Ozturka, G., Halild, M., Akcicekf, F., Doventasb, A., Kepekcie, Y., Inceg, N. and Karana, M. 2015. Geriatrics education is associated with positive attitudes toward older people in internal medicine residents: a multicenter study. *Archives of Gerontology and Geriatrics*. 60: 307–310.

Türgaya, A.S., Şahinb, S., Şenuzun Aykarc, F., Sarid, D., Badire, A. and Canli Özerf, Z. 2015. Attitudes of Turkish nursing students toward elderly people. *European Geriatric Medicine*. 6: 267–270.

Turner, A., Nikolova, S. and Sutton, M. 2016. The effect of living alone on the costs and benefits of surgery amongst older people. *Social Science & Medicine*. 150: 95–103.

Uchino, B.N. 2009. Understanding the links between social support and physical health: a lifespan perspective with emphasis on the separability of perceived and received support. *Perspectives in Psychological Science*. 4: 236–255.

Uchino, B.N., Bowen, K., Carlisle, M. and Birmingham, W. 2012. Psychological pathways linking social support to health outcomes: a visit with the 'ghosts' of research past, present and future. *Social Science & Medicine*. 74: 949–957.

UK Department for Work and Pensions. 2009. *UK Family Resources Survey 2007/8*. London.

UK Office for National Statistics. 2013. *UK General Lifestyle Survey 2011*. London.

United Nations. 2002. *World population ageing: 1950–2050*. New York: UN Department of Economic and Social Affairs, Population Division.

United Nations. 2015. *Women's flagship report: progress of the world's women*. See http://progress.unwomen.org/en/2015/ (accessed 7 Feb 2016).

Ussher, J., Wong, T. and Perz, J. 2011. A qualitative analysis of changes in relationship dynamics and roles between people with cancer and their informal carer. *Health*. 15(6): 650–667.

Vaillant, G. 1977. *Adaptation to life*. Boston, MA: Little Brown.

Vaillant, G.E. and Milofsky, E. 1980. Natural history of male psychological health: IX empirical evidence for Erikson's model of the life cycle. *American Journal of Psychiatry*. 137: 1348–1359.

Van de Water, D. and McAdams, D.P. 1989. Generativity and Erikson's 'belief in the species'. *Journal of Research in Personality*. 23: 435–449.

Van Dussen, D.J. and Weaver, R.R. 2009. Undergraduate students' perceptions and behaviors related to the aged and to aging processes. *Educational Gerontology*. 35: 342–357.

Van Haitsma, K. 2000. The assessment and integration of preferences into care practices for persons with dementia residing in the nursing home. In R. Rubinstein, M. Moss and M. Kleban (eds), *The many dimensions of aging*. New York: Springer, 143–163.

Van Haitsma, K.S., Curyto, K., Abbott, K.M., Towsley, G.L., Spector, A. and Kleban, M. 2015. A randomized controlled trial for an individualized positive psychosocial intervention for the affective and behavioral symptoms of dementia in nursing home residents. *Journals of Gerontology, Series B: Psychological Sciences and Social Sciences*. 70: 35–45.

van Wijngaarden, E., Leget, C. and Goossensen, A. 2015. Ready to give up on life: the lived experience of elderly people who feel life is completed and no longer worth living. *Social Science & Medicine*. 138: 257–264.

Versey, H.S., Stewart, A. and Duncan, L. 2013. Successful aging in late midlife: the role of personality among college-educated women. *Journal of Adult Development*. 20: 63–75.

Versey, S. 2015. Managing work and family: do control strategies help? *Developmental Psychology*. 51(11): 1672–1681.

Victor, C.R. and Bowling, A. 2012. A longitudinal analysis of loneliness among older people in Great Britain. *Journal of Psychology*. 146(3): 313–331.

Vladeck, B.C. 1980. *Unloving care: the nursing home tragedy*. New York: Basic Books.

Voas, D. and Doebler, S. 2011. Secularization in Europe: religious change between and within birth cohorts. *Religion and Society in Central and Eastern Europe*. 4: 39–62.

Vogel, N., Schilling, O.K., Wahl, H.-W., Beekman, A.T.F. and Penninx, B.W.J.H. 2013. Time-to-death-related change in positive and negative affect among older adults approaching the end of life. *Psychology and Aging*. 28: 128–141.

Vuorisalmi, M., Sarkeala, T., Hervonen, A. and Jylhä, M. 2012. Among nonagenarians, congruence between self-rated health and proxy-rated health was low but both predicted mortality. *Journal of Clinical Epidemiology*. 65: 553–559.

Wadensten, B. 2005. Introducing older people to the theory of gerotranscendence. *Journal of Advanced Nursing*. 52: 381–388.

Wadensten, B. 2010. Changes in nursing home residents during an innovation based on the theory of gerotranscendence. *International Journal of Older People Nursing*. 5: 108–115.

Wahl, H.-W., Heyl, V. and Schilling, O. 2012. Robustness of personality and affect relations under chronic conditions: the case of age-related vision and hearing impairment. *Journals of Gerontology, Series B: Psychological Sciences and Social Sciences*. 67: 687–696.

Watkins, R., Cheston, R., Jones, K. and Gilliard, J. 2006. 'Coming out' with Alzheimer's disease: changes in awareness during a psychotherapy group for people with dementia. *Aging and Mental Health*. 10: 166–176.

Watson, D., Clark, L.A. and Tellegen, A. 1988. Development and validation of brief measures of positive and negative affect: the PANAS scales. *Journal of Personality and Social Psychology.* 54(6): 1063–1070.

Watt, A., Konnert, C. and Speirs, C. 2015. The mediating roles of primary and secondary control in the relationship between body satisfaction and subjective well-being among middle-aged and older women. *Journal of Gerontology: Psychological Sciences and Social Sciences.* doi: 10.1093/geronb/gbv098.

Webster, J.D. 1993. Construction and validation of the Reminiscence Functions Scale. *Journal of Gerontology.* 48: 256–262.

Webster, J.D. 2002. Reminiscence functions in adulthood: age, race, and family dynamics correlates. In J.D. Webster and B.K. Haight (eds), *Critical advances in reminiscence work: from theory to application.* New York: Springer, 140–152.

Webster, J.D. 2003. An exploratory analysis of a self-assessed wisdom scale. *Journal of Adult Development.* 10: 13–22.

Webster, J.D. and Haight, B.K. (eds) 2002. *Critical advances in reminiscence work: from theory to application.* New York: Springer.

Webster, J.D., Westerhof, G.J. and Bohlmeijer, E.T. 2014. Wisdom and mental health across the lifespan. *Journals of Gerontology, Series B: Psychological Sciences and Social Sciences.* 69: 209–218.

Weiss, D. 2014. What will remain when we are gone? Finitude and generation identity in the second half of life. *Psychology and Aging.* 29: 554–562.

Wells, Y., Foreman, P., Gething, L. and Petralia, W. 2004. Nurses' attitudes toward aging and older adults: examining attitudes and practices among health services providers in Australia. *Journal of Gerontological Nursing.* 30: 5–13.

Westerhof, G.J., Bohlmeijer, E.T. and McAdams, D.P. 2016. The relation of ego integrity and despair to personality traits and mental health. *Journals of Gerontology, Series B: Psychological Sciences and Social Sciences.* doi: 10.1093/geronb/gbv062.

Westerhof, G.J., Bohlmeijer, E.T., van Beljouw, I.M.J. and Pot, A.M. 2010a. Improvement in personal meaning mediates the effects of life review intervention on depressive symptoms in a randomized controlled trial. *Gerontologist.* 50: 541–549.

Westerhof, G.J., Bohlmeijer, E.T. and Webster, J.D. 2010b. Reminiscence and mental health: a review of recent progress in theory, research and interventions. *Ageing and Society.* 30: 697–721.

Wettstein, M., Schilling, O.K., Reidick, O. and Wahl, H.-W. 2015. Four-year stability, change, and multidirectionality of well-being in very-old age. *Psychology and Aging.* 30: 500–516.

Whisman, M. 2010. Loneliness and the metabolic syndrome in a population-based sample of middle-aged and older adults. *Health Psychology.* 29: 550–554.

Whitehead, B.R. and Bergeman, C.S. 2012. Coping with daily stress: differential role of spiritual experience on daily positive and negative affect. *Journals of Gerontology, Series B: Psychological Sciences and Social Sciences.* 67: 456–459.

Whitley, E., Popham, F. and Benzeval, M., 2016. Comparison of the Rowe–Kahn model of successful aging with self-rated health and life satisfaction: the West of Scotland Twenty-07 Prospective Cohort Study. *Gerontologist.* 56. doi: 10.1093/geront/gnv054.

Wiese, B., Freund, A.M. and Baltes, P.B. 2000. Selection, optimization, and compensation: an action-related approach to work and partnership. *Journal of Vocational Behavior.* 57: 273–300.

Wilkinson, P.J. and Coleman, P.G. 2010. Strong beliefs and coping in old age: a case based comparison of atheism and religion. *Ageing and Society.* 30: 337–361.

Williams, S.W., Zimmerman, S. and Williams, C.S. 2012. Family caregiver involvement for long-term care residents at the end of life. *Journals of Gerontology, Series B: Psychological Sciences and Social Sciences.* 67: 595–604.

Wilson, R.S., Boyle, R.A., Segawa, E., Yu, L., Begeny, C.T., Anagnos, S.E. and Bennett, D.A. 2013. The influence of cognitive decline on well-being in old age. *Psychology and Aging*. 28: 304–313.

Wilson, R.S., Kreugar, K., Arnold, S., Schneider, J., Kelly, J., Barnes, L. and Bennett, D. 2007. Loneliness and risk of Alzheimer's disease. *Archives of General Psychiatry*. 64: 234–240.

Wilson, R.S., Segawa, E., Boyle, P.A., Anagnos, S.E., Hizel, L.P. and Bennett, D.A. 2012. The natural history of cognitive decline in Alzheimer's Disease. *Psychology and Aging*. 27: 1008–1017.

Windle. G. 2011. What is resilience? A review and concept analysis. *Reviews in Clinical Gerontology*. 21: 151–169.

Windsor, T.D., Burns, R.A. and Byles, J.E. 2013. Age, physical functioning, and affect in midlife and older adulthood. *Journals of Gerontology, Series B: Psychological Sciences and Social Sciences*. 68: 395–399.

Wink, P. and Dillon, M. 2002. Spiritual development across the adult life course: findings from a longitudinal study. *Journal of Adult Development*. 9: 79–94.

Wink, P. and Helson, R. 1997. Practical and transcendent wisdom: their nature and some longitudinal findings. *Journal of Adult Development*. 4: 1–15.

Wink, P. and Schiff, B. 2002. To review or not to review? The role of personality and life events in life review and adaptation to older age. In J.D. Webster and B.K. Haight (eds), *Critical advances in reminiscence work: from theory to applications*. New York: Springer, 44–60.

Winnicott, D.W. 1965. *The maturational processes and the facilitating environment*. London: Hogarth Press.

Wolff, J., Schüz, B., Ziegelmann, J., Warner, L. and Wurm, S. 2015. Short-term buffers, but long-term suffers? Differential effects of negative self-perceptions of aging following serious health events. *Journals of Gerontology: Psychological Sciences*. doi: 10.1093/geronb/gbv058.

Wong, P.T.P. and Fry, P.S. 1998. *The human quest for meaning: a handbook of psychological research and clinical applications*. Mahwah, NJ: Lawrence Erlbaum.

Wong, P.T.P. and Watt, L.M. 1991. What types of reminiscence are associated with successful aging? *Psychology and Aging*. 6: 272–279.

Woods, R., Aguirre, E., Spector, A.E. and Orrell, M. 2012. *Cognitive stimulation to improve cognitive functioning in people with dementia*. The Cochrane Library. Wiley, UK: Chichester.

Woods, R. and Clare, L. 2008. Psychological interventions with people with dementia. In R. Woods and L. Clare (eds), *Handbook of the clinical psychology of ageing*. Chichester, UK: Wiley, 523–548.

Wortmann, J.H. and Park, C.L. 2008. Religion and spirituality in adjustment following bereavement: an integrative review. *Death Studies*. 32: 703–736.

Wrosch, C. and Miller, G.E. 2009. Depressive symptoms can be useful: self-regulatory and emotional benefits of dysphoric mood in adolescents. *Journal of Personality and Social Psychology*. 96: 1181–1190.

Wrzus, C., Müller, V., Wagner, G.G., Lindenberger, U. and Riediger, M. 2014. Affect dynamics across the lifespan: with age, heart rate reacts less strongly, but recovers more slowly from unpleasant emotional situations. *Psychology and Aging*. 29: 563–576.

Wurm, S. and Benyamini, Y. 2014. Optimism buffers the detrimental effect of negative self-perceptions of ageing on physical and mental health. *Psychology and Health*. 29(7): 832–848.

Wurm, S., Wolff, J. and Schüz, B. 2016. Primary care supply moderates the impact of diseases on self-perceptions of aging. *Psychology and Aging*. 29: 351–358.

Yang, Y. and George, L.K. 2005. Functional disability, disability transitions and depressive symptoms in late life. *Journal of Aging and Health*. 17: 263–292.

Young, L.M., Baltes, B.B. and Pratt, A. 2007. Using selection, optimization and compensation to reduce job/family stressors: effect when it matters. *Journal of Business and Psychology*. 21: 511–539.

Zacher, H. and Frese, M. 2011. Maintaining a focus on opportunities at work: the interplay between age, job complexity and the use of selection, optimization and compensation strategies. *Journal of Organizational Behavior*. 32: 291–318.

Zaninotto, P., Falaschetti, E. and Sacker, A. 2009. Age trajectories of quality of life among older adults: results from the English Longitudinal Study of Ageing. *Quality of Life Research*. 18: 1301–1309.

Zautra, A.J., Finch, J.F., Reich, J.W. and Guarnaccia, C.A. 1991. Predicting the everyday life events of older adults. *Journal of Personality*. 59: 507–538.

Zhang, S-Y., Edwards, H., Yates, P., Li, C. and Guo, Q. 2014. Self-efficacy partially mediates between social support and health-related quality of life in family caregivers for dementia patients in Shanghai. *Dementia and Geriatric Cognitive Disorders*. 37: 34–44.

Zhang, S-Y., Edwards, H., Yates, P., Ruth, E. and Guo, O. 2013. Preliminary reliability and validity testing of a self-efficacy questionnaire for Chinese family caregivers. *Aging & Mental Health*. 17: 630–637.

Zhang, X., Chen, X., Ran, G. and Ma, Y. 2016. Adult children's support and self-esteem as mediators in the relationship between attachment and subjective well-being in older adults. *Personality and Individual Differences*. 97: 229–233.

Zigmond, A. and Snaith, R. 1983. The hospital anxiety and depression scale. *Acta Psychiatrica Scandinavica*. 67(6): 361–370.

Zinnbauer, B.J., Pargament, K.I. and Scott, A.B. 1999. The emerging meanings of religiousness and spirituality: problems and prospects. *Journal of Personality*. 67: 889–919.

INDEX